The Short Oxford History of Europe

The Early Middle Ages

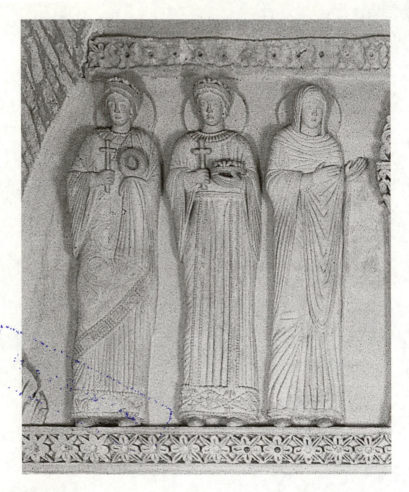

Figure 1 Stucco relief from the eighth-century church of Santa Maria in Valle, Cividale

The Short Oxford History of Europe

General Editor: T. C. W. Blanning

The Early Middle Ages

Europe 400–1000

Editor: Rosamond McKitterick

170101

OXFORD
UNIVERSITY PRESS

OXFORD
UNIVERSITY PRESS

Great Clarendon Street, Oxford OX2 6DP

Oxford University Press is a department of the University of Oxford.
It furthers the University's objective of excellence in research, scholarship,
and education by publishing worldwide in

Oxford New York

Athens Auckland Bangkok Bogotá Buenos Aires
Cape Town Chennai Dar es Salaam Delhi Florence Hong Kong Istanbul
Karachi Kolkata Kuala Lumpur Madrid Melbourne Mexico City Mumbai
Nairobi Paris São Paulo Shanghai Singapore Taipei Tokyo Toronto Warsaw

with associated companies in Berlin Ibadan

Oxford is a registered trade mark of Oxford University Press
in the UK and in certain other countries

Published in the United States
by Oxford University Press Inc., New York

British Library Cataloguing in Publication Data

Data available

Library of Congress Cataloging in Publication Data

Data available

ISBN 0–19–873173–6 (hbk)
ISBN 0–19–873172–8 (pbk)

1 3 5 7 9 10 8 6 4 2

Typeset in Minion
by RefineCatch Limited, Bungay, Suffolk
Printed in Great Britain by
T.J. International Ltd, Padstow, Cornwall

General Editor's Preface

The problems of writing a satisfactory general history of Europe are many, but the most intractable is clearly the reconciliation of depth with breadth. The historian who can write with equal authority about every part of the continent in all its various aspects has not yet been born. Two main solutions have been tried in the past: either a single scholar has attempted to go it alone, presenting an unashamedly personal view of a period, or teams of specialists have been enlisted to write what are in effect anthologies. The first offers a coherent perspective but unequal coverage, the second sacrifices unity for the sake of expertise. This new series is underpinned by the belief that it is this second way that has the fewest disadvantages and that even those can be diminished if not neutralized by close cooperation between the individual contributors under the directing supervision of the volume editor. All the contributors to every volume in this series have read each other's chapters, have met to discuss problems of overlap and omission, and have then redrafted as part of a truly collective exercise. To strengthen coherence further, the editor has written an introduction and conclusion, weaving the separate strands together to form a single cord. In this exercise, the brevity promised by the adjective 'short' in the series' title has been an asset. The need to be concise has concentrated everyone's minds on what really mattered in the period. No attempt has been made to cover every angle of every topic in every country. What this volume does provide is a short but sharp and deep entry into the history of Europe in the period in all its most important aspects.

T. C. W. Blanning

Sidney Sussex College
Cambridge

Editor's Preface

When the six of us agreed to try to write about the history of Europe in the period 400–1000 in 80,000 words, we knew it was a challenge and some might think it was foolhardy. Quite how difficult but also how enjoyable it would be became increasingly apparent as we settled down to writing. With such a long period to discuss, our perspective is what might be termed the Boeing 767 view of early medieval Europe. We have not attempted to be comprehensive, for that was clearly impracticable. We have emphasized, therefore, what we think are the most important elements within the period and have tried to make generalizations that are sufficiently valid in relation to the surviving evidence and on which we are more or less agreed. A homogeneous view of this crucial period in Europe's history is not possible, but we have endeavoured at least to provide one that is coherent. The six authors have worked very closely together on this book. We exchanged and discussed our original synopses and, once our drafts were written, met for a full day in Cambridge to discuss all the chapters and the distinctive interpretations they offered, moving paragraphs from one chapter to another and deciding what should be discussed where. Thus, in addition to many small exchanges between us all, Chris Wickham and Jonathan Shepard contributed a number of paragraphs to the Introduction, notably those concerning Byzantium, Jean-Pierre Devroey provided the section on finances to the chapter on politics and Rosamond McKitterick offered material on Carolingian and Ottonian culture and we have all contributed to the Conclusion. We circulated our revised and final versions thereafter so that all six of us are indeed the authors of this book: it represents a truly collaborative effort.

As Editor I wish to thank my fellow authors for all their hard work, frank criticism, and good cheer, especially during the inevitable interruptions to writing time. I am indebted to Caroline Burt for her help with the Chronology, and to Lucy McKitterick and Laurent Terrade for their help with the translation of Jean-Pierre Devroey's chapter from French into English. Collectively the six authors benefited greatly from the candour and learning of each other as well as the many friends and colleagues who were willing to read and comment on our chapters, especially David McKitterick, Yitzhak Hen, Christina Pössel, David Pratt, Barbara Rosenwein, Thomas Noble, and Julia Smith. We wish to thank our anonymous referees of the original proposal made to Oxford University Press, whose scepticism about the feasibility of our particular enterprise was a useful stimulus. We are also very grateful to our General Editor Tim Blanning, whose brain children this series and this volume are, and to Ruth Parr and our special editors, Andrew Maclennan and Fiona Kinnear, and Jo Stanbridge at Oxford University Press for their advice and support.

Rosamond McKitterick

Cambridge
August 2000

Contents

List of Illustrations

List of Maps

List of Contributors

MAYKE DE JONG is Professor of Medieval History at the University of Utrecht. After earlier publications on early medieval monasticism, notably *In Samuel's Image: Child Oblation in the Early Medieval West* (Leiden, 1996), she has now turned her attention to the interface of politics, ritual, and exegesis in the Carolingian world. She has edited a special issue of *Early Medieval Europe*, 7 (1998), on 'The power of the word: The influence of the Bible on early medieval politics', and two collaborative volumes: (with Esther Cohen) *Medieval Transformations* (Leiden, 2000) and (with Frans Theuws and Carine van Rhijn) *Topographies of Power in the Early Middle Ages* (Leiden, 2001). Her forthcoming book will address the dynamics of penance in the politics of the reign of Louis the Pious.

JEAN-PIERRE DEVROEY is Professor of Medieval History at the Université Libre de Bruxelles and a member of the Académie royale de Belgique. In addition to many seminal articles on the economy of the early middle ages he has published editions of the Carolingian polyptychs, notably *Le Polyptyque et les listes de Cens de l'abbaye Saint-Remi de Reims (IXe–XIe siècles)* (Reims, 1984) and *Le Polyptyque et les listes de biens de l'abbaye de Saint-Pierre de Lobbes (IXe–XIe siècles): Édition critique* (Brussels, 1986), and *Études sur le grand domaine carolingien* (Aldershot, 1993). He is currently writing a book on *Peasant Economy and Societies in Carolingian Europe*.

ROSAMOND MCKITTERICK is Professor of Medieval History at the University of Cambridge and Fellow of Newnham College. She is a Korrespondierendes Mitglied of the Monumenta Germaniae Historica. Her work includes *The Frankish Church and the Carolingian Reforms, 789–895* (1977), *The Frankish Kingdoms under the Carolingians, 751–987* (1983), *The Carolingians and the Written Word* (1989), *Books, Scribes and Learning in the Frankish Kingdoms, Sixth to Ninth Centuries* (1994), *The Frankish Kings and Culture in the Early Middle Ages* (1995), and the edited volumes *The Uses of Literacy in Early Mediaeval Europe* (1990), *Carolingian Culture: Emulation and Innovation* (1994), *The New Cambridge Medieval History, II. c.700–c.900* (1995) and (with Roland Quinault) *Edward Gibbon and Empire*

(1997). She is currently completing a book on *The Migration of Ideas in Early Medieval Europe* and a new study of Charlemagne's reign is in preparation.

JONATHAN SHEPARD was until recently Lecturer in Russian History at the University of Cambridge and a Fellow of Peterhouse. His various contributions to Byzantine, Russian, Scandinavian, and Balkan history include the synthesis (with Simon Franklin) *The Emergence of Rus 750–1200* (1996), which has now also been published in Russian, and the edited collection (with Simon Franklin) *Byzantine Diplomacy* (1992). He is currently completing *Byzantium between Neighbours, 812–c.1050.*

CHRIS WICKHAM is Professor of Early Medieval History at the University of Birmingham, a Fellow of the British Academy, and a Corresponding Fellow of the Accademia Nazionale dei Lincei. His books include *Early Medieval Italy: Central Power and Local Society* (1981), *The Mountains and the City: The Tuscan Appennines in the Early Middle Ages* (1988), *Land and Power: Studies in Italian and European Social History, 400–1200* (1994), and *Legge, pratiche e conflitti* (Rome, 2000).

IAN WOOD is Professor of Early Medieval History at the University of Leeds and was recently Visiting Professor at the University of Vienna. His publications include *The Merovingian Kingdoms, 450–751* (1994) and *The Missionary Life: Saints and the Evangelisation of Europe, 400–1050* (2001). Among his edited works are (with Evangelos Chrysos) *East and West: Modes of Communication* (1999). He is the general editor for the series *The Transformation of the Roman World.* This is the outcome of the European Science Foundation's research project of the same name of which he was a coordinator.

Figure 2 Stilicho, *magister militum*, and his wife Serena (the niece of Emperor Theodosius I), and his son Eucherius

Introduction

Rosamond McKitterick

When the poet of the Paderborn epic in 799 referred to Charlemagne as the *pater Europae*, father of Europe, he gave an ancient classical name to a new Christian territory, embodied, for the poet at least, in the rule and realm of the Frankish ruler. In this volume we have elected to take the long view of historical developments within an even greater geographical extent than the European kingdoms over which Charlemagne ruled. The definition of Europe between 400 and 1000 is ambiguous. In many ways it was coterminous with Latin Christendom. But Latin Christian Europe was dynamic, polymorphous, and constantly expanding and thus does not fit neatly for long into any one political mould. Further, westerners knew of the existence to the east of another, well-established, form of Christian order. As we shall see, Latin Christendom had moreover crucial contacts with other areas, themselves affected by, or affecting, western European civilization. These include Scandinavia, the Celtic areas of western Britain and Ireland, the Slavic regions of the Balkans and eastern Europe, the Islamic Middle East and North Africa, and Byzantium. A sense of a shared 'Roman' imperial past and a common Christian religion did not create an integrated Europe in any political or ecclesiastical sense, but the forces straddling, if not binding together, this politico-cultural magnetic field were strong. We shall follow the particular themes of this Short Oxford History, namely, politics, society, economy, religion, culture, and links with the wider world, through the entire period with the appropriate geographical diversity and a comparative element between the earlier and later parts of the period. Unlike the other volumes in this series, we have integrated military matters and warfare, which were so entrenched in social and political structures in this period, into the chapters on politics, economics, and society where they can be discussed in context. We have added a separate chapter on religion, for the institutional foundations of the Christian church, as well as the crucial developments in faith and ritual and the definition of relations with other religions to be observed in Europe subsequently, were established in this period. This is not, therefore, a narrative history but a set of thematic interpretations. In this introduction, however, I provide, after a discussion of modern historiographical debates and the original sources, a brief narrative of the principal developments within Europe between 400 and 1000. The reader is also directed to the detailed chronological table and the guide to further reading at the end of this book.

Context

The period between c.400 and c.1000 has been seen in the past as a transitional period, overly Franco-Germano-centric in emphasis, between the supposedly coherent world of the Roman empire and its provinces and the disparate world of medieval Europe, where local differences assumed far greater significance. More recent perspectives, however, stress two things. First, there is the great diversity of the Roman world of late antiquity. Secondly, a strong coherence was lent to the successor states of early medieval Europe by the institutional religion of Latin Christianity and a rich but distinctive blend of classical, Christian, and non-Roman culture. Major issues for this period remain the collapse of the western Roman empire in the fifth century; its replacement by Germanic political and military elites, the unification and expansion of the Frankish kingdoms and their ultimate reintegration (largely via cadet lines and marriage) into the local aristocratic power-bases in the tenth-century successor states within the areas we now label Germany, France, Benelux, Switzerland, Austria, and Italy. Nevertheless, the relationship between central power and the localities in the lands west and east of the Rhine, and the sheer variety of polities across Europe warn us that the old simplistic understanding, governed by developments in what became France and Germany, is inadequate.

This volume takes into account, therefore, the diversity of Ireland;

the gradual unification of the English kingdom in the tenth century; the small Christian kingdoms of northern Spain; the emergence of kingdoms such as Denmark, Norway, Poland, Hungary, Croatia, Bulgaria, the Kievan Rus, and Bohemia and their adoption and exploitation of Christianity; the complexities of Byzantine politics throughout the period; and the strength of the maritime communities based around the Mediterranean, Irish, Baltic, and North Seas. Dominant themes of this period, which the subsequent chapters will explore in detail, are the continuity and discontinuity with the Roman world and the ways these can be examined. A major preoccupation for much of this period is the degree to which a particular culture or society (in this case, Rome) as observed in its forms of government, ideologies of rulership, social organization, and intellectual and cultural preoccupations, can provide such an overwhelmingly powerful model that societies with which it came into contact (in this case, the barbarian successor states of western Europe) sought consciously to emulate it. The strength of the Roman heritage in many different contexts and the degrees of continuity and discontinuity with the Roman world need to be explored further. How and why have historians perceived this period in the shadow of Rome? Why has the earlier period in particular been seen in such stark terms of cultures in conflict? Why was the traditional picture one of a civilized Roman empire overrun by barbarian tribes?

Yet anyone writing the history of western Europe in a six-hundred-year period must also be concerned with unconscious emulation and assimilation, continuities as well as discontinuities, selection and rejection, and new influences. How can the barbarian successor kingdoms and their peoples be defined? How can notions of identity and self-consciousness be identified? These questions are considered in the context of the broad areas of political development, social groups, the economy, religion, intellectual traditions, and cultural developments. Many themes within these broad categories, such as literacy, memory and orality, the role of women and gender, the working of law and justice, perceptions and representations of the past, belief and its expression, or ethnicity and identity are of crucial importance. How can we document the cultures of power at central and local levels, the role of courts, lordship, kingship, 'queenship', and the family? Further questions arise concerning the modern perception of the later part of the period as dominated by the Carolingians. What is the legacy of the whole period between 400 and 1000 for the political, social, economic, and cultural development of Europe as a whole? What are the consequences of the expansion of Europe to the north and east and with whom did the peoples of Europe come into contact? Further, given the preoccupation with the year 1000 in relation to interpretations of the history of medieval Europe, and common notions of periodization, it is necessary to consider the validity of the year 1000 as a dividing line of any kind in the 'formation of Europe'.

Evidence

How does one fit together an interpretation of the history of this period that makes sense in terms of the surviving evidence? What questions are appropriate to that evidence? Although the surviving sources are not nearly so abundant as for more modern periods, to focus on the relative paucity of bureaucratic remains or the lack of personal details about so many men and women of this period is to miss the point. There is still a remarkable quantity and variety of evidence, from the scruffiest potsherd and remains of a rural settlement to gold crowns and ruins of a palace complex, and from a scrap of a local legal document, recording the transfer of a small field by a devout farmer to a local monastery, to the massive output of royal chanceries, letters, sophisticated treatises on images and doctrine, narrative histories, and universal encyclopaedias. As for any period of history, we are dependent to a considerable degree on chance and random selection for the survival of our evidence. Excavation by the French antiquarian Chifflet uncovered the rich grave of Childeric, father of Clovis, the first king of the Franks, in 1653. His drawings, and a few items missed by the thieves who broke into the palace of the Louvre in 1831 and stole all the gold, are all we now have to tell us of the political status of Childeric in northern Gaul at the end of the fifth century. The correspondence between the first three Carolingian rulers and the popes in Rome in the second half of the eighth century depends on one late ninth-century manuscript copied at Cologne and now in the Österreichische Nationalbibliothek. Confirmation of the mint at Quentovic (near Rouen) for the so-called imperial coinage of Charlemagne exists in the unique specimen portraying the ruler as a Roman emperor and a ship with a bird at the masthead, now in the Fitzwilliam Museum in Cambridge. Allied bombs in 1944 exposed the grave of a young Merovingian prince underneath the late medieval Cologne cathedral. Finds of building structures and tools from the Viking period found at L'Anse aux Meadows in Newfoundland have confirmed thirteenth-century stories that the Vikings had discovered America by about 1000. New material continues to come to light. Thus, the current 'millennium' excavations in the Nerva Forum in Rome have uncovered a fine early ninth-century town house. The vast ninth-century monastic complex at San Vincenzo al Volturno in central Italy has been steadily revealed by archaeologists over the past twenty years.

Other categories, such as documents recording legal transactions, the deliberations of legal assemblies, books, letters, and historical narratives, were deliberately preserved in an effort to make lasting records. Wherever the institutions in which these records were deposited have survived undisturbed, as at the monastery of St Gallen in Switzerland, so too have the documents. At St Gallen, over eight hundred charters, that is, single-sheet documents recording legal transactions from the eighth to the tenth centuries, are preserved in their original form. Similarly, St Gallen's library still houses the books produced by the monks of St Gallen in the early middle ages. Archives such as those of Saint-Denis, Fulda, Lorsch, Canterbury, and Farfa have similarly preserved a range of documentation of crucial importance for high politics as well as for the history of local society. Yet the selections made from historical records by subsequent generations and decisions made by contemporaries in, say, the eleventh and twelfth centuries, mean that much was also deliberately cast into oblivion. Thus, the historian of this period is as much concerned with what has or may have been destroyed and forgotten as with what is still remembered. Still other texts and objects, such as letters, jewellery, graves, contributions to political and intellectual debates, the written inventories of an estate's resources known as polyptychs, poems, and weapons, were designed for contemporaries but have become rich veins of material for modern historians of this period. As a matter of course, early medievalists have become accustomed to tackling a wide variety of material and written evidence for the light it may shed on the past.

The survival to the present day of these sources is similarly dependent as much on chance as on deliberate conservation. Modern historians of late antiquity and the middle ages owe an enormous debt, for example, to the antiquarians and curiosity hunters of the early modern period who gathered objects and recorded the appearance of artefacts and buildings. Further, scholars since the Renaissance have searched for and printed many texts from manuscripts they discovered. Men such as Poggio Bracciolini and his colleagues in the Renaissance, and Jean Mabillon, Humphrey Wanley, Ludovico Muratori, and Etienne Baluze in the seventeenth and eighteenth centuries, developed scholarly methods for the categorization, dating, and authentification of the sources on which we are still thoroughly dependent. Indeed, some of the editions of texts we still use are those made in the seventeenth and eighteenth centuries. Many of these were reprinted in an astonishing enterprise in Paris in the middle of the nineteenth century known as the Ateliers Catholiques. This book factory was run by the Abbé Migne and produced the *Patrologia Latina* and *Patrologia Graeca*. Migne's printers set older editions in close-packed, double-columned reprints from stereotypes on steam-driven presses. The story goes that the printing was done by a motley group of proscribed priests, petty criminals, and vagrants kept off the streets, all on minimal wages, and that the Ateliers were under constant police surveillance. One of the other most important and indispensable repositories of historical texts for the early middle ages is the series of publications of the Monumenta Germaniae Historica. The MGH was founded in 1819 (and is still active) in order to produce new scholarly editions of the texts relating to the medieval history of 'Germany', a region so generously defined as to embrace the whole of Latin Christian Europe from Ireland to Hungary and Poland.

National enterprises for the preservation of historical sources in libraries and in scholarly editions were, of course, linked with nationalistic wishes to record the past of a particular region and to foster the political as well as the historical identity of the people of that region. This was as true of the so-called 'national' histories written in the early middle ages as of the use made of the medieval past by many subsequent generations. One has only to think of François Hotman's *Francogallia* (1573), which attempted to prove the derivation from Frankish tradition of the consultative assembly and the dependence of the king upon his people, or the cult of King Alfred by the Victorians. Twentieth-century examples also spring to mind, such as the

Council of Europe exhibition on Charlemagne, planned in the aftermath of the Second World War and the beginnings of the European
Community and finally staged in 1965; the anniversary celebration of
the conversion of the Rus in 1988; the extraordinary circumstances
surrounding the papal visit to France in 1996 to celebrate the 1500th
anniversary of the baptism of Clovis, first Christian king of the
Franks; the Paderborn exhibition of 1999 to celebrate the meeting
there between Charlemagne and Pope Leo III in 799; and the Council
of Europe exhibition on Otto the Great planned in Magdeburg for
2001. All these reflect the varied propagandistic, celebratory, political,
and academic exploitation of the early medieval past. Yet underlying
many of these commemorations remains the sense of a common
cultural and political inheritance across Europe and the imperative
need for all of us in the modern world to understand it fully.

All categories of sources, moreover, present images of their own
societies in a variety of media—art, buildings, coins, religious symbols, political tracts, historiography, law, and a plethora of other
kinds of text—which it is for modern readers to analyse. One striking
feature of the early middle ages is the extent to which knowledge and
subsequent discussion of the barbarian kingdoms of early medieval
Europe have been shaped by the narrative histories written in these
kingdoms one or two centuries after their establishment. Once
labelled 'national' histories, these narratives provide, in their different
ways, a long and distinctive past for a particular people. They played a
crucial role in defining that people's identity both at the time they
were written and subsequently. In the eyes of modern historians these
texts mirror the process of ethnogenesis, that is, the construction and
metamorphosis of political or professional groups into ethnic groups
and the birth of a 'people'. The early medieval narratives also proposed a special perspective for the peoples about whom they wrote,
quite apart from the selection of events and personalities on which
attention has been concentrated ever since. Gregory of Tours (d. 594),
for example, writing in Gaul in the later sixth century, started his
vigorous narrative with the Creation, Adam and Eve, and a selective
account of Old Testament history and the early Christian church
before he chronicled the violent deeds of the Frankish kings and
bishops of Gaul.

Gregory does so very cleverly and thereby makes the Franks the
new Chosen People in a direct line from the Children of Israel. By

contrast, Jordanes the Goth (d. 552), and the Lombard Paul the Deacon (d. 799) from northern Italy provide accounts of the Goths and the Lombards which stress the ancient Germanic origins of the people. Bede (d. 735) in his *Ecclesiastical History of the English People* emphasizes above all the Christianity of the English and their kings and the church's connections with Rome. The narrators of Frankish history in the eighth, ninth, and tenth centuries similarly focus on the identity and triumphs of the Christian Franks. The histories written in England and Germany in the later ninth and the tenth centuries celebrate the emergence of strong united kingdoms under the kings of the house of Wessex and of the 'Ottonian' or Saxon rulers, respectively.

All these writers, drawing on oral and written tradition and social memory, constructed an immensely influential and powerful image of their society and its events. They created what can be recognized as attempts to establish an agreed version of their pasts. Anyone studying the early middle ages, therefore, has to exploit all other available sources in order to provide a counterweight to the extent to which the narrative sources have set the agenda for our understanding of the past they portray.

To a great degree, moreover, the extant sources are primarily those of the social elites, though local charter evidence and the material evidence permits some indication of people in the lower strata of society. It is important not to underestimate the authority of the written word and the levels of pragmatic literacy in the various kingdoms of western Europe. Texts had many practical uses as well as symbolic force in early medieval Europe. Old assumptions about literacy being the preserve of a small clerical elite simply do not accord with the great variety of uses of literacy that have now been identified in the material surviving from the early middle ages. Patterns of literacy in the Roman world persisted side by side with new ways of exploiting writing in the Germanic kingdoms. The strongly textual culture of the early middle ages provided secure foundations for the subsequent further expansion of literacy in the later middle ages. Nevertheless, what survives is a predominantly, though not exclusively, elite perspective of the course of events in early medieval Europe. Literate skills were concentrated in the leading lay and clerical groups. Although ecclesiastical institutions have been best able to preserve records of the past, moreover, it is by no means the case that all our material is from clerical writers or clerical sources. The growing recognition of the sheer volume of material relating to secular society as well as the degree to which lay and clerical interests and activities were intertwined is something which is stressed and elaborated in every chapter in this book.

The majority of the extant written sources for the period are in Latin. In the areas once part of the Roman empire, Latin was effectively the vernacular and it gradually evolved into the various Romance languages of western Europe. There were also the vernaculars such as Irish, Old English, Old Norse, Frisian, Old Saxon, Old High German, Hebrew, and the Slav languages, and in the east a host more such as Greek, Coptic, Arabic, Syriac, Armenian, and Aramaic. Apart from Arabic Spain, Latin, whether as first or second language of the people, was the language of liturgy, learning, and the law in the west (though in Ireland, Scandinavia, and England the laws were in the vernacular). This created coherence and an ease of communication across political boundaries, just as the Christian religion, itself a remarkable amalgamation of different traditions, helped to forge a common culture.

Inevitably there can be dispute about how to interpret particular texts or objects. So too, it is difficult to gauge the influence the time and place of production or the author's or craftsman's intentions may have had on the information a text or object purports to contain. We offer our particular interpretations of the evidence with emphases and details on which we are agreed, but we wish to stress that it would be unrealistic to expect a comprehensive treatment of the period. The fine line between a coherent account which omits some things and a jumble of information is one we have tried not to cross. What we have tried to convey is a sense of the principal developments and the complexities and excitements of this period, and some of the new interpretations of it.

Events

The remaining task of this introduction is to provide the basic chronological framework for the period *c.*400–*c.*1000.

To write the history of the period between the fourth and sixth centuries and of the 'fall of the Roman empire' and the 'barbarian invasions' was once a simple matter. The sack of Rome by Alaric and his Goths in 410, luridly described in far-off Palestine by Jerome, who cribbed his details from the biblical account of the sack of Jerusalem, could be taken as the leitmotif for barbarian behaviour. The deposition of Romulus Augustulus, the 'last emperor in the west', in 476 could be taken as a neat break. It was not difficult to add in concepts of decline and decadence (encouraged by some contemporary and localized ecclesiastical comment) and emotional rhetoric about the ravening barbarian hordes pouring out of the Germanic forests across the Rhine and Danube, destroying Roman civilization as they came. The notion of a Dark Age that descended upon Europe proved very resilient and perversely attractive. But, of course, it was not as simple as that.

The establishment of the early barbarian kingdoms

The growing strength of the Huns in the region north of the Black Sea in the late fourth century appears to have encouraged, if not forced, other groups, identified in Roman sources as the Vandals, Sueves, Alans, and Goths, to advance into Roman territory. In the east, the Goths, for example, were permitted by the Roman authorities to cross the Danube and settle in Thrace in 376. In rebellion against their dreadful living conditions, they inflicted a heavy defeat on the Romans at Adrianople in 378. Thereafter they were established as federates (supporting defensive troops for the Romans).

This federate arrangement and the use of tribal groups either as mercenaries or as regular sections of the Roman army were in fact the commonest forms of relations between the Roman authorities and the 'barbarians'. The word 'barbarian' itself originally simply meant a non-Greek speaker, a man who could only make the sound 'ba-ba'. It came to mean non-Latin speaker, non-Roman or foreign. In the extensive frontier regions, moreover, and most particularly in the Rhine and Danube areas, daily contact between the Roman garrisons and their supporting networks of administration involved the peoples settled in the area and thus ensured a steady interchange.

This was enriched by the supply of provisions, gear, tools, news, building materials, luxuries, and livestock. Recent studies and the increasingly abundant archaeological evidence have emphasized the mixed nature of the societies in these frontier zones.

Similarly, in the west, Sueves, Alans, Burgundians, and Franks appear to have crossed the Rhine by the beginning of the fifth century (groups and individuals had done so for more than a century earlier) and it seems likely that most were settled under federate troop arrangements within the Roman provinces of Gaul, Germany, and Spain. It was also as invited troops that Alaric and his Visigoths first assisted Stilicho, then commander-in-chief of the western Roman army and related by marriage to the emperor Theodosius II, in a campaign in Illyricum. But the campaign was called off, and pleas by Alaric to be paid fell on deaf ears. Only after a series of fruitless negotiations to secure payment for his army, did Alaric finally sack Rome in 410 and leave Italy to seek employment for his warriors elsewhere. Eventually the Visigoths, after a brief period of fighting for the Romans in Spain, were established in south-west Gaul in 418 by the praetorian prefect. In due course they expanded over the area south of the Loire and took over the rulership of the whole region. The Vandals, on the other hand, invaded North Africa and by 450 had established control and captured most of the coastal provinces, including Carthage. The Huns in the meantime, famous for their ferocity in battle and under the leadership of Attila, attacked both the eastern and the western empires. Attila was decisively beaten by the Roman troops on the Catalaunian plains in 451 and died of a violent nosebleed soon afterwards. Hunnic power dwindled rapidly thereafter.

In the course of the fifth century the political life and administrative arrangements of the western (Latin) empire and eastern (Greek) empire were increasingly divided, and the central control of the western emperor became less effective. This process was assisted by the apparent lack of interest on the part of the emperor in the affairs of the various western provinces. The Emperor Honorius, for example, failed to replace the legions withdrawn from Britain early in the fifth century. There is a particularly marked diminution of contact and interest maintained between Italy, on the one hand, and Gaul and Spain, on the other, from the middle of the fifth century onwards. So dissatisfied with the situation were the people in southern Gaul indeed, that in the 450s the Visigothic military rulers and members of the Gallo-Roman senatorial aristocracy joined forces to elevate the Gallo-Roman Avitus to the imperial throne. Within Italy itself the rapid succession of emperors, who with few exceptions were but the puppets of factions, enabled the commanders-in-chief of the Roman armies, many of whom were, more often than not, themselves of barbarian origin (such as Stilicho, Ricimer, or Odoacer) to become de facto rulers.

In Italy, Odoacer's assumption of control and deposition of the 16-year-old emperor Romulus Augustulus in 476 was simply one of a succession of political coups and interregna. Despite the existence of another western emperor, Julius Nepos, who took refuge in Dalmatia and did not die until 480, Odoacer simply ruled as 'king' in Italy in the name of the eastern emperor, Zeno. Theodoric the Ostrogoth invaded Italy at the request of Zeno, got rid of Odoacer by treacherously inviting him to dinner to discuss terms and then murdering him, and took control in 493. His rule as king of the Goths and Romans in Italy was recognized by the eastern emperor Anastasius, Zeno's successor. Theodoric ruled the peoples of Italy peacefully for the next thirty years, though the three decades after his death saw the violent efforts of the Byzantines to reconquer Italy. The Gothic wars of the first half of the sixth century enabled the Lombards, another Germanic group from Pannonia (roughly equivalent to present-day Hungary) who had originally served as mercenaries for the Byzantine armies in Italy, to invade and settle in the Po plain and set up their own northern kingdom based at Pavia, but with duchies in Spoleto and Benevento in central Italy as well. The Byzantines retained control of the north-east portion around Ravenna until the eighth century and also of the southern tip of Italy until well into the tenth century. The pope had his own small territory of the 'Republic of St Peter' around Rome and by the later eighth century had succeeded in casting off even any lingering or nominal deference to Byzantium.

In southern Gaul the Visigoths who had assumed complete control in the south, once the central authority of the western Roman empire ceased to exist, were ousted in 507 by the Franks from the north. From the second decade of the sixth century, therefore, the Visigoths ruled only in Spain over a mixed population of Hispano-Romans and Visigoths until defeated in their turn by the Arabs and Berbers in 711.

Some of the Visigothic ruling elites were able to retreat to found the northern Christian kingdoms of Spain. It was from Leon and Castile, centuries later, that the Reconquista started, culminating with the expulsion of the Arabs from Spain in 1492.

In northern Gaul the Franks under the Merovingian rulers—Clovis, his sons, and grandsons—in the sixth century systematically expanded their territory by military conquest of Visigothic Aquitaine and Provence, of the Burgundian kingdoms, and of the Rhineland Frankish kingdoms. In partnership with the Gallo-Roman aristocracy and the episcopate, they created a strong polity securely based on the foundations of the Roman provincial administration they had taken over. Even within Gaul, however, some areas such as Brittany, Bavaria, Frisia, Rhaetia, and the territories of the Alemans (in what is now southern Germany and Switzerland) remained independent, though it was a Frankish family, the Agilolfings, who appear to have established their rule in Bavaria. There are indications that in England at least Kent, among the new territorial kingdoms based on various Anglian and Saxon tribal units, was in some way subservient to the Merovingian kings. Certainly links between Frankish Gaul and England were strong, particularly in the spheres of trade and the work of the church, as they were with Ireland.

In all these emergent kingdoms of western Europe the local reactions to the political shock of the demise of the western emperor were very different. But in no case was there a brutal and immediate imposition of an alien political system on a conquered people. To a considerable degree the incoming Franks, Vandals, Visigoths, Sueves, Burgundians, Ostrogoths, Lombards, and the like had intermarried with and adopted the language and mores, institutions, and culture of the people among whom they had settled, often long before the end of the fifth century. Although many of the Germanic peoples were Arian rather than Catholic Christians, and had been Christian, moreover, before they settled within the empire, most accepted orthodox Christianity in due course. No doubt the strongly entrenched Catholic ecclesiastical hierarchies of the former Roman provinces exerted considerable pressure on them to do so. Assimilation and transformation were very gradual processes. Many Roman traditions and institutions also disappeared or simply became redundant in the process, not least the arenas and amphitheatres for the circuses and games once supported by the state and municipal authorities.

It is all very well to speak of settlement, transformation, and the like, but where did the notion of invasion, coupled with the violent destruction of the western Roman empire, originate? In part it is due to contemporary observers, recording local short-term crises, dramatic takeovers, and upheaval. Commanders were changed; the rulers were replaced. The military elites, full of those identified as non-Romans and foreign troops, played a major role. Some, such as the Vandal regime in Northern Africa, were decidedly aggressive towards the Catholic Romans in their midst. Elsewhere the picture is more complicated. Occasionally we get a glimpse of what it was like to see the world ostensibly change before one's eyes. Sidonius Apollinaris (d. 479x486) in Gaul, for example, speaks of the often conciliatory policies adopted by his Roman contemporaries in terms of containing the power of the Visigoths. But of Euric (d. 484), the Visigothic ruler, he says that the king may in fact be able to 'protect the dwindled Tiber', that is, help to conserve the trappings of Roman civilization prized by Sidonius and his contemporaries. In Italy, Romulus Augustulus' deposition was not a signal for anarchy. Rather Odoacer and Theodoric both continued the pattern of Roman government and bureaucracy. In northern Gaul, Childeric, father of Clovis, appears to have acted as military governor of a Roman province and Clovis succeeded to his father's power in 481, ruling Romans and Franks and supported by Remigius, archbishop of Rheims and his ecclesiastical colleagues.

Major physical upheaval was rare, as distinct from the beginnings of slow but ultimately radical changes in society and political organization, as we shall see in subsequent chapters. In Italy, the real disruption, as it was to a lesser extent in Spain and Africa, was not the Vandals or Goths but the Byzantine reconquest. Yet as it turned out, Byzantium was unable to consolidate its conquests. Byzantine rule was replaced, in North Africa and Spain at least, by the Arabs. The picture of forceful barbarian invasion in the fifth century may have been influenced by some Byzantine historians of the sixth century, overanxious to justify Justinian's wars of reconquest in the western empire. In the archaeological record it is primarily in association with the Byzantine wars of reconquest that layers of destruction are to be observed.

Byzantium

The crisis for the Byzantine empire came in the seventh century, with the long war against the Persians and then, in 636–642, the conquest by the Arabs of two-thirds of the lands of the empire and probably three-quarters of its wealth. Byzantium was left with the Aegean Sea, and the Anatolian plateau to its east, which was both poor and exposed to Arab raiding. Most of the Balkans, too, was temporarily lost in this period to the Slavs. This was retraction on a massive scale. Everything had to be refigured as a result. The Arab conquests eventually effected far more of a transformation in the east than the earlier settlements of Germanic peoples within the Roman empire had effected in the west. It is also important to remember that Arab presence made itself felt in the west, most crucially in the Spanish peninsula and the establishment there of Arab rule after 711, but also in the small colonies, trading settlements, and pirate camps scattered throughout the Mediterranean, especially in Sicily, southern Italy, Corsica, and Sardinia.

As a result of never ceasing to tax, Constantinople remained rich and populous, and money was available to fund the extensive civilian bureaucracy there; but the army, too, remained partly salaried, and imperial hegemony over its structures was correspondingly far greater. The Byzantines maintained territorial armies, with precisely delimited geographical remits, whose structure was quite unlike the armed aristocratic clienteles of the west. Consequently, political practice was different. Even after 700, the major dangers to emperors were coups by bureaucratic or military factions, in a classic Roman tradition rather than the decentralization and potential break-up of the contemporary Carolingian world. The mystique of the Byzantine imperial court, increasingly elaborated under such emperors as Justinian, Heraclius, or Basil I, helps to account for this cohesiveness in the absence of particularly abundant Byzantine economic or military resources. Indeed, regional separatism was barely a problem for the Byzantines at all until long after 1000, if we except some of the seventh- and eighth-century outposts of the empire in Italy such as Rome, Naples, and Venice, which did slip out of Constantinople's control. It is also probable that the coherence of imperial power, and the relative unimportance of military elites, was maintained for a long time in the lands nearest the capital, in the northern Aegean and in what is now north-west Turkey, which were also among the richest parts of Byzantium. The parts of the empire most like the west, Anatolia and (later) the Balkans, were also the most marginal and the poorest.

The emergence of the Carolingians

The period from the seventh century to the beginning of the eleventh century in western Europe is dominated by the Frankish expansion within Europe led by the Carolingian family and their successors. The leading males of the Carolingian family had succeeded in monopolizing the senior position of mayor of the palace in Austrasia (the eastern part of the Merovingian kingdom in the lower Rhine, Moselle, and Meuse regions) by the end of the seventh century. A judicious series of marriages enhanced their personal wealth and they gradually extended their power and influence over Neustria, that is, the area between the Seine and the Loire, and Burgundy (the upper Rhône and Saône river valleys and western present-day Switzerland).

The steady series of Frankish conquests led by the Carolingian rulers Charles Martel, Pippin III, and Charlemagne in the course of the eighth century, during which Alemannia, Frisia, Aquitaine, the Lombard kingdom of northern Italy, Septimania, Bavaria, Saxony, and Brittany were added to the Frankish heartlands in Gaul, created a vast empire. Expansion ceased for a time from about 803, with military strategies thereafter concentrated on defence and consolidation. With the Treaty of Verdun in 843, the territory was divided into separate kingdoms for the benefit of Charlemagne's grandsons, but the empire remained under the various members of one family.

The consolidation of Carolingian strength and creation of solidarity among the elite within the kingdom was made possible by the warrior leadership the Carolingian rulers offered. They rallied Frankish forces against outside threats such as those offered by the Frisians, Saxons, Avars, and Arabs in the eighth century, and by the Vikings and Magyars in the ninth and tenth centuries. Although such raids and incursions considerably disrupted the political life of the different regions of the empire, they had little lasting impact on it as a territorial or cultural entity. The spread of Carolingian education and culture (see below, Chapter 5), the foundation of new bishoprics and new monasteries, and the creation of Frankish and Christian frameworks for social and political life were important and enduring achievements. The personnel of these bishoprics and monasteries as well as the leading lay magnates played a crucial role in the kingdom, both in their own institutions and in the assemblies convened by the ruler.

As a political system, the Carolingian empire is a conscious emulation of the Roman past, not least because it re-created within its boundaries much of the old former territory of the western Roman empire itself. It was the late Roman Christian empire above all, and in particular the Christian emperors Constantine and Theodosius, who provided the strongest inspiration for the Frankish rulers. Such inspiration is reflected visibly, moreover, in the physical structures of many Carolingian church buildings such as the palace chapel at Aachen modelled on the church of San Vitale in Ravenna. Other churches emulated the great fourth- and fifth-century basilicas of Rome.

The protection of the papacy, moreover, became an increasingly urgent task. In 754, the Carolingian king, Pippin III, had become the protector of the Holy See. This was a role that enhanced both the king's prestige and, in his family's eyes at least, his legitimacy. The relationship culminated in the crowning of Charlemagne as emperor by Pope Leo III in Rome on Christmas Day 800. It was an office which carried with it the rulership of northern Italy and protection of Rome. Until well into the tenth century, one of the Carolingian rulers held the title of emperor and he was at least nominally the superior of his brothers, cousins, and nephews. The imperial coronation was thus of great symbolic significance with real if limited practical effect, even though when first conferred in 800 it had seemed simply an extra title redolent of the strong Roman heritage of the Franks. Certainly as far as Charlemagne was concerned it made no difference to his actual power. Nevertheless the relationship thus created between the western rulers and the papacy was to have ramifications and repercussions throughout the middle ages, particularly once the papacy started to develop the implications of the papal office and papal authority and ideology vis-à-vis secular power from the 1050s onwards.

The tenth century

In the tenth century the political and economic contacts between the Scandinavian and Slavic peoples and the older established kingdoms of western Europe, Britain, and the eastern Mediterranean intensified. Viking adventurers established farming communities and trading centres in Russia at Staraia Ladoga, Kiev, and Novgorod and far across the north Atlantic in Iceland, Greenland, Newfoundland as well as north of Britain in the Orkneys, Shetlands, Hebrides, and on the Isle of Man, in Ireland, northern and eastern England, and western France in what became Normandy. The peoples to the north, east, and south of the Frankish kingdoms, notably the Obodrites, Sorbs, Moravians, Bohemians, Poles, Bulgars, Slovenes, and Magyars interacted with their Frankish and Byzantine neighbours in both the political and ecclesiastical spheres, with support sought or imposed for particular contenders for political leadership or the infiltration of Christian missionaries. It was, indeed, primarily in their rivalry over the exertion of influence in the Slavic regions that the west European kingdoms and the Byzantine empire had the most contact.

The Carolingian empire was divided into many smaller kingdoms and duchies. New kingdoms such as those of Burgundy, Poland, Hungary, Croatia, Bulgaria, quite apart from those of Denmark, Norway, Scotland, Wales and Ireland, and the Venetian Republic, had emerged by the end of the tenth century. The Ottonian rulers in Germany built a new empire which stretched from the Baltic to the Mediterranean and Otto I emulated Charlemagne in being crowned emperor in Rome in 962. The new Capetian dynasty in France which replaced the Carolingian family in 987 ruled over a disparate set of semi-autonomous territorial principalities. Yet many ties, symbolic and real (not least those of marriage among the ruling elites), continued to bond the whole together, most notably in those territories which had once been part of the Carolingian polity. The achievement and legend of Charlemagne himself proved powerful inspirations for his many successors.

Figure 3 Charles the Bald, king of the west Franks (840–877), enthroned

1

Politics

Rosamond McKitterick

The politics of Europe in the early middle ages have rarely been considered as a whole. Rather, separate considerations of the many regions of Europe, on the one hand, and on the other, a predominantly franco-centric perspective from which generalizations have been made, have tended to influence interpretations and understanding of political developments overall. Only a systematic and detailed comparison of the various polities of western Europe could determine how valid generalizations about the politics of medieval Europe might be. This would be far beyond the remit of this chapter. An attempt needs to be made, nevertheless, to analyse the political structures, behaviour, and ideologies of western Europe in this six-hundred-year period. I shall do so in terms of political control and cultures of power, and determine what these polities had in common as well as the many changes over time.

Above all, the very particular political and social emphases of this period need to be seen, first, in the context of the gradual transformation of the Roman world in the earlier part of the period. Secondly, from the eighth century onwards, the exercise of political authority by the Franks was determined both by their conquests and expansion east and north into areas which had not been part of the Roman empire and by the incorporation of new peoples to be governed. The limits of the Frankish kingdoms of the Carolingian rulers in the north and east were virtually also those of Latin Christianity for the later third of this period. In the west and south, however, there are also the Christian kingdoms of Britain, Ireland, Benevento, and northern Spain to be considered. Further, there are the areas where Latin and Greek Christianity each tried to exert an influence, such as Moravia and Bulgaria. In the Ottonian period of the later tenth century, moreover, there was a further expansion of Latin Christendom into Scandinavia, Poland, and Hungary, while the Kievan Rus were converted to Christianity from Byzantium. The extent of the Frankish realm certainly contributed substantially to the configuration of later medieval Europe and to the orientations of its politics. Yet it is important to note that the Frankish frontiers were inherited from those the Carolingian rulers subjected to Frankish rule rather than being the outcome of deliberate strategic choice. In other words, the Franks adapted to existing configurations even if we cannot now reconstruct these with any precision.

The Frankish empire at its height stretched from Brittany to Carinthia, from the Pyrenees and northern Italy to the North Sea and the Baltic. It comprised many different people. Thus, relations between the centre and these (from a Frankish perspective) peripheral regions are of central importance for our understanding of government from the eighth century onwards. The frontiers remained regions of interchange and channels of communication for military leaders and local officials, merchants, pilgrims, and the local populations, just as they had been in the Roman empire. Nevertheless, the peoples on the peripheries of the Frankish realms in their turn had independent relations with the peoples to their north, south, west, and east. Expansion of territory and the consolidation of political control also brought new contacts and required new efforts within the peripheral regions to maintain peace and stability. The narrative sources in particular are full of accounts of embassies and special meetings to arrange truces or conclude peace between warring bands. Of the consummate skill with which early medieval rulers conducted relations with their neighbours (the Byzantine rulers are the best documented), and the degree to which there were formal protocols and 'intelligence' brought to bear on 'foreign relations', we can occasionally gain glimpses in the archaeological and literary records of the period.[1]

Beyond the Frankish sphere of control but still in interaction of some kind with it were Scandinavia, the British Isles, Moorish Spain, the papacy, Byzantium, the Balkans, and eastern Europe. Due both to the enormous area under Frankish jurisdiction in the ninth century, and to the contacts with their neighbouring polities, Frankish influences in both the practice and the ideology of ruling are as

---

[1] See Chapter 6.

crucial an element of the political formation of Europe as the Roman legacy. Indeed, the emergence of particular rulers and styles of rulership that we can see in such regions as Croatia or Denmark in the ninth and tenth centuries was a direct outcome of contact with the Franks.

Late Roman political structures

The *Notitia Dignitatum*, a 'list of all ranks and administrative positions both civil and military' describes, rather unsystematically, the elaborate administrative structures of the Roman empire at the end of the fourth century and thus the beginning of the period covered in this book. Such was the extent of the empire, that 'delegation was an inescapable corollary of autocracy'.[2] So, possibly, was corruption. The civil administration of the empire was divided into provinces, each administered by a governor. His responsibility embraced local affairs of finance, justice, and administration. A province was divided into dioceses supervised by a *vicarius*. The dioceses themselves were grouped into four huge prefectures, each one under a powerful civil official called the praetorian prefect. Each had overall responsibility for the administration of the empire in Gaul (including Britain and Spain), Italy (including Africa), Illyricum (the Balkan region), and the east, respectively. All these officials were served by hierarchies of bureaucrats dependent on extensive written communications and records for the documentation of their work. Yet the career of a military general such as Aetius, equally renowned for his negotiations with the Burgundians and Goths and for his defeat of Attila the Hun on the Catalaunian plains in 451, is an indication of how the military leadership within a province or prefecture could overlie, or be combined with, its civil counterpart. This was perhaps to be expected in a system in which the emperor himself, more often than not, emerged from the ranks of the army and where the commander-in-chief of the Roman army was the principal support for the emperor's position, notably in the fifth century in the west.

<hr>

[2] C. Kelly, 'Empire building', in G. Bowersock, P. Brown, and O. Grabar (eds.) *Late Antiquity: A Guide to the Postclassical World* (Cambridge, Mass., and London, 1999), pp. 170–95, at p. 176.

There was also a close relationship between war and political power. Internal civil wars were an even greater threat to stability and imperial security than the peoples on the frontiers. Many of the peoples just beyond the empire in the frontier regions were recruited to swell the ranks of the armies of contenders for political power within the empire and many of their leaders in consequence rose to civil and military prominence within the empire. These included Stilicho the Skirian (d. 408), *magister militum* of the Roman army and nephew-in-law of the Emperor Theodosius who invited Alaric and the Goths to Illyricum to act as mercenaries on a Roman military campaign and who is allegedly buried in a magnificent tomb in the church of San Ambrogio in Milan. Gundobad, king of the Burgundians (474–518) was formerly *magister militum* of the Roman army. King Euric the Visigoth (466–484) ruled both the Goths settled by the Roman authorities in Aquitaine and the Gallo-Romans. Childeric, father of Clovis, king of the Franks (d. 481), whose sumptuous grave was uncovered at Tournai in 1653, appears to have been the provincial governor of the second Belgic province in northern Gaul at the end of the fifth century.

The early medieval kingdoms of Europe

With the demise of central Roman government, the structures of provincial government and their methods of documentation which persisted in the west, with the barbarian leaders assuming civil responsibilities, aided by Roman officials, combined with the military leadership of the war-bands. Consequently, the structures and methods of the imperial bureaucracy associated with the provincial governorship also persisted within the early barbarian kingdoms. Thus, Sidonius Apollinaris, a Gallo-Roman aristocrat living in the Auvergne, refers to the rule of the Gothic kings, Theodoric and Euric in southern Gaul, and tells us of his colleagues Leo, who 'every day in the councils of the king gathered information about the world's affairs',[3] and Syagrius who had mastered German, translated letters,

---

[3] Sidonius Apollinaris, *Poems and Letters*, ed. and trans. W. B. Anderson (London and Cambridge, Mass., 1963), II, Ep. IV. 22, p. 147.

and was 'the new Solon of the Burgundians in discussing their laws'.[4]

In the east, as will be seen below, the Roman system was also continually adapted, especially from the seventh century onwards, to accommodate the new political situation. Elsewhere, those areas which were developing outside the Roman imperial system, such as Scandinavia, the Slav lands, and Ireland had their own forms of leadership in time of war and peace, and their own methods of regulating a community's behaviour and preserving order and justice. These were no doubt effective in their own terms. By the time they are described in the written records, however, the influence of classical and Christian antiquity as mediated through the Christian church can be observed, such as the strong mark of the Old Testament on the laws and conceptions of kingship in Ireland. This makes it difficult to reconstruct the pre-Christian organization with any confidence. Further areas outside the former Roman empire are recorded in the first instance by observers from within the Romanized area who translate what they see into terms familiar to them and write, moreover, in a Latin already carrying extra connotations. Thus, Frankish references to the Slavs or Scandinavians are of limited value in constructing the political structures of these regions before the introduction of Christianity or the establishment of contacts with the rest of Europe.

Despite the enduring strength of the Roman legacy, the emergent political structures of Europe in the sixth, seventh, and eighth centuries should be understood on their own terms. It is a mistake to see the kingdoms of early medieval Europe either as a messy version of the late Roman social and political patterns or as rudimentary versions of that which existed in Europe from the eleventh century onwards.

Nevertheless, the political arrangements of the early barbarian successor states were a consequence of the peculiar circumstances of the fifth century and of the immediate aftermath of the deposition of the last Roman emperor in the west in 476. Regions that had hitherto been under Roman rule now lacked any attempt at guidance, exploitation, or control from a central government. The local populations were a mixture of people born there, military garrisons, and families originally from elsewhere in the empire who had become landowners and office-holders in the local civil and ecclesiastical

---

[4] Ibid., Ep. V. 5, p. 183.

hierarchies. Together they were left to their own devices. The precise ways in which political leaders and institutions emerged in the fifth and sixth centuries, however, is often obscure. In Britain, for example, there is little besides surmise, modern reconstructions arguing backwards from a situation from a century and more after Roman central government ceased to be effective, and from a wealth of archaeological material. The imposition of a clear structure of kingdoms in England before the eighth century was the work of historians from the eighth century onwards, who no doubt found it difficult to imagine any other political arrangements. Bede at least, however, was aware of the complexities of the existing arrangements.[5] The archaeological evidence from England indicates that small kingdoms were beginning to crystallize only from about 600 onwards.

On the Continent the evidence is more substantial and the takeover of administration and government by local elites, the army, and the army's barbarian federates and allies is clear. It was a situation in which the leaders were those who had wealth and who could rely on armed might. In the earliest written sources from the barbarian successor states these new rulers are identified as the kings of people who now occupied formerly Roman provinces and ruled over a mixed population.

There is a lack of clarity in the primary evidence and lively dispute among modern historians about the origins and identities of these peoples—Romans, 'Gallo-Romans', 'Hispano-Romans', 'Romano-Britons', Picts, Scots, Franks, Goths, Lombards, Burgundians, Sueves, Alemans, Vandals, Angles, Saxons, and so on. Such identities were not a matter of biological ethnicity but were in part constructed retrospectively, that is, invented; they are part of a process described by modern scholars as ethnogenesis. Such cultural construction is to be observed most notably in histories written from the sixth century onwards, such as Jordanes on the Goths, which narrated the origins of the different peoples. The legendary origins of the royal families provided a crucial focus. Their victories over rivals for power, won with the help of their loyal followers, on behalf of the people over whom they ruled, consolidated the sense of loyalty and political belonging. Yet law and the extent of the political power and jurisdic-

---

[5] James Campbell, 'Bede's reges et principes', Jarrow Lecture, 1979 (Jarrow, 1980) reprinted in *Essays in Anglo-Saxon History* (London, 1986), pp. 85–98.

tion of a particular ruler, as will be seen below, assisted in the process of the construction of political identities regardless of ethnic origin. In other words, in ethnogenesis we are dealing not with objectively existing 'tribes' but with identities created by texts.

Comparisons might be drawn between these early kingdoms and a commonwealth of nations, each gradually seeking independence from the old imperial, provincial, or colonial structures to which they had once been subject. Archaeological evidence cannot help in establishing identity, though what can be discerned are major changes in the lifestyle and the nature and concentration of the material evidence. Indeed, to persist in a search for old identities such as 'Roman' or 'non-Roman' at the expense of the new is like worrying about the proportion of eggs, cheese, and flour in a soufflé when eating it. Rather we should seek to understand how these groups of peoples together ordered their society.

As we might expect, their methods of government were a combination of inherited structures and procedures and innovations designed to adapt to local and immediate circumstances. Thus, the barbarian kingdoms fitted, more or less, into the former Roman administrative structures of provinces, assisted by the *civitas* divisions (that is, the administrative area of a city with its dependent territory) which were taken over by the church to define episcopal dioceses. Just as the extent of the Roman imperial administration's jurisdiction had defined the territorial limits of the empire outlined in documents such as the *Notitia Dignitatum* referred to above, so the degree of each ruler's jurisdiction defined his kingdom in the early middle ages. It is important to note, however, that the kings were generally (but not always) called kings of peoples rather than of a territory. Only gradually in the course of this period were polities defined in clear terms of territory and explicit geographical sensibility. The most striking instance, and one which set a precedent, was the division of the Frankish empire at the Treaty of Verdun in 843 between the three surviving sons of the Emperor Louis the Pious.

Louis the German got everything east of the Rhine and on [the western] side of it he got the civitates and districts of Speyer, Worms and Mainz; Lothar got the lands between the Rhine and the Scheldt where it runs into the sea, and inland by way of Cambrai, Hainault, the regions of Lomme and of Mézières and the counties which lie next to each other on the western side of the Meuse down as far as where the Saône runs into the Rhône, and down the

Rhône to where it flows into the sea, likewise with the counties situated on both sides of it. Beyond these limits, though, all he got was Arras, and that was through the generosity of his brother Charles. Charles [the Bald] himself was given everything else as far as Spain.[6]

In this case the kingdoms were defined in terms of regions in relation to major rivers, *civitates* (that is, dioceses), and counties. The division created the middle kingdom of Lotharingia, an area over which disputes were constant and not finally settled until 1945.

Small units, such as the diocese or the county (or *pagus* in the Frankish realms) were administered by officials acting for the king. Other administrative units were devised in due course, such as the ealdordoms, shires, and hundreds in England or the *themes* in Byzantium. The military element in these divisions varied. The count or his equivalent would often have judicial duties, charge of the mint and of the upkeep of roads and bridges, and the obligation to summon the army for military campaigns. Counts could be appointed to the office from elsewhere or they could be local men. Towards the tenth century there is an increasing tendency for these countships to be hereditarily vested in a particular family and to be associated also with the land held by the count. In the marcher or peripheral limits of kingdoms, especially those of the Franks, the counts of the march probably had a greater weight of responsibility for defence and relations with those outside their own rulers' jurisdiction.

The king

At the head of the administration of all the early medieval polities was the king. He was the leader of the army. He assumed responsibility for the maintenance of justice and peace. As Roman emperors had done before him, he issued legislation and did so with the agreement and advice of all his leading men. From the beginning, moreover, the king enjoyed a relationship with the church similar to that of the Roman emperors. That is, his authority came from God and he was

---

[6] *Annals of St Bertin*, ed. R. Rau, *Quellen zur karolingischen Reichsgeschichte* 2 (Darmstadt, 1972), p. 60; English trans. J. L. Nelson, *The Annals of St-Bertin* (Manchester, 1991), p. 56.

responsible for the welfare and the salvation of his people. In 589, for example,when inaugurating the change from Arian Christianity to Catholicism in his kingdom, Reccared, king of the Visigoths in Spain, affirmed, that 'Omnipotent God has given us charge of the kingdom for the profit of its peoples and has entrusted the rule of not a few peoples to our Royal care.'[7] This special responsibility became greatly enhanced under the Carolingian rulers and was transmitted to subsequent generations. A concern for the moral welfare of the subjects, correct forms of worship, thought, and devotion, and the promotion of education and learning in order to encourage right thinking and understanding of the Christian faith became essential elements of the ideology of Christian kingship. Rulers admonished and exhorted their subjects to join in their effort to realize their vision of a Christian realm in which justice and order prevailed.

What was expected of a king in the early middle ages? The whole answer to this question might be different if one were discussing, say, Gundobad of the Burgundians in the late fifth century and early sixth century, Æthelberht of Kent in the sixth century, Egica of the Visigoths in seventh century Spain, or Charlemagne at the end of the eighth century. This is not merely because circumstances were so obviously different, but also because the primary sources we have vary so greatly.

By the time written accounts of rulers in the barbarian successor states were made, in the sixth century and thereafter, some change in the expectations of rulership from the fifth century might be assumed. It is possible also to gain some notion from the recorded actions of kings, especially in narrative histories, what they, and possibly their subjects also, assumed they could do. In this way practice could provide a model for theory, and theory could elaborate the practical possibilities of coercion and control within a political system. The earliest opportunities to observe the barbarian rulers in action are through the law codes attributed to them and the earliest narratives about them. These include Victor of Vita's condemnatory accounts of the Arian Vandal rulers' persecution of Catholics in fifth-century North Africa; Gregory of Tours's *Histories*, with his vivid portraits of the axe-happy Merovingian Frankish rulers of the sixth

---

[7] Reccared, profession of faith at the Third Council of Toledo, 589, ed. G. Martínez Díez and F. Rodríguez, *La Colección canónica hispana 5. Concilios Hispanos: segunda parte*, Monumenta Hispaniae Sacra, Serie Canónica 5 (Madrid, 1992), p. 54; English trans. J. N. Hillgarth, *Christianity and Paganism, 350–750* (Philadelphia, 1986), p. 90.

century; and Isidore of Seville's *History of the Goths, Sueves and Vandals*, full of adulation for the Visigothic kings once they had become Catholic in 589. The authors nevertheless make important assumptions about the power of the ruler and the spheres of his activities.

In their laws, the kings of early medieval Europe come closest to emulating Roman rulers. Yet it is the warrior element of kingship in the early middle ages which provides much of the explanation of how kingship worked. Leadership, tactical ability, judgement, decisiveness, and a winning streak inspired both trust and loyalty. So much of the effectiveness of political control might be attributed to the subjects' feeling of security, or of being in strong hands. A successful ruler would exploit all means of good government as a means of exerting that control. He could also, of course, overstep the conventions of good government, resort to fear and tyranny, and remove himself from the bounds of the law.

The queen

Within the household, the king was supported by the queen. Her role and the degree to which it may have altered during this period is still being assessed, but it may be closely related to whether or not kingship was hereditary in the kingdoms. In many kingdoms, notably that of the Visigoths and, to a lesser extent, that of the Lombards, kingship was in principle elective and dynasties did not secure the throne. Elsewhere, most successfully in Frankish Gaul under the Merovingians and then the Carolingians, a dynastic succession from father to one or more sons (by partible inheritance) or, as in Ireland, the succession of one son of the king, was established from at least the late fifth century onwards. In still others, such as the Anglo-Saxon kingdoms, rulers appear to have been chosen from males in a leading kin group and only gradually in the course of the later ninth century did the dynastic succession of the house of Wessex from king to king's son become the norm. This remained the custom for the kings of England. Only the Picts, possibly, diverged from the European pattern of male descent with their apparently matrilinear succession to the kingship, though this is much debated.

Some political and inheritance systems, therefore, such as those of the Anglo-Saxons, the Irish, and the Visigoths, apparently gave far less prominence to the role of the queen than did those of the Franks or the Greeks. This, however, may be due to the different perceptions afforded by the existence of narrative sources. The importance of Queen Theodelinda and possibly Gundeperga of the Lombards in Italy in the seventh century should also be noted. In the Frankish and Byzantine realms, the queen's position was in part due to her ability to produce male heirs. In Byzantium the term for the reigning emperor's consort was the *Augusta*. She was normally the wife of the emperor but occasionally a widower would make his daughter or even some other woman the *Augusta*, so important was it to have a female persona in the ceremonial and court life. Overall in the western polities of Europe, however, she also appears to have been responsible for the domestic affairs of the household, with officials under her, and to have held the pursestrings for matters to do with the provision of the court. Furthermore, as many charters, letters, and narrative references make clear, the queen also had a role as mediator, peace-broker, patron, and even as co-conspirator, as in the cases of Goiswintha, queen of the Visigoths reported by Isidore of Seville to have plotted with Bishop Uldida against the Catholic party of King Reccared, or Rosamond, queen of the Lombards, who successfully plotted to have her husband, King Alboin, murdered.[8]

A queen had, after all, her own special way of reaching the king's ear. Forceful personalities were able to exploit the potential for influence and power that their position as king's wife afforded. This extended to the ecclesiastical sphere as well, in terms of friendships with clerics, the endowment of churches and monasteries, and the patronage of particular scholars. In this respect early medieval queens emulated the cultural activities of the Theodosian empresses of the fifth century. This can be observed as much with Theodelinda, queen of the Lombards in the sixth century as with Judith, wife of the Emperor Louis the Pious in the ninth century.

It is striking, moreover, how many queens were left as regents (whether de facto or de iure) for their young sons or grandsons in this period: Amalasuintha of the Ostrogoths was regent for Athalaric

---

[8] Paul the Deacon, *Historia Langobardorum*, II. 28, ed. G. Waitz, *Monumenta Germaniae Historica* (hereafter *MGH*) *Scriptores rerum germanicarum* 48 (Hanover, 1878), pp. 104–5.

in the sixth century and Brunhild, Balthild, and Nantechild of the
Franks for Theudebert II and Theuderic II, Chlothar III, and Clovis
II, respectively, in the sixth and seventh centuries; the Empress Irene
ruled for Constantine VI (d. 797) in Byzantium (and eventually over-
threw and replaced him); Adelaide and Theophano ruled on behalf of
Otto III (d. 1002) during his infancy in Germany in the late tenth
century. Other female members of the royal house, such as the king's
daughters, sisters, and aunts can occasionally be documented extending political influence and patronage in very similar ways to those of
the queen herself. Ostensibly politically neutralized by marriage to
lesser nobles or being committed to the religious life, many noble and
royal women nevertheless achieved positions of considerable influence. The most striking instances are Gisela, Gisela the younger, and
Rotrud, the sister and daughters of Charlemagne, presiding over the
royal convent of Chelles but maintaining close associations with the
royal court. The female kin of Otto I of Germany in the tenth century
governed wealthy convents such as Quedlinburg and Gandersheim.
These convents functioned as five-star hotels for the royal entourage.[9]
The royal women thus played a crucial role in the royal itinerary and
the government of the Saxon kingdom.

Power and responsibility: consensus

The political behaviour of the peoples of the early middle ages can be
reconstructed from both their actions and their expectations
recorded in the primary sources. The narrative accounts, such as the
so-called national histories of the Franks, Goths, Lombards, and
Anglo-Saxons, and the extensive series of annals from all parts of
western Europe have been highly influential in determining much of
our current understanding of the cultures of power in this period.
These sources stress two things above all: consensus and closeness to
the ruler.

Hitherto, consensus has most often been discussed by modern historians in the context of Frankish rule and has sometimes, wrongly,

[9] See J. W. Bernhardt, *Itinerant Kingship and Royal Monasteries in Early Medieval Germany, c.936–1075* (Cambridge, 1993).

been regarded as an aspect of late Roman political influence rather than as an original feature of early medieval govenment. Consensus throws light on political practice, on the relationship between the ruler and the nobility and on the different tensions of mutual dependence, cooperation, opposition, and self-interest in the relations between the king and his magnates. It is difficult to elaborate general principles about the way Carolingian politics worked, let alone politics in the other regions of Europe. Most of the Frankish and Italian capitularies, for example, can be seen as direct responses to particular problems rather than as a formulation of policy. Further, it is clear that politics at a local level mirrored political behaviour centrally, with the *potentes*, powerful men, actively participating in government at every level.[10]

Kingship is a political system in which the personal ability, talent, and resources of the ruler are as important as the system itself. To some degree, as the many minorities, interregna, or regencies that can be documented in all the early medieval kingdoms attest, the system could sustain an individual as king who was personally unable to gain the consent of the wider political community for what he wanted to do. But one king or a run of kings who sought to exploit the system too much or, more commonly, who lacked the toughness to exploit it enough, as we see in the case of the Visigoths and the Merovingian Franks, respectively, could provide the downfall of an individual or dynasty, even though kingship as an institution remained.

Three examples can serve to illustrate how a choice of ruler was made and the thinking behind the resources made available to him. In the eighth century, Paul the Deacon gave a remarkable account of the choice the Lombards made in 584 in favour of a king after ten years of the rule of many dukes ' . . . those who were then dukes gave up half of their possessions for royal uses that there might be the means from which the king himself and those who should attend him and those devoted to his service throughout the various offices might be supported.'[11] When Pippin III made himself king in 751 it was, so the annalist who tells of the matter reports, 'with the consent and

---

[10] See M. Innes, *State and Society in the Early Middle Ages, 400–1000* (Cambridge, 2000).

[11] Paul the Deacon, *Historia Langobardorum*, III, 16, ed. Waitz, p. 123; English trans. W. D. Foulke, *Paul the Deacon, History of the Lombards* (Philadelphia, 1907 and 1974), p. 114.

advice of all the Franks'.[12] In 888, when the legitimate ruler Charles [*Simplex* (straightforward, simple)] was but a baby, the west Frankish nobles elected one of their number, Odo, count of Paris to be king, whose reputation as a warrior offered them the hope of effective leadership against the Vikings.[13]

Loyalty was something to be won and retained, but it could also be both bought and institutionalized. Gift-giving in the form of gold, jewellery, weapons, or animals, grants of land and offices could all build up a cohort of faithful men around a king as well as building up their own power. Followers electing a king were also proclaiming themselves as his loyal supporters. Charlemagne chose to require a formal oath from his followers, both while he was king of the Franks and afresh after his famous coronation as emperor in Rome in 800. The oath, explicit in his case and echoed under his successors, neatly expresses the ties of mutual obligation and duty that bound man and lord to each other. The following extract is a typical example of the emphases of such an oath:

I shall be your faithful helper, as much as my knowledge and powers allow, with the help of God, without any deception or revolt, in counsel and in aid, according to my function and my person, so that you will be able to maintain and exercise your authority which God has given you at His will and for your own salvation and that of your faithful subjects.[14]

The court and closeness to the king

Closeness to the king (*Königsnähe*) was also a crucial element of political behaviour. Being a duke or a count, or holding more generic royally conferred titles such as *vir inluster* (in Francia) or *vir magnifi-*

---

[12] *Annales regni francorum*, ed. F. Kurze, MGH, *Scriptores rerum germanicarum* 6 (Hanover, 1895), p. 8 (entry for the year 749); English trans. B. Scholz, *Carolingian Chronicles* (Ann Arbor, 1970), p. 39.

[13] Richer, *Histoire de France (888–995)*, I, 5, ed. Robert Latouche (Paris, 1967), p. 16.

[14] Extract from the oath to Charles the Bald, king of the west Franks (840–877) at Quierzy in 858, ed. A. Boretius and V. Krause, MGH, *Capitularia regum francorum* II (Hanover, 1897), no. 269, p. 296; partial English trans. D. Herlihy (ed.), *The History of Feudalism: Selected Documents* (London, 1970), p. 88. See C. E. Odegaard, 'Carolingian oaths of fidelity', *Speculum*, 16 (1941), pp. 284–96 and his *Vassi et Fideles in the Carolingian Empire* (Cambridge, Mass., 1945), appendix IV, pp. 75–9.

cus (in Italy) were important privileges; so was being close to the king in a personal sense. Both brought not only status but royal protection and support for the private acts of such aristocrats (such as their court cases) but also more direct material benefits such as treasure and land. It was to the advantage of the 'elite' as a whole that kings should remain able to enforce their wills so that these practices could continue. All the same, as factional struggles continued in every royal court, one could very easily be on the losing side, and have to give up wealth and status and in many cases one's life. Kings, particularly Merovingian and Visigothic kings, were not shy of killing those who were suspected of disloyalty or who were otherwise out of favour. Enjoying *Königsnähe*, therefore, was both risky and not necessarily permanent. Losing factions sometimes found themselves fighting the king, or else switching loyalty from one king to another if there were alternatives. There were alternatives in Francia with its tradition of dividing the kingdom or England with its many small kingdoms. Across Europe, moreover, there are records of many political exiles and men claiming diverse origins offering service to foreign kings far from their original home. A rune stone put up by Gulli in Västergöt-land in eastern Sweden in the late Viking age commemorates his wife's brothers 'Æsbiorn and Iuli, very tough lads [who] met their deaths on active service in the East'.[15] Cultures of power were a combination of intimacy and responsibility. The king's communal activity with his court, such as feasting, hunting, and horseracing, and his association with the queen were essential aspects of early medieval kingship. Einhard said of Charlemagne how the king enjoyed swimming in the hot springs at Aachen with members of his court, so that at any one time 'a hundred or more men might bathe with him'.[16] Louis the Pious keenly enjoyed hunting, especially 'in the month of August, when the deer are very fat, he spent his time hunting them until the time to hunt wild boars came'.[17] Many royal

---

[15] R. I. Page, *Chronicles of the Vikings: Records, Memorials and Myths* (London, 1995), p. 87.

[16] Einhard, *Vita Karoli*, c. 22, ed. R. Rau, *Quellen zur karolingischen Reichsgeschichte* 1 (Darmstadt, 1974), p. 194; English trans. P. E. Dutton, *Carolingian Civilization: A Reader* (Peterborough, Ontario, 1993), p. 36.

[17] Thegan, *Gesta Hludowici imperatoris*, c. 19, ed. E. Tremp, *MGH, Scriptores rerum germanicarum* 64 (Hanover, 1995), p. 204; trans. Dutton, *Carolingian Civilization*, p. 146.

residences or palaces seem to have been partly intended as hunting lodges, such as Thionville in the Ardennes or Tamworth in the kingdom of Mercia. The Lombard courts and royal families of the eighth century, as well as those of the Carolingians and Anglo-Saxons in the ninth century and the Ottonian rulers of the tenth century, quite apart from those of Byzantium and the emirs of Córdoba, were also, at different times, noted for their culture, promotion of scholarship and learning, and active patronage of the arts. In such patronage especially, the households of bishops and leading members of the aristocracy emulated them.[18]

Within kingdoms, there were often civil wars between rival claimants. In these circumstances, losing factions became much harder to coerce. Tenth-century kings were less able to extend their direct political control over the full theoretical and territorial extent of their kingdoms than their predecessors had been in France and Italy, and thus were less of a focus for aristocratic interest. In Germany they were far more directly able to impose their will in their territories, but they did not directly control more than portions of their kingdom. Only in kingdoms such as England and Leon Castile (both imitative of Carolingian patterns and also relatively small) were tenth-century kings actually more able to exert direct control over their subjects and enforce their authority than before, though the difficulties of governing kingdoms which had recently expanded in size, such as tenth-century England, should not be underestimated. In most parts of Latin Europe, however, real holders of public power in the tenth century, the foci of *placita* (judicial assemblies) and the upholders of peace, were dukes and counts rather than kings. They did this in a Carolingian manner but they operated on far smaller a scale.

Officials and assemblies

Men gathered at the court acted as advisers to the king and officers within the palace. One way to understand early medieval government is not to categorize it, its officials or its structures and their spheres of

---

[18] See below, Chapter 5.

jurisdiction too narrowly. Under the earlier barbarian rulers, clerics and laymen together were in charge of public affairs, even if each had their own distinct areas of responsibility. The Visigothic church councils, for example, legislated against political conspiracy and rebellion and the Anglo-Saxon kings of Northumbria and Mercia convened the meetings to receive the papal legates in 786. In the administration of the Ostrogothic kingdom of Italy reflected in the *Variae* of Cassiodorus,[19] and in the Lombard kingdom before 774, on the other hand, the clergy do not appear to have played a direct role in political life. Whereas many of the other law codes refer to the assistance of clerics, bishops, or abbots, the Lombard laws refer only to judges and advisers in a manner which makes their secular character without doubt.

Under the Carolingians, the versatility of public officials is particularly apparent. A court notary could also be a scholar and a cleric. A bishop could run his diocese spiritually and materially but also serve as a royal adviser, *missus* (see below), and ambassador. A count could be a *missus*, judge, lead a section of the army on campaign, run his own estates, be a scholar, and a patron of the church. Clerics played an important role in government. Laymen supported the church and some even held abbacies, at least in the ninth century. This was a matter of rewarding them for their service. They would enjoy the revenues accruing from a monastery but would also be required to take due care of the brethren and protect their interests. There was a role for clerics and laymen alike in the expansion of the Frankish kingdom and consolidation of Frankish rule. Each had similar ambitions rewarded in a similar way which resulted in the same manifestations of power and wealth.

Although the common cause of clerics and laymen in the political arena is best documented in the Frankish sources, it is likely that very similar ambitions prevailed elsewhere. It is striking, for instance, how ecclesiastical and secular concerns were entwined in the Toledan councils of the Visigothic kingdoms, how emphatic a role is played by the bishops of Armagh, London, York, and Canterbury in Ireland and England, how material the contribution of the Italian clergy was in

---

[19] Cassiodorus, *Variae*, ed. T. Mommsen, *MGH, Auctores Antiquissimi* 121 (Hanover, 1894) and A. Fridh, *Corpus Christianorum Series Latinorum* (Turnholt, 1973); English trans. S. J. B. Barnish, *Cassiodorus: Variae*, Liverpool Translated Texts for Historians 12 (Liverpool, 1992).

the consolidation of Frankish rule after the Carolingian conquest of the Lombard kingdom, and how heavily the Ottonian rulers of Germany relied on their lay and ecclesiastical magnates. Even Offa of Mercia tried to create his own archbishopric (of Lichfield) within his kingdom, just as Boris, khan of the Bulgars, negotiated with the papacy for his own patriarch.[20]

In most of the early medieval kingdoms, moreover, we can posit the existence of a group of officials responsible for administration with notaries working for them. The latter drew up the official documents expressing the ruler's decisions and wishes and responding to petitions. Much of this evidence is in the form of royal charters, whose format, derived from Roman official documents in itself is indicative of the strength of the Roman heritage. In the kingdoms of the Ostrogoths, Vandals, Burgundians, Lombards, and Visigoths, there are references to, and later copies of, their recourse to written documents in government and in legal transactions. Original documents from before the eighth century only survive from the Merovingian kingdoms of the Franks (in direct continuation of the Roman provincial administration) and the Anglo-Saxons (to whom documentary practices were reintroduced by the Christian missionaries from Italy and Gaul in the seventh century). These originals retain extra information not preserved in the later copies. All kings depended on a group of officials to carry out administrative functions both at court and elsewhere in the kingdom.

A Frankish royal writing office with archchancellor and notaries can be documented throughout the eighth, ninth, and tenth centuries. This in its turn was emulated by counts and dukes in such emergent duchies and principalities as Burgundy, Flanders, Lotharingia, Normandy, Aquitaine, Saxony, Bavaria, Spoleto, and Tuscany in the tenth and eleventh centuries, quite apart from the independent kingdoms of England, northern Spain, and central and eastern Europe. A royal writing office undoubtedly existed in England by the tenth century, if not much earlier. The Franks also instituted a palace chapel with chaplain and staff (who may have served a dual function as notaries). Angilram, bishop of Metz (d. 791) and Archbishop Hildebold of Cologne (d. 818) even had to be granted papal permission to be absent from their dioceses in order to serve the king at court as

---

[20] See below, p. 229.

chaplains. The degree to which the royal courts of the various barbarian kingdoms, most spectacularly those of the Carolingians, issued
oral and written instructions and texts is very striking and attests to
the high levels of pragmatic literacy in early medieval Europe. It was a
society in which writing and administration were embedded in social
and political practice.

A direct outcome of the major expansion eastwards of the Carolingian rulers was the reorganization of both secular and ecclesiastical
administration beyond the court, and the intimate cooperation
between them at every level. In Francia, the king secured lines of local
communication and administration first of all through the network
of counts acting as agents in the localities. Secondly, there is the
Frankish institution of the *missi dominici*, probably in the latter part
of the eighth century, reorganized in 802, and whose duties appear to
have merged with those of local princes by the end of the ninth
century. The *missi* were royal agents acting in pairs, one count and
one bishop, in charge of an area known as a *missaticum*. Together,
the *missi* would arbitrate and investigate that affairs were being run
properly and justice preserved. One *missus* was Theodulf, bishop of
Orleans, who addressed a poem to judges warning them against
bribery and favouring the rich in judgments.[21] Paschasius Radbert
describes the confidence placed in the overriding authority of the
Frankish *missus*, Wala, in Italy by those seeking justice.[22]

In most other kingdoms similar arrangements to the Frankish
system of counts as royal agents were in place, or were introduced,
though the degree to which written administrative methods were
either appropriate or required varies enormously. In Iceland, for
example, the *goðar*, the leading landowners of the 'republic' discussed matters of common concern at the *thing*. In eastern Brittany
the local leaders in the parishes were the *machtierns*, who presided
at meetings and sometimes initiated legal proceedings in the village
communities. In Lombard Italy, on the other hand, structures were
more formal. Local officials known as *gastalds* served either in a

---

[21] Theodulf of Orleans, *Contra Iudices*, ed. E. Dümmler, *MGH, Poetae Latini aevi
Carolini* I (Hanover, 1881), pp. 493–517; extracts in English trans. P. Godman, *Poetry of
the Carolingian Renaissance* (London, 1985), pp. 162–6.

[22] Paschasius Radbert, *Epitaphium Arsenii*, ed. E. Dümmler, *Abhandlungen der
königlichen Akademie der Wissenschaften zu Berlin, phil.-hist. Klasse* 2 (Berlin, 1900),
pp. 1–98.

city instead of a duke or count or as the administrator of royal property in a city territory. At the other end of the Mediterranean in Byzantium, by contrast, there was an elaborate central bureaucracy staffed with civil servants and in the provinces units known as *tourmai* and *banda*. These were essentially military in character, their heads being under the direction of the *strategos* (commander of the *theme*), but some officials reported back to the central administration, and most of the senior ones seem to have received their pay from the capital.

No doubt corrupt, inefficient, or lazy officials were among these local officials and royal agents, but a system should not be judged on its effectiveness in terms only of those who abused and failed it.[23] Essentially the administrative systems of the early medieval kingdoms, with the stress on carrying out the king's will and securing order and justice at a local level, appear to have been adaptable to local conditions as well as susceptible of elaboration by any king seeking a greater measure of control.

The royal presence was a physical manifestation of the king's power. The court was where the king was. In the Irish, Scottish, English, Lombard, Visigothic, Bulgar, or Danish kingdoms, with such places as Tara and Dublin, Dunkeld, Winchester, London, York, Pavia, Toledo, Pliska, or Jelling functioning as both residence and capital (and often as ecclesiastical centres as well), the king's seat was a central location of his power, and the location of a central administration (if any) as well as a palace complex. Many early medieval kings, in principle at least, however, were also itinerant. An itinerant court stayed at urban and rural palaces and hunting lodges. Thus, Charlemagne and Louis the Pious stayed at Thionville, Aachen, Frankfurt, Paderborn, and Regensburg, among others. Elaborate planning for food, fodder, and bedding had to be done. The king and his entourage were also the guests of bishops and abbots in the great sees and monasteries of the realm. The Plan of St Gallen provides an indication of the quarters for distinguished guests, as does the newly excavated ninth-century monastery of San Vincenzo al Volturno in

---

[23] The more negative emphases of scholars such as F. L. Ganshof, *Frankish Institutions under Charlemagne*, trans. B. Lyon and M. Lyon (New York, 1970), have been ameliorated in more recent work: see Innes, *State and Society*, and J. L. Nelson, 'Literacy in Carolingian government', in R. McKitterick (ed.), *The Uses of Literacy in Early Mediaeval Europe* (Cambridge, 1990), pp. 258–96.

central Italy. These royal monasteries were an essential part of the topography of royal power.

A major means of government and decision making was the assembly. These were great public meetings of lay and ecclesiastical magnates, both at the central and at the local level. At them, disputes were settled, petitions heard, decisions reached, and laws made. Assemblies were often timed to coincide with the mustering of the army in the spring before a military campaign. The Visigothic kings in the seventh century in large part governed through the huge and elaborate councils which regularly met in their capital at Toledo.[24] Church councils were venues for the lay elites to meet as well. By the late seventh century the judicial assembly known as the *placitum* had developed in Francia, which would continue until at least 1000 as a regular venue for disputing, heard by a public community which included some at least of the local landowners and leading men. This sort of political practice had strong Roman elements, not least its constant association with the terminology of the *publicum*, public power.

The agendas and decisions of these assemblies in the eighth and ninth centuries are presented in the capitularies, conciliar records, and single-sheet charters recording legal decisions. These give an ample indication of the variety of business discussed at them. The Council of Frankfurt in 794, for example, stated the Frankish rejection of the theological notion of Adoptionism (that Christ is the adopted son of God), and of the Byzantine position on religious images, regulated weights and measures, and offered directives on ecclesiastical discipline and lay religious observance. The general capitulary of 802 stressed many different aspects of royal authority, the punishment of crimes, and the administration of justice. In the kingdom of Italy in the tenth and eleventh centuries over 300 records of the hearings of judicial assemblies witness to the public discussion of legal cases and disputes, presided over by emperors or their local representatives.[25] The *Althing* in Iceland c.1000 made its celebrated decision to accept Christianity. The English royal charters with their listings of leading lay and ecclesiastical magnates acting as witnesses, indicate that gatherings of

---

[24] See below, p. 137 (Ch. 4).

[25] C. J. Wickham, 'Justice in the kingdom of Italy in the eleventh century', *La Giustizia nell'alto Medioevo (secoli IX–XI)*, Settimane di Studio del Centro Italiano di studi sull'alto Medioevo (Spoleto, 1997), pp. 179–250.

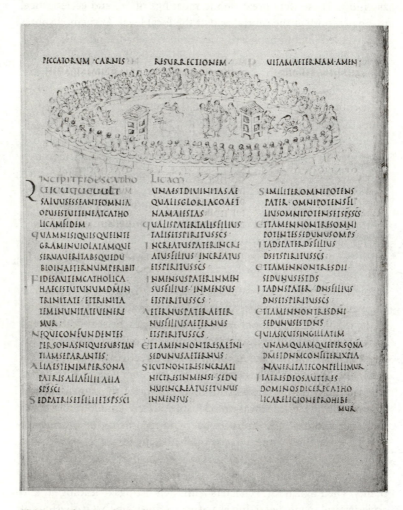

Figure 4 The Utrecht Psalter: A Carolingian assembly

the leading men of the kingdom, summoned by the king as a way of extending political control, were not uncommon. Further, the many different laws emanating from the various barbarian kingdoms are the outcome of deliberations of the kings and their magnates.

Law

Many elements of the legal and judicial system elaborated in the various early medieval kingdoms, and of the institutions and methods of government introduced or consolidated by the Carolingian rulers, provided a lasting legacy and model in the medieval and early modern periods. Modern scholars' emphasis on developments in the eleventh and twelfth centuries has led to forgetfulness of the fundamental nature of the early medieval achievement for the subsequent development of Latin Europe in every sphere. The church was an integral part of that achievement. Not only did its personnel share in the business of government and administration; its spiritual ideals were an essential part of the political ideology of the secular rulers. Religious and intellectual concerns were as much the business of the secular rulers as they were of the clerics. Later distinctions between 'church' and 'state' are of no relevance in the early medieval period. It is notable that many leading ecclesiastics insisted on the rule of law and helped to maintain it. Hincmar, archbishop of Rheims from 840 to 882, for example, stated as follows:

Since it is declared that all must know the laws and conform to their decisions, no layman, whatever his position, can claim exemption from their authority. Thus there are laws that kings and *ministri rei publicae* must enforce in the administration of their provinces and there are also capitularies of Christian kings and of their predecessors legally promulgated by them with the general consent of their *fideles* and these equally must be observed. St Augustine says of these laws 'It is right for men to debate them while they are being formulated but once they are agreed upon and accepted judges no longer have the option to dispute them but only to implement them.[26]

[26] Hincmar of Rheims, *De ordine palatii*, c. 3, ed. T. Gross and R. Schieffer, *MGH, Fontes iuris germanici antiqui* 3 (Hanover, 1980), pp. 46–7; I am grateful to Jinty Nelson for allowing me to use her translation. An alternative English version, reprinted from Herlihy, *History of Feudalism*, p. 213 is available in Dutton, *Carolingian Civilization*, p. 488.

Continuity with the Roman world is most apparent in the context of law and the associated matters of legal transaction and the use of writing for legal record. There was no 'decline and fall' of Roman law, but a gradual process of adaptation. Early medieval law in the west comprises, first of all, Roman law in the form of the Theodosian Code. This Code was written in Latin in 438. Various abridgements were made of it in the early middle ages, the most widely disseminated of which was the so-called *Breviary of Alaric* or *Lex Romana Visigothorum*. The *Corpus iuris civilis* of Justinian (534), also in Latin, was known but not referred to much at all in the west before the eleventh century, though it was the standard codification of Roman law in the east and Greek translations and digests of it began to be made and used for teaching in the law schools of Byzantium from the seventh century onwards. Secondly, there is the group of texts known collectively, if somewhat misleadingly, as the Germanic *leges* of the Burgundians, Visigoths, Alemans, Bavarians, Lombards, Anglo-Saxons, Franks, Saxons, and Frisians. These, apart from the Anglo-Saxon laws in English, are also in Latin and mostly based on Roman law in structure and form. Some of the content, moreover, arises out of late Roman legal practice or a development from it. Elements of possibly non-Roman social practice and new legislation were also incorporated. Most of the initial codifications of the *leges* are associated with rulers and their chief advisers.

Further, there is the ecclesiastical law of the church. Biblical laws and regulations naturally had a strong influence on subsequent ecclesiastical legislation. The ecclesiastical provisions agreed at the major councils of the early church, papal decisions, and Roman imperial law dealing with ecclesiastical matters of organization and discipline is collectively referred to as canon law. Various individual compilations of canon law in relation to local perceptions of what was needed were made in the early middle ages. Some purport to function as collections for the Frankish and Visigothic kingdoms, like the *Vetus Gallica* of *c.*700 or the *Hispana*, *c.*700, respectively. An attempt was made to impose uniformity at the end of the eighth century with a text associated with the pope but promoted by the Frankish ruler, known as the *Dionysio-Hadriana*. More compilations were formed in the tenth and eleventh centuries, the most influential of which, by Regino of Prüm (d. 915) and Burchard of Worms

(965–1025), played a role, together with the earlier collections, in the formal codification of canon law in the twelfth century. North of the Alps from the middle of the eleventh century onwards there is a rich and lively, if discordant, tradition in opposition to even more emphatic efforts on the part of the popes to create uniformity and enforce their authority.

Lastly there is new royal legislation, most notably the laws of the English kings from the end of the ninth century onwards and the laws in the form of capitularies produced by the Carolingian rulers in the late eighth and the ninth century. An abridgement of the Carolingian capitularies of Charlemagne and Louis the Pious by Ansegisus, possibly acting in an official capacity, was made in the 820s and widely disseminated throughout the Carolingian empire.

Discussion of the law and its function in the middle ages has focused in particular on the role of written law. But the extent to which the written law acted as a constant source of reference and guidance for legal decisions in practice, made by judges and with the advice of groups of men with a judicial function who served in the courts (such as the *rachimburgii* of Merovingian Gaul), can only occasionally be deduced from the charters, dispute settlements (largely about land), and *placita* records. Legal norms may have existed in the memory of each man in the community, but it is more likely that the preservation of legal decisions in writing led in due course to the development of a group of specialists in the law, such as those who have been identified in northern Italy in the tenth century.

In the late Roman period there had been divergence between law in action and law in the books. The same was the case in the early medieval period. There was probably a constant process of adaptation, change, and interpretation of the law in relation to existing and changing social conditions. There are many Carolingian prescriptions, requiring judges to judge according to the written law rather than following their own supposedly arbitrary judgment. This of course implies that many judges chose not to refer to the law books but may, nevertheless, have meted out judgment in terms of accepted legal norms. There are also many extant copies of the barbarian *leges*, dating predominantly from the late eighth, the ninth, and the tenth centuries, suggesting a wide dissemination of the *leges* in company with Carolingian capitulary legislation throughout western Europe.

Many surviving manuscripts indicate that individuals made collections of law for their own use. But a significant group of Frankish legal codices reflects the activity of a small group of scribes presided over by the head of the royal writing office, the *cancellarius*, and associated with the royal court. Thus, the initial responsibility for copying and disseminating the decisions of the king and the assemblies in the early middle ages was probably assumed by the king and his writing office. We also find collections in both England and Francia associated with particular leading ecclesiastics.

The proliferation of copies of the *leges* and capitularies, of canon law, and of the Theodosian Code in its full and various abridged versions would also appear to indicate an understanding of the authority of the written law. These texts witness to an attempt to understand that authority in relation to legal procedures and judicial decisions within a political system whose leaders guaranteed the working of justice and the law. Roman law, the *leges*, and Carolingian capitularies all inspired later formulations of law for the monarchies of western Europe and the growing profession of lawyers in the eleventh and twelfth centuries. Within the early medieval kingdoms, moreover, law is neither a defining trait nor a characteristic of ethnic identity so much as a mark of political allegiance and social alignment. It is a statement of political rather than of biological identity.

Legal transactions between individuals and institutions were recorded in charters. These recorded the settlement of property disputes, sales, exchanges, gifts, rents, and the manumission of slaves. They attest to procedures prescribed and recorded in writing. In charters, we may also observe the continuation of Roman practices, gradually adapted over time. They are written in Latin with distinctive formulae in relation to particular transactions (some of which were put together for the assistance of legal clerks in collections known as formularies). In legal disputes, therefore, the written law, custom, charters, and memory, that is, written and oral testimony, are drawn on. Both are closely interrelated and interdependent.

The charter evidence provides the strongest thread of continuity in social interaction and legal transactions right through the period from *c*.550 into the eleventh and twelfth centuries. Charters mirror how men and women clung to their rights and established claims to their land and inheritance. The donations to religious institutions, moreover, express the pious devotion which served to bind spiritual and worldly concerns together in a world where the monasteries were firmly embedded in the local communities. All over Europe the basic patterns were established in all the early medieval kingdoms in terms both of the functions of the charters and of the social organization supporting their production and use in the localities. Subsequently, the use of charters, along with Latin script, was introduced into the newly conquered and Christianized areas of Europe such as Scandinavia and Bohemia.

The resources and practicalities of government: finance and the army

It is with the rewards or payment for assisting the ruler in government that the greatest difference between the Roman system and that of the kingdoms of western Europe in the early middle ages gradually becomes apparent. Although the Visigoths maintained a tax system and so, until c.600, did the Franks, there are no signs that it was more than a subsidiary aspect of royal power. The important rewards for service and loyalty were now in land, not money; and above all, titles like count or duke were useless if they could not be backed up by private landowning and clienteles of military dependants. Even the armies of each kingdom were little more than collections of armed private clienteles of this kind. These clienteles, too, expected to be rewarded principally in land. It was probably, as a result, more expensive to be a powerful aristocrat in 650 than in 400; and aristocratic interest came to be directed at least as much towards the creation of local power-bases as towards state service. Thus was begun the pattern of the politics of land that would dominate in the middle ages up to 1250 at least, though it should also be stressed that we know far too little about plunder, gifts, and rewards in kind—treasure, military gear, livestock, and slaves—apart from land. One gave out land to gain loyalty, but consequently had ever less to give, and less negotiating power in the future as a result. Kings and magnates, furthermore, had the same sorts of resources, and thus played on the same ground. This could easily favour the considerable decentralization of power.

Kings had slimmer material resources and became less able directly to require their subjects to do exactly what they wanted them to do in much of Europe after 900 or so.

The Roman empire had maintained an unwieldy and elaborate tax system, based mainly on landed property and its agricultural exploitation. It is estimated that the tax demands may have exceeded half of the agricultural surplus (after subsistence needs were met) of the empire. Tax was not the state's only resource; in late antiquity and Byzantium the imperial administration may have been self-sufficient throughout the empire in terms of its estates and its products, though there is no evidence that this was the case. Yet taxes were essential to cover public expenditure, the maintenance of roads and bridges, the deployment of the standing army, and pay for the soldiers.

Money was the form in which public revenue could be collected and spent. The stability of the coinage was therefore a major factor in public finance. After the period of inflation at the end of the third century and the depreciation in value of the *denarius*, taxes were levied in kind and, in the late fifth century, in gold. Tax was doubly regressive. The poor paid significantly more tax than the rich; the farming-out of tax collection left a far from negligible portion of the money gathered in the hands of the *curiales* (city councillors) recruited from the ranks of the municipal aristocracies, who acted as tax gatherers. Each city was required to produce the tax raised from the surrounding countryside. Thus, tax extortion became the direct rival of private rents.

The evolution of tax and coinage in the eastern and western empires diverged markedly in the early middle ages. In the east the state retained its direct interest in striking good coinage, for the tax in gold was one of the links in the cycle of exchange (including taxes and salaries paid by the state) in which commerce played a minimal role. In the west the new rulers endeavoured to leave the collecting of taxes and some of the administrative framework of the Roman fiscal system in place. Remuneration for public service and the upkeep of the military elite, however, was increasingly underpinned by the distribution of land rather than by payments in gold and silver. Coinage, therefore, became less complex.

The burden of indirect taxes, however, increased during the whole of the middle ages. The taxation of transport and of sales of merchandise, for example, was the exclusive prerogative of the king and his agents until the middle of the ninth century. It formed a weighty contribution to the royal treasury. Further, immunity was an essential part of the system of the government's delegation of certain tasks to an intermediate group. Immunity placed an individual, his possessions, and his dependants outside the bounds of interference from public officials. The obligations of the immunist towards the king remained complete in principle, but matters to do with taxes, justice, and raising an army from the population at large tended to be delegated by the king to a holder of an immunity. The granting of an immunity was an extraordinary act of self-restraint by the ruler and his agents.[27] Yet paradoxically it was also a demonstration of royal authority and an affirmation of royal status. Immunities were most often granted to ecclesiastical institutions. Thus, they also constituted a secular manipulation of the boundaries of sacred space. In the practical sphere, it is possible that in the course of the early middle ages, the mechanisms of immunity completely disrupted the system of land taxes, for the land tax had disappeared by the early seventh century. Documented immunities postdate this disappearance but there may be no causal connection. Services due from an immunist and the principle of public taxation were two totally separate systems. Some continuity from late antiquity is evident in the role of the lay and ecclesiastical magnates as indispensable agents of government. With the demise of a permanent standing army, for example, it was no longer the imposition of taxes, but war and military organization which devolved to the magnates.

From the end of the seventh century, kings relied upon the growing solidarity of the political elites inspired by military success. In Francia from the time of Charles Martel (714–741) and even more so under Pippin III (741–768) and Charlemagne (768–814), military campaigns and the progressive expansion of territory constituted an increasingly regular and dominant aspect of Frankish life and a continued increase of landed wealth. Historians have rightly insisted upon the increasing strength of the Frankish army, of professional warriors, armed and usually mounted, whose livelihood was assured with the granting to them of royal and church estates in benefice.

---

[27] See B. Rosenwein, *Negotiating Space: Power, Restraint and Privileges of Immunity in Early Medieval Europe* (Manchester, 1999).

The remarkable extent of military and public expenditure entailed a degree of logistical and economic organization without precedent in western Europe since the fifth century. The sheer efficiency of the military and administrative organization is exemplified in the major campaigns, on two fronts simultaneously, against the Saxons and the Avars at the end of the eighth century; in the impressive, if ultimately abortive, attempt to connect the Main/Rhine and Danube by a canal between the Rednitz and Altmühl rivers; and by the obligations laid on the totality of the dependent manses of the church of Reims to cooperate in order to provide transport and labour for the building of the palace at Aachen at the beginning of the ninth century.

Although they continued to rule through the magnates as intermediaries, the Carolingian rulers sought also to endow the church with new resources and new tools. The political economy of the Carolingian period was dominated throughout the eighth century and the first third of the ninth century by the need to centralize and place the supply of labour, agricultural implements, and food products at the king's disposal. Among the most important of the new resources of the ruler was the new method of management of the royal and ecclesiastical estates.[28]

In the absence of the permanent standing army of the Roman empire, and in contrast to the small standing forces maintained by Byzantium, army service in the west was organized in principle by the general levy on all freemen. This was maintained in theory until the ninth century. Charlemagne introduced at the turn of the eighth century a system whereby actual service was only required of men in possession of a certain amount of allodial land. In 808 the amount was fixed at four manses.[29] Other men would combine resources in order to equip a man at arms, or, no doubt more usually, to pay substitute taxes to a magnate acting as intermediary. The commonest form of dues paid to the ruler, alongside military service and other duties required by the ruler, was the annual gift rendered by the magnates to the king (*annua dona; eulogiae*) which was a non-Roman custom.

The principal medium for the payment of these dues was the *denarius* or silver penny. It first made its appearance as a unit of

---

[28] See below, Chapter 3.   [29] See below, Chapter 3.

currency in Neustria in about 670 and soon thereafter in Anglo-Saxon England. It was the same weight as the gold *tremissis* it replaced (1.3g or 20 grains of barley) and therefore of considerably less face value which may well have facilitated commercial exchange at a local level, though this is much disputed. The Carolingian rulers reformed the weight to 1.7g or 20 grains of wheat. The monetary system of western Europe had evolved towards monometallism, at first based on an increasingly debased gold coinage and in due course on silver. Coinage issues gradually changed from Roman imperial coinage and imitations of imperial coinage. Eventually the distinctive coins of the Visigothic, Lombard, English, and Frankish rulers were produced, though the degree of political control exerted over the mints and coinage varied considerably in the different kingdoms. In Merovingian Gaul, for example, it was primarily a local coinage, from more or less private mints with small outputs, though there may have been more overall control of the coinage than is now apparent. Nevertheless, by the eighth century, royal control of coinage is clear. The interregional circulation of coinage in the northwest of Europe was dominated by Frisian and to a lesser extent, Anglo-Saxon pennies whose main impetus for production appears to have been commercial.

Decrees concerning coinage are linked by the Franks with measures against the abuse of tolls (that is, private individuals appropriating them for their own use), the adulteration of weights and measures, counterfeit coinage, and control of markets. By counterfeit coinage was meant not so much the striking of imitations from base metal (for which there is in fact very little extant evidence) as coins struck in mints not controlled by the king. There were also severe punishments for refusing to accept good money. Such a rejection (which may seem very odd to us) possibly hides more complex elements of resistance to royal control in the population at large.

Judging from the pattern of minting and coin finds, the eastern part of the Frankish kingdom from the reign of Louis the German onwards (840–876) enjoyed an essentially non-monetary economy. There are other differences between the regions east and west of the Rhine, pointed to by Adriaan Verhulst, such as the recourse to labour services and a lack of emphasis on rents in money. Nevertheless, money clearly circulated regularly and rapidly, stimulated by commercial activity, especially in the North Sea area. The Franks were very successful in preventing the circulation of foreign money within the Frankish realm. Indeed, in the reign of Louis the Pious western Europe enjoyed what can only be described as a single European currency, with foreign coin excluded from the Carolingian empire. Only England and Benevento, of the coin-producing polities, were outside the system. In England's case, however, their money, reformed by King Offa of Mercia in the late eighth century, was of the same weight of silver. The important trading centre at Venice produced Louis's *Christiana religio* coinage in its mint alongside similar issues of its own, presumably in order to facilitate trade.[30] Coinage in both England and Francia was used as a means of affirming royal authority, though the volume of production of early medieval coinage is still in question.[31] Coinage could also be a way of raising tribute payments quickly though in some cases tribute was also paid partly in wine, livestock, and grain. The tributes paid to the Vikings, moreover, meant that precious bullion left the country. From the last third of the ninth century, control of the monetary system was both diverted to and acquired by the great lay and ecclesiastical magnates who resorted on a massive scale, as other rulers had done before them, to the depreciation of the metal content as well as the weight of the coinage. From about 900, the fate of money is a fair indication of the different political developments within the kingdoms of the Christian west. In Germany, for example, the Saxon rulers disseminated the minting of coinage in the regions east of the Rhine and it was gradually extended to the new polities such as Poland, Hungary, and Bohemia, but minting was organized through local magnates. In France, regional standards of weight had developed by the end of the tenth century. Anglo-Saxon England, on the other hand, retained and even increased strong royal control over the coinage. By the middle of the tenth century, indeed, England had the most sophisticated, albeit self-contained, monetary system in the whole of contemporary western Europe.

Although family treasure does not appear to be an element of

---

[30] S. Coupland, 'Money and coinage under Louis the Pious', *Francia*, 17/1 (1990), pp. 23–54.

[31] See M. Blackburn, 'Money and coinage', in R. McKitterick (ed.), *The New Cambridge Medieval History*, II. *c.700–c.900* (Cambridge, 1995), pp. 538–62.

contested state power in the Lombard or Visigothic kingdoms, it was essential in Francia. After the death of Pippin II and his son Grimoald in 714, for example, Ragamfred the mayor of the palace of Neustria and Radbod, king of the Frisians, kidnapped Pippin's widow Plectrude together with the Pippinid family treasure. Charles Martel was eventually able to retrieve the latter in 717. Further, Charlemagne made full use of the Avar treasure after 796 as a means of making sumptuous gifts to impress such neighbouring rulers as Offa of Mercia, and to reward his faithful men at court. Nevertheless, the distribution and control of offices, such as countships, abbacies, and bishoprics rather than the royal treasury became the main foci of the political rivalries and conflicts of the ninth and tenth centuries.

Political ideology

Much of this chapter has dwelt on the realities of rulership and government, in so far as these can be reconstructed. But there were also powerful ideals at work in the practical responses to the exercise of political power. Even the apparently light-hearted weekly order in the duty of an Irish king in the Críth Gablach in fact embodies many of the underlying expectations of political behaviour discussed above as well as ideals of rulership:

Sunday for drinking ale, for he is no rightful ruler who does not provide ale
  for every Sunday
Monday for judgement, for the adjustment of the *tuatha*
Tuesday for playing chess
Wednesday for watching deerhounds at the chase
Thursday for the society of his wife
Friday for horse-racing
Saturday for judging cases.[32]

---

[32] Críth Gablach, c. 41, ed. D. A. Binchy, *Críth Gablach*, Mediaeval and Modern Irish Series 11 (Dublin, 1941), p. 21; English trans. E. MacNeill, 'Ancient Irish law: The law of status and franchise', *Proceedings of the Royal Irish Academy*, 36 C (1923), pp. 265–316, at p. 304. The *tuatha* are the political and jurisdictional units of the kingdom. See W. Davies, 'Celtic kingships in the early middle ages', in A. Duggan (ed.), *Kings and Kingship in Medieval Europe* (London, 1993), pp. 101–24.

In late antiquity the power and presence of the emperor were implicit. The majesty of the emperor himself was greatly enhanced, from the time of Constantine onwards, with an insistent monarchical ideology bolstered by the Christian vision of a hierarchical heaven ruled by an omnipotent divinity. Elaborate ceremonies celebrated the arrival (*adventus*) and triumphs of the emperor. The exaltation of the emperor was increasingly enmeshed in a strict protocol for entering his presence. These were recorded, on the one hand, in such works as Eusebius' *Life of Constantine* and his *Ecclesiastical History* (the latter known in the west in the Latin translation made by Rufinus, d. 411). Further, the ideologies of political and legal power were articulated in the Theodosian Code of Roman law, put together in 438 and used in the west until the eleventh century. Emphatically Christian imperial and royal ideology enjoyed great influence thereafter. It was given visual expression in paintings and sculpture and elaborated not only by the church in liturgical ritual, but by the rulers and their advisers in the staging of the king's arrival, presiding over the court, and court ceremonial.

The image of the king therefore combined highly charged symbolism and association with divine authority with the more pragmatic and domestic business of ruling men and women, maintaining the balance of relations with them and with the chief advisers and officers. The earliest post-Roman royal portraits surviving, apart from earlier images on coinage from Spain, England, Francia, and Italy, are manuscript illuminations from the middle of the ninth century. There the ruler is represented with symbols of his office and the hand of God over his head. In depictions of Charles the Bald (840–877) (Plate 3) and of the Ottonian rulers of Germany (Plate 11), there are representations of the lay and ecclesiastical magnates of the kingdom, personifications of the royal virtues—prudence, justice, fortitude and temperance—and of the provinces or regions over which the king ruled.[33] Such links with God-given authority and the responsibility of the Christian ruler to support the Christian religion become a familiar aspect of medieval ruler portraits: Queen Emma and King Cnut, royal patrons of New Minster, Winchester in the

---

[33] See H. L. Kessler and P. D. Dutton, *The Poetry and Paintings of the First Bible of Charles the Bald* (Ann Arbor, 1997) and H. Mayr-Harting, *Ottonian Book Illumination: An Historical Study* (London, 1991).

eleventh century, for example, are depicted in the *Liber Vitae* of New Minster (British Library Stowe 944, fo. 6ʳ) presenting a golden cross to the abbey.[34]

These portraits reflect, moreover, much that is also expressed in the inauguration or coronation rituals which began to be incorporated into the Frankish and Anglo-Saxon liturgies in the course of the ninth century. In their turn these were formalized and specific rituals that had their roots in earlier masses for the king, such as the prayers in the seventh-century Visigothic liturgy for the king going out to battle. Such prayers and gestures are dramatic expressions of the role of the king as God's deputy in securing justice and peace for the Christian people. Both the Visigoths and the Franks, in emulation of the Old Testament, anointed their kings with holy oil. In the case of the Franks the anointing was a ritual devised by the Frankish clergy to enhance the position of the new Carolingian ruler Pippin III on his usurpation of the Merovingian dynasty. Anointing new kings as part of elaborate liturgical rituals in due course became standard European practice.[35] Kings further enhanced the wider consciousness of their status and of that of their families by instituting commemorative prayers on particular family anniversaries to be observed in the monasteries and churches of their realms.

The ideology of Christian rulership, and occasionally also of the ideal of the harmony, if not the unity of the Christian empire, was also adumbrated in more conventional form in treatises, often known as mirrors of princes. Several from the ninth century survive. They drew heavily on earlier models of Christian rulership, not least those of Augustine, and on biblical models. In their turn these treatises influenced the formulation of political thought thereafter. Yet early medieval texts, notably the historical writing and legislation of the period, also reinforce the importance of political fidelity and lordship, or political virtue and mutual obligation between the ruler and his faithful men. As Janet Nelson has stressed, 'political thought is embodied not only in theories but in contemporaries' *ad hoc*

---

[34] S. Keynes (ed.), *The Liber Vitae of the New Minster and Hyde Abbey Winchester*, Early English Manuscripts in Facsimile 26 (Copenhagen, 1996), plate v.

[35] See R. A. Jackson, *Ordines Coronationis Franciae: Texts and Ordines for the Coronation of Frankish and French Kings and Queens in the Middle Ages*, 1 (Philadelphia, 1995).

responses to political problems and perceived discrepancies between ideals and realities.'[36]

Certainly there are many contrasts and variations in the cultures of power and manifestations of political control across Europe throughout the early middle ages. Yet there were also fundamental similarities in the development from the autocratic system of the late Roman empire through the early barbarian kingdoms to conceptions of the realm as a territorial and sociological entity, the *ministerium* of the Christian ruler, and the sharing of power and responsibility, to a greater or lesser degree, between the aristocracy (lay and ecclesiastical) and the king.

[36] Janet L. Nelson, 'Kingship and empire in the Carolingian world', in R. McKitterick (ed.), *Carolingian Culture: Emulation and Innovation* (Cambridge, 1994), p. 65.

Figure 5 Beatus of Liebana, Commentary on the Apocalypse

2

Society

Chris Wickham

In this chapter two histories, those of landowning aristocracies and peasantries, respectively, will be counterposed. This is not because the two classes were entirely distinct (less, in some areas, than in any period of history from 200 BC to the present), but because if one does not keep them apart, peasant societies risk exclusion altogether as a result of their poor documentation, even though they made up perhaps 95 per cent of the population. In the framework of that basic opposition, I shall discuss three groups of European societies separately: the post-Roman societies of the west; the still-Roman society of the east; and the non-Roman societies of the north. It is hard not to be schematic in a discussion of the social history of 600 years, but this separation will, I hope, allow at least some equilibrium between the recognition of often huge local or regional differences in early medieval Europe and the establishment of comprehensible general trends.

The concentration on aristocrats and peasants involves some omissions. I shall concentrate on lay society and, as far as possible, on secular aspects of social action; ecclesiastics and religious activity will be discussed in Chapter 4. Similarly, artisans and merchants will be dealt with, as economic forces above all, in Chapter 3, for they were relatively few in number after the end of the Roman empire, and did not form a particularly well-defined social category (or categories) on their own. Artisanal work is well attested in early medieval archaeology, especially that of metal-workers and potters. Artisans, however, usually worked part-time, and in social terms can be assimilated to the peasantry or, in the case of a few elite occupations such as goldsmiths and moneyers, to the aristocracy.[1] Even in societies where urbanism survived, such as northern Italy, agriculture was the economic base of nearly the whole of society; this chapter aims to reflect that fact.

Roman aristocracies

Our starting-point must be the late Roman world, which was still prosperous and stable in 400. Late Roman aristocrats were roughly divisible into four overlapping categories. Firstly, there are the senatorial families, who could be hugely rich, as with Probus, who in the early 420s paid 1,200 pounds of gold just for his praetorian games, a ritual marking the beginning of his formal political career, or with Pinianus and Melania, a young couple who adopted ascetic Christianity in the first decade of the fifth century and sold off estates in Italy, Sicily, North Africa, Spain, and even Britain, as well as huge quantities of clothes and jewellery.[2] Secondly, there is the government elite of the empire. Many of these were from senatorial families, and many more became so. They were largely focused on the capitals, Ravenna (after 401) for the west and Constantinople for the east, though there were still plenty in older centres too: Rome, Antioch, and elsewhere. Thirdly, there were the families of the city councillors (*curiales*) of the many hundreds of cities of the empire, the urban aristocracy who had put up the second-century temples and other public buildings which still so often survive, and who were, from the fourth century onwards, enthusiastically endowing churches, the buildings of the new state religion, Christianity. This local aristocratic stratum felt itself under

---

[1] A good survey of the range of crafts and artisans can be found for England in C. J. Arnold, *An Archaeology of the Early Anglo-Saxon Kingdoms*, 2nd edn. (London, 1997), pp. 67–100. For western Europe as a whole, see R. Doehaerd, *The Early Middle Ages in the West* (Amsterdam, 1978), pp. 159–69, a convenient brief survey based mostly on written sources. Merchants could be rich and influential, but were even more socially marginal, as outsiders, often foreigners, potential (indeed, sometimes actual) spies: for a list of references, ibid., pp. 169–82, and more in detail, D. Claude's articles in *Untersuchungen zu Handel und Verkehr der vor- und frühgeschichtlichen Zeit in Mittel- und Nordeuropa* (Göttingen, 1985), vols. 2 and 3, pp. 9–99.

[2] Olympiodorus, frag. 41. 2, ed. and trans. in R. C. Blockley, *The Fragmentary Classicising Historians of the Late Roman Empire*, 2 (Liverpool, 1983), pp. 204–7; *Vie de Sainte Mélanie*, cc. 11, 19–20, ed. and trans. D. Gorce (Paris, 1962), pp. 146–9, 162–71. Probus was regarded by Olympiodorus as of less than average wealth.

threat by 400, as its traditional tax-collecting role was undermined by functionaries of the more centralized late Roman state, but its collective wealth was not much diminished. Overall, *curiales* formed the main group of landowners under the Roman empire, and their lands, which tended (unlike those of senators) to be restricted to the territories of single cities, were more likely to survive the radical decentralization that accompanied the break-up of the empire in the west. Fourthly, there was the army, a partially separate hierarchy, whose leaders were nonetheless major players in the political scene. Many of these were of senatorial origin, but there was always space at the top of the military hierarchy for able men of lesser families, particularly from frontier areas and indeed, increasingly, from Germanic communities beyond the frontier. Such new men were not only ignorant of Virgil but their Latin (or, in the east, Greek) was often itself considered faulty; for these reasons, they were regularly the target of the social and cultural snobbery of the civilian elites (including the writers of all our sources), but they were not the less Roman for that, and not a few of them became emperors.

Several points need to be made about these different aristocratic groups, taken as a whole. First is the fact that the majority of the members of this class, including the richest and highest-status of them, were civilian, not military, figures: the Roman imperial aristocracy was one of the very few in the history of the pre-industrial world (the only major one outside China) not to be dominated by military prowess. Its cultural markers were not valour, horsemanship, hunting, but, rather, education and comfort. Roman civilian aristocrats had to know Virgil by heart (in the east, Homer), and to be able to turn out a passable lyric or oration themselves; they also valued good-quality houses, full of marble, mosaic floors, frescoed walls, and underfloor central heating: respectively, the source of the literary and the archaeological remains that have awed subsequent generations right up to the present day. They also valued expensive and flashy food and clothing. In this they were not atypical of subsequent aristocracies, even if a Roman senator would soon have tired of the obsessive roast meat diet of his western medieval noble descendants.

Secondly, there was a close association between aristocratic status and imperial office-holding. Even members of the richest senatorial families were fully legitimated only by holding a series of offices, either in the old ceremonial capital, Rome (as with Probus' praetorship) or in the administration. Not that all family members needed to be officials, or indeed could be, for there were not enough offices to go around. Even when they rejected them, as for example if they opted for ascetic Christianity, they nonetheless kept 'their own rank', as Gregory of Tours said about an early fifth-century senatorial saint, Paulinus of Nola.[3] But it would not have been possible for a family to remain of full senatorial status if, for example, it had rejected all office and retired to its lands; and for the curial stratum such a choice was actually illegal. One alternative was certainly to join the church: bishops were usually from either senatorial or *curialis* families. As time went on, the ecclesiastical hierarchy became a parallel one, ever more attractive to curial families in that it was tax-exempt. But the episcopate was closely tied into imperial values as long as the empire lasted; bishops and *curiales* cooperated in governing the cities of the fifth century.

A third point is, precisely, this urban focus for the aristocracy. Only the military hierarchy was partially immune from having to operate on an urban stage in its public activity. Roman cities were full of public arenas for political action: the forum, the ceremonial buildings around it, the baths for less formal meetings, and by now the cathedral. This was often on the forum, thus further reinforcing the importance of the town centre, although equally often carefully situated in a corner of the town walls, as an alternative ceremonial focus. 'Civilized' behaviour—knowing Virgil, etc.—meant, precisely, city-dwelling behaviour. Not that one never went into the countryside. In the late empire, in particular, every major western family had at least one lavishly furnished rural estate, or 'villa' as we call them, in which aristocrats routinely spent the summer months. Large numbers of these have been found by archaeologists. But this sort of life was not considered as an alternative to the city; it was called *otium*, 'rest' (with its opposite the effectively urban-based *negotium*, 'business'). The Gaulish senator Sidonius Apollinaris (c.431–485) put it well in his extensive letter-collection of the 460s and 470s: one went to lavishly appointed estates like his own Avitacum in the Auvergne, with its portico overlooking a lake and its private bath-house, to talk to one's

---

[3] Gregory of Tours, *Liber in gloria confessorum*, c. 108, ed. B. Krusch, *MGH, Scriptores rerum merovingicarum* 1.2 (Hanover, 1885), pp. 817–18; trans. R. van Dam, *Gregory of Tours: Glory of the Confessors* (Liverpool, 1988), pp. 108–11.

guests, in the summertime, but in the autumn one was due back in town (in his case, Clermont), if one was not to be despised as a peasant. Sidonius does not mention Avitacum's agrarian functions, even though it must have had them, for they would have been the basis of his own wealth; an open interest in wealth-creation was considered déclassé. 'If you cultivate an estate in moderation, you own it; if you do it too much, it owns you,' he wrote to Syagrius, a friend whom he suspected of too little interest in urban life. This could have been said by any traditionalist Roman aristocrat. Such an equation between city and culture/civilization was inherited by the city-based episcopate, who by the late fifth century were among its staunchest defenders. Sidonius, indeed, at the end of a successful public career, became bishop of Clermont in 469, and helped defend it against Visigothic armies in 471–475. His friend Mamertus, bishop of Vienne, in the same period developed the public church rituals known as Rogations, essentially processions in the city, described in striking language by Sidonius in another letter, to fortify the citizen body after a series of disasters.[4]

One must not, nonetheless, take Sidonius too much at face value. He is a good example of this urban lifestyle and imagery, not only because he expresses it well, but also because he wrote at a moment of change. Sidonius chose to write as part of an endless tradition of poetry-loving, toga-clad, bath-frequenting civilian aristocrats. But not everyone followed his example. Syagrius, for one, did not. We do not know how typical his rejection of the city was, but it was probably not uncommon. Nor, however, did Sidonius' brother-in-law Ecdicius, who was military-minded enough to be prepared to defend Clermont with a private army. Nor indeed did Ecdicius' father Avitus (who actually became emperor in 455–456, thus launching Sidonius' public career): Avitus was capable in his youth of riding after a Hunnic horseman in Roman army-service who had casually killed his slave, and killing the Hun in single combat, a highly martial image, as Sidonius himself records in a praise poem. When the Visigoths took over southern Gaul in the 470s, the aristocracies began to have to choose new roles. Some of their members put on the robes of the

[4] Sidonius Apollinaris, *Epistolae*, 2. 2, 1. 6, 8. 8, 7. 1, ed. and trans. W. B. Anderson, *Sidonius: Poems and Letters*, 2 vols. (Cambridge, Mass., 1936), vol. 1, pp. 416–35, 362–7; vol. 2, pp. 336–41, 286–93.

church, as bishops or aspirant bishops, as did Sidonius and Mamertus; some put on armour, as generals in the armies of the new Romano-Germanic kingdoms; some, like Sidonius' own son, did both.[5] There was, however, decreasing space for a specifically civilian lay aristocracy, except for a few people in the immediate administration of kings. Sidonius, for all his confident traditionalism, was in the last generation of its splendour. By the sixth century, many things had changed.

Early medieval western elites

Let us continue with the aristocracy of the western Roman provinces into the post-Roman world, the period 500–750, to see how different they were from the Roman tradition. We can find the same sort of patterns in Frankish Gaul, Visigothic Spain, or, a little later, Lombard Italy from 568/569 onwards, and I shall take my examples from all three regions. In each case, a major marker of the secular aristocracy was by now military activity, which indeed by the seventh century was often a requirement for bishops as well. Even central government administrators could be given a belt (*balteus* or *cingulum*) by kings as a sign of military service (though in the Roman world *cingulum* and *militia* had already meant civilian public service in the abstract). It could not be concluded, however, that this sort of formal investiture 'created' military and aristocratic status, as dubbing to knighthood did in north-western Europe in the twelfth century. In fact, this period is perhaps the least explicit in western history for exactly what made up aristocratic status, the status of being *nobilis*, as aristocrats were sometimes called. Wealth (in land) was one element, certainly; military office-holding another; descent a third; closeness to the king (see Chapter 1) a fourth; an array of typical aristocratic behaviour patterns a fifth. We need to keep these separate, at least in our minds, if we are to understand aristocratic society in the early medieval west. Although in practice they have to be described together, they were considerably less inseparable than they would be in later periods.

[5] Sidonius Apollinaris, *Carmen* 7, lines 246–94, *Poems and Letters* vol. 1, pp. 138–41; for Sidonius' son Apollinaris, Gregory of Tours, *Decem libri historiarum*, 2. 37, 3. 2, ed. B. Krusch, *MGH, Scriptores rerum merovingicarum* 1.1 (Hanover, 1885), pp. 88 and 98; trans. L. Thorpe, *Gregory of Tours: The History of the Franks* (Harmondsworth, 1974), pp. 154 and 162–3.

It may be most helpful to begin with descent. Who was of clearly high status in the west in, say, the seventh century? One clear answer is former Roman aristocratic families, the group called 'senatorial' families by Gregory of Tours in the 570s–580s, although the senate as an institution was by now confined to Rome itself, and in terminal decline even there. We can trace their descent well into the seventh century in Gaul in some cases, as with Avitus' and Sidonius' family in Clermont, although less well in Spain and Italy, for the evidence is less good there.[6] These families maintained their status in part because of their continued landed wealth, but in great part because of their ancestry: they could command respect. It is interesting, however, that they were also better defined as a descent group than were the new Germanic aristocracies who came in with the conquest. In Italy, Lombard named male-line blood-aristocratic families (*genera*) are not documented after the 640s, and the concept may have rapidly fallen into disuse as they ran out of male heirs; only in Bavaria do such families, there called *genealogiae*, last into the eighth century. In Francia, by contrast, the earliest law code, the *Pactus legis Salicae* of *c.*500–510, only refers to free Franks, and makes no reference to aristocratic status of any kind.[7] In the Frankish lands, indeed, it has as a result often been argued that the early medieval aristocracy was a new service aristocracy, owing their wealth and position exclusively to Clovis and his sons. This is unlikely, for they are pretty firmly rooted, probably by 500–520 if we consider the dates of the rich founding graves of Merovingian-period cemeteries, and by 550 at the very latest. Yet the argument at least shows how hard it would be to claim that there was any explicitly characterized aristocracy of blood in Francia, at least until the major sixth-century families themselves put down roots. But these had slightly different family structures, as we shall see in a moment.

Landowning was, on the other hand, a constant. In eighth-century Italy, wealth and *nobilitas* were in effect synonyms, as Paul the Deacon

---

[6] For Clermont, see I. N. Wood, 'The ecclesiastical politics of Merovingian Clermont', in P. Wormald (ed.), *Ideal and Reality in Frankish and Anglo-Saxon Society* (Oxford, 1983), pp. 34–57.

[7] *Edictus Rothari*, Prologue, ed. F. Beyerle, *Leges Langobardorum 643–866* (Witzenhausen, 1947), pp. 2–4; trans. K. F. Drew, *The Lombard Laws* (Philadelphia, 1973), pp. 39–40; *Lex Baiwariorum*, 3. 1, ed. E. von Schwind, *MGH, Leges nationum germanicarum* 5.2 (Hanover, 1926), pp. 313–15; trans. T. J. Rivers, *Laws of the Alamans and Bavarians* (Philadelphia, 1977), p. 129.

tells us.[8] In Francia, the equivalence was less explicit, but was doubt-less regarded as equally normal. Whether Germanic aristocrats seized land directly, or were assigned it by kings as part of a formal land-settlement, or gained it through office-holding or later royal largesse, they certainly possessed it, in every successor state. Some of these possessions were huge, too, by any criteria except those of the richest fifth-century senators. Wademir, a landowner living in or near Paris, who made his will in 690, had thirty-three estates, scattered across the whole Paris area, down to Angers on the Loire, and even as far as Cahors in central Aquitaine. Bertram bishop of Le Mans in his will of 616 listed even more, some hundred estates scattered across a dozen dioceses. It has been plausibly argued that Bertram was of partially Roman descent, as well as maybe related to two Merovingian queens; it is as significant, however, that he was a close follower of King Chlotar II, and gained much of this land in the aftermath of that king's rapid conquest of all the other Frankish kingdoms in 613.[9] By now, ethnic descent was less important than *Königsnähe*; but both were transmuted into landed wealth, and thus the possibility of independent local power.

If one compares Francia with the Visigothic and Lombard king-doms, one conclusion seems clear: Frankish aristocrats were the rich-est. Wademir and Bertram are part of a group of hugely wealthy aristocrats, based between the Loire and the Rhine, who have no known parallels elsewhere. In the eighth-century documentation for Lombard Italy, landowners rarely held more than half a dozen estates each, even when they were royal associates: even middling Frankish aristocrats may have outclassed them. The situation is less clear in Spain, but our fragmentary evidence hints at a similar small scale for all but the greatest noble families. This would allow for an accumulation of wealth and a range of exchange activity in Francia that could not be matched elsewhere after 650 or so, as we shall see in Chapter 3. It also made life more difficult for Merovingian kings, who had to face the most serious faction-fighting of any Germanic

---

[8] Paul the Deacon, ed. E. Dümmler, *MGH, Poetae aevi carolini* I (Hanover, 1881), p. 48.
[9] Wademir, in H. Atsma and J. Vezin (eds.), *Chartae Latinae Antiquiores* XIII (Olten and Lausanne, 1981), n. 571, pp. 94–9, with facsimile; for Bertram, see the text and the hypotheses about family origins in M. Weidemann, *Das Testament des Bischofs Bertram von Le Mans vom 27 März 616* (Mainz, 1986).

kingdom. Riding that tiger was hard, and it is not surprising that the Merovingian kingship was the one to suffer the most serious political crisis, in the mid- to late seventh century. Royal resources remained sufficiently great in Francia, however, for the Carolingians to bounce back from 718 onwards, and to establish themselves as the most powerful dynasty in the west. Indeed, once they had asserted their authority over the factions, and once they had confiscated the lands of losing opponents, they could benefit from the wealth and local power of their aristocracies as well.

These Frankish, Italian, and Spanish aristocracies were above all military. They aimed for positions in royal government that were above all defined in military terms, as dukes and counts, that is to say provincial and local army-leaders and judges. They attached themselves to each other, and to kings, in clienteles tied together by oaths of loyalty that had a strong military element. Their image of proper behaviour allowed for a great deal of violence: not only bravery in war but also revenge-killing was considered entirely honourable, even by kings and churchmen. Gregory of Tours chronicled some more unpleasant sadism in his aristocratic neighbours, which he did criticize; he remarked rather sourly that aristocrats in general were only interested in honour, plunder, money, and court cases.[10] But these latter characteristics were more often tolerated than criticized by our commentators, including on other days Gregory himself. They were normal. So was aristocratic display. Elites wore a great deal of wealth on their person, for effect: gold and gems on fine leather and silk clothing was common among aristocrats of both sexes, for example. When St Eligius of Noyon (d. 660) was the court goldsmith for the Frankish king Dagobert in the 630s, he was so holy that he gave his gemmed silk clothes, his gold bracelet, and even his belt of office to the poor and to redeem captives. But he was not too holy to wear them at all, and when he gave them away the king gave him new

[10] Revenge as normal: for example, Gregory, *Decem libri historiarum*, 9. 19, ed. Krusch, pp. 432–4; trans. Thorpe, *Gregory of Tours*, pp. 501–2; *Vita Landiberti* 11–17, ed. B. Krusch, *MGH, Scriptores rerum merovingicarum* 6 (Hanover, 1913), pp. 364–70; Rothari, *Edictum*, 74, ed. Beyerle, p. 26; Paul the Deacon, *Historia Langobardorum*, 4. 51, ed. G. Waitz, *MGH, Scriptores rerum germanicarum* 48 (Hanover, 1879), pp. 174–6; trans. W. D. Foulke, *Paul the Deacon: History of the Lombards* (Philadelphia, 1907), pp. 205–8. Gregory on aristocrats: *Decem libri historiarum*, 5. 3, ed. Krusch, pp. 196–8; trans. Thorpe, *Gregory of Tours*, pp. 255–8; *Liber Vitae Patrum* 6.1, ed. B. Krusch, *MGH, Scriptores rerum merovingicarum* 1.2 (Hanover, 1884), p. 680.

ones. This clothing rhetoric was respected even by peasants, one should note: when the Visigothic king Leovigild gave an estate to a real ascetic, Nanctus, two of the estate-workers killed him because he was dressed in rags with his hair unkempt: such clothing was unworthy of a *dominus*.[11] Eating and drinking to excess was normal, too. Indeed, participating in royal banquets—being a *conviva regis*—was a particularly important aspect of *Königsnähe*.

Clothing and eating were not solely attributes of military identity, but it may be because of military traditions that they did not seem to have been matched by good housing. With the decline of cities as political foci at the end of the empire, urban living was no longer essential for aristocracies, and where towns were not strongly rooted, as in northern and central Gaul or inland Spain, elites came largely to live in the countryside. Only in Italy did cities clearly keep their former role as living quarters for the aristocracy. But nothing has ever yet been found by archaeologists for early medieval Francia or Italy to match the great rural villas of late Rome, which had gone by 600 everywhere—by 450 in northern Gaul. In Spain, too, only one probably seventh-century example is known, at Pla de Nadal outside Valencia.[12] Nor do literary sources tell us much about aristocratic residences, even casually, though they tell us often enough about the wonders of church architecture. Lay aristocrats seem to have spent their wealth on personal adornment, food, and—above all—buying loyalty from armed followers with money and land, rather than on the permanent buildings favoured by Roman civilian aristocrats or by early medieval churchmen.

The picture just presented has very little parallel to that of the civilian aristocracy of the Roman empire, except in the importance of landed wealth. Yet many of the ancestors of the military aristocrats of the seventh century will certainly have been Roman. Indeed, in places like Aquitaine, where few Germans settled for long, most or all of

---

[11] *Vita Eligii* 1. 10–12, ed. B. Krusch, *MGH, Scriptores rerum merovingicarum* 4 (Hanover, 1902), pp. 676–80. *Vitas sanctorum patrum Emeritensium*, 3. 10–15, ed. A. Maya Sánchez, *Corpus Christianorum* 116 (Turnhout, 1992), pp. 21–4; trans. A. T. Fear, *Lives of the Visigothic Fathers* (Liverpool, 1997), p. 57.

[12] E. Juan and I. Pastor, 'Los visigodos en Valencia. Pla de Nadal: una villa aulica?', *Boletín de arqueología medieval*, 3 (1989), pp. 137–79. Some earlier villas did continue into the seventh century in Spain, however; the best studied is Vilauba in northern Catalonia, for which see R. F. J. Jones et al., 'The late Roman villa of Vilauba and its context', *Antiquaries Journal*, 62 (1982), pp. 245–82, at pp. 271–2.

them were Roman in origin. But even Aquitainian aristocrats are not visibly different from those elsewhere, as texts such as the eighth-century *Vita Pardulfi* show.[13] Why was this picture so different? Above all it was because the form of the state had changed. The material basis for aristocratic activity, in any pre-industrial society, is land; but its institutional forms and cultural identity are always related to the wider structures of political power. The Roman empire was a very strong political system, funded by tax-raising; not only titles, status, and privilege but also money were available as a result of state service. Being a part of this system, and playing by its rules, was profitable, and, above all, stable: possession of a given title meant what it said, as the basis for secure position, and for the patronage powers that derived from it. Only in the final decades of the empire did less formal elements of local power, such as private armies, become more than occasionally necessary for aristocrats. None of this was true in the post-Roman world. As we saw in Chapter 1, the tax system was in sharp decline in the sixth century, and landowning became the basis of both royal and aristocratic wealth and power; all elements of political position were only worth anything if they were backed up by the control of land. Politics became more decentralized as a result, for local power became more and more important; it also became more direct, because if one could not impress one's immediate armed entourage, one had no chance of impressing anyone else. Again, kings and aristocrats were here in the same boat, and tended to behave in the same ways.

The other thing that changed was, of course, that the states of the post-Roman world, and the legitimacy they sought, had come to be seen as Germanic. Such legitimations were not necessarily old; recent research shows that collective identities among Germanic peoples were very fluid indeed before their armies took over Roman provinces. The 'ethnogenesis' of hitherto mixed groups, united only by their leaders, into theoretically homogeneous communities of Franks or Lombards was actually a result of that conquest, a little like the way warm toffee crystallizes into fixed shapes when it is submerged in cold water. Such a crystallization process was effective, however; as long as a kingdom lasted, its king and its court would be Frankish,

[13] *Vita Pardulfi*, cc. 9, 17, ed. W. Levison, *MGH, Scriptores rerum merovingicarum* 7 (Hanover, 1919–20), pp. 29–30 and 35.

Visigothic, Lombard, Burgundian, Alaman, Bavarian. Such kings were also, at least nominally, the rulers of a people in arms, who included the peasantry. They ruled by assembly, as a result: through the great public meetings, both at the central and the local level, often called *placita*, at which disputes were settled and laws were made, which were described in Chapter 1. This sort of political practice had strong Roman elements, but the imagery attached to it was ethnic. To participate in secular politics, one came increasingly, at least by the seventh century, to have to be seen to *be* a Frank, Visigoth, or whatever was locally appropriate. Naming practices changed to match. Gregory of Tours's great-uncle was one of the first Roman senators to be associated with Frankish government service; he was called by the Germanic name Gundulf.[14] By the seventh century Roman names in Francia were decidedly fewer; by the eighth, in a second process of ethnogenesis, all the inhabitants of the lands north of the Loire were called, and seem to have considered themselves to be, Franks. The same thing happened in Italy and Spain. With these changes, a wider aristocratic identity changed as well: all secular aristocrats became local lords with a military training, whatever else they also were.

Aristocratic families were widely-based: family attachment was through female as well as male lines, as late Roman family structures had been before them. A good deal of attention was paid to marriages, as the key means of extending clan identity sideways, and this in turn means that the location of women was of some importance to families. This did not in itself bring much female autonomy, but it is probably in this context that another social role developed for aristocratic women, at least in Francia, namely, the control of nunneries. These could become semi-autonomous religious foci for quite wide family groups, as were Nivelles in north-west Francia and Faremoutiers east of Paris for the two major Frankish clan groupings of the seventh century. Membership of the Frankish royal families, both the Merovingians and the Carolingians, was by contrast restricted to the male line, but the wives and mothers of kings were often from the aristocracy. Here, too, such women could gain a considerable political role, for themselves and through them for their families, particularly

---

[14] Gregory, *Decem libri historiarum*, 6. 11, ed. Krusch, p. 281; trans. Thorpe, *Gregory of Tours*, p. 342; *Vita Arnulfi*, c. 3, ed. B. Krusch, *MGH, Scriptores rerum merovingicarum* 2 (Hanover, 1888), p. 433.

in time of royal minorities, when mothers were generally queens-regent. When, in the tenth century, male-line family structures became a feature of the aristocracy as well, this sort of genealogical centrality produced a notable group of powerful mothers, in every part of Latin Europe. We should not mistake this set of influential women for a proof of female independence and autonomy: queenly power was often contested, and all the evidence we have for female autonomy shows it to have been both fragile and circumscribed. The public space was seen as male above all; female self-assertion in it was regularly criticized. Gregory of Tours lived at the time of two power-ful queens-regent, Brunhild and Fredegund: he reserves much of his venom for Fredegund, who was his enemy. But even more signifi-cant is his relative silence about Brunhild, his patron; female public activity was too problematic for him to be able to praise it. Women, however influential, were supposed to operate in private, inside the household. But they did get into the public arena on at least some occasions.

The local power-bases of aristocracies were, as we have seen, cru-cial. They were also highly diverse. No two areas of Europe were alike in their social structures, and this meant that local power had to be differently constructed in each. Between Nivelles and Liège, for example, hardly anyone is known to have held land in the seventh and eighth century who was not part of, or dependent on, the network of families we call the Pippinids, the ancestors of the Carolingians. Local power was here straightforward and uncontested. By contrast, around a major royal power-centre such as Paris in the same period, we find a variety of large-scale landowners jostling for power in the same space: major aristocratic families, rich suburban monasteries (Saint-Denis and Saint-Germain-des-Prés), and the king himself. Here, power was more competitive, and more mediated: both through the foundation of private monasteries, and through aristo-crats simply seeking to make their presence felt in the royal palaces that clustered north of the city. Perhaps more common than either of these two patterns, however, was a still more fragmented one. Around Lucca, the best-documented city in eighth-century Italy, documents show us a variety of aristocrats, urban-dwelling in this case, with very scattered landowning, intercut not only by other aristocratic land but also by the lands of the peasantry. No local lord could establish uncontested power in this sort of environment. Rather, he would use his lands to build up clienteles and thus support and influence. His aim would be to come to the attention of the king and become his personal follower, with the possibility of gaining more wealth as a result, or else becoming duke or indeed bishop of the city. This constant competitive game at the local level, with half a dozen major players, could absorb aristocrats for generations. It was also of course much less dangerous to royal power than were local power-points like the Liège area, at least unless the aristocratic factions of different localities joined together in wider groupings.

I have taken most of the above examples from the pre-Carolingian period, but it needs to be said as a conclusion to this section that the Carolingians changed few of these patterns. What the four generations of unitary Carolingian power between 718 and 840 did was to focus aristocratic attention firmly on the mayor of the palace/king/emperor and his court as the only serious venue for large-scale political action. This was all the more attractive because Frankish expansion into Aquitaine, Catalonia, Saxony, Bavaria, and (above all) Italy provided unmatched patronage opportunities for the Carolingian family, with a host of new counties, duchies, and royal lands to be given out. Once it became clear how profitable this could be, by the mid-eighth century, factional violence dropped back considerably, and did not return until the 830s, when the empire had ceased to expand. By then, the rules and the ideology of politics had changed considerably, as can be seen in other chapters; but aristocratic society and values remained much the same. Two changes are worth signalling: first, in the framework of a powerful and aggressive state, large landowners increased their wealth considerably, often at the expense of their poorer neighbours; second, as a result of this, aristocrats had many more personal dependants, and the rituals of dependence became rather more developed, notably those associated with sworn loyalty, oaths of vassalage as they were sometimes called in ninth-century Francia and Italy. I shall return to the implications of these developments later.

Byzantium and the Arabs

The Roman empire 'fell' in the west in the fifth century, but not in the east. Most of the eastern empire lay outside Europe, for it consisted of the whole of the eastern Mediterranean, but its capital Constantinople was and is a European city, and indeed, after the early sixth century, was unquestionably the largest city in Europe for the rest of the early middle ages. In the sixth century it dropped its residual Latin-speaking tradition, and westerners as a result usually called it the empire 'of the Greeks'; less accurately, we call it Byzantium. Throughout the fifth and sixth centuries, the picture I have drawn of Roman aristocracies was still valid for the east, with only a little modification (senatorial families, for example, were less rich); cities, too, remained active and prosperous social centres.

The crisis for the Byzantine empire came in the seventh century. One of the clearest casualties was, once again, the Roman tradition of civilian aristocratic society. Tax revenues had been cut to a quarter, but a large army was more necessary than ever; by the eighth century, we can see it on the Anatolian plateau. A new military elite grew up, based on the frontier region, which by the ninth century had developed its own culture: partly Greco-Roman in origin, partly Armenian, but above all proudly devoted to the frontier warfare of the period, and to the sort of military prowess that would have been very recognizable to a ninth-century Frank, as in the frontier epic *Digenes Akritis*, which may in parts have a ninth- or tenth-century base.[15] This military aristocracy also eclipsed most of the civilian strata. The senatorial and curial aristocracies more or less disappeared; urban life (outside Constantinople, Thessaloniki, and a handful of other centres) was by now weak, and its leaders must have gone for the most part either to the army or to the capital. Even in Thessaloniki, seventh-century city officials seem to have become restricted to the bishop and the local imperial representative, the eparch. In the *Miracles of St Demetrius*, a seventh-century text devoted to the city's patron, high-born civilian notables do appear, but they are by

---

[15] *Digenes Akritis*, ed. and trans. E. Jeffreys (Cambridge, 1998).

contrast much more vaguely characterized.[16] A real network of civilian elites was confined to Constantinople, and to the still substantial palace bureaucracy there. There came, in fact, to be a sharp political and (still more) cultural division between the bureaucrats of the capital, still imbued with a traditional Greek culture, both pagan and Christian, and the army men of the provinces; they were still at loggerheads when the Turks invaded Byzantine territory in the 1060s.

There are obvious similarities to the west in this picture, as well as fundamental differences. In the east as in the west, faced with decentralization, endemic military insecurity, and a new form of the state, civilian aristocratic structures were squeezed out. As they declined, so did much of the traditional identity of their members. Roman naming practices disappeared very quickly. If in Francia or Italy former Roman aristocrats were by 700 called Waldelen or Lanprand instead of Claudius or Florentinus, in Byzantium they came to be called John or Peter, generic names in the Christian tradition. It is actually harder to trace aristocratic family continuity across the seventh century in the east than in the west, and ancestry clearly mattered very little to the new Byzantine elites, particularly the military ones. Continuities in landowning presumably mattered rather more, though we do not have documents for this period, so we cannot check. A landed military elite dominated by 700 in both east and west, with little link to the past, whatever its genealogical origins, and with similar values; in both, it became ever more firmly rooted with time. It must be recognized that the structure of Byzantium's territorial armies, with their precisely delimited geographical remits, was quite unlike the armed aristocratic clienteles of the west. This was the result of a very different economic basis for the state, and had in turn different political consequences, as we saw in the Introduction. But even in that context, some analogous patterns of social development can be seen. The stabilization of the aristocracy had, for example, similar consequences in both east and west. The Carolingians legislated in the ninth century to try to safeguard the lands of the free peasantry, at risk from the military aristocracy. So, in the tenth century, did Byzantine emperors. They were both equally unsuccessful; aristocratic hegemony at local level was in practice unassailable. By

---

[16] *Miracula sancti Demetrii*, ed. P. Lemerle, *Les plus anciens recueils des miracles de Saint Démétrius* (Paris, 1979–81).

900 military families in the east had acquired surnames and a dynastic identity, too, which had its parallels in turn in the west a century later.

The Arab empire lies for the most part outside the remit of a book on Europe. Actually, in the ex-Byzantine lands of the Arab world such as Syria and Egypt, some Roman social patterns survived rather better than they did in the Byzantine empire itself, notably a city-dwelling tradition and a local civilian aristocracy, even if this aristocracy had far less status than the military elites of the Arabs themselves. The Arabs continued to tax, too, even if their fiscal structures slowly diverged from Roman traditions. When the Arabs conquered most of Spain, in 711, they re-established some of these patterns there. The Visigoths had taxed, but their army was certainly landed. Under the Arabs, taxation was swiftly re-established as the basis of the state, which gained a measure of stability under the Umayyad dynasty, from 756 onwards. Exactly what Arab Spain was really like is not easy to see, unfortunately, because its documents are almost wholly lost; the societies of the tiny Christian polities clinging to the northern mountains are actually better known. What we know about Arab Spain recalls Byzantium rather than the Visigoths, however. There seems to have been the same sort of balance between a largely civilian, bureaucratic culture in the capital, Córdoba (another large city, though smaller than Constantinople), dedicated to tax-raising, and a more militarized frontier aristocracy in the relatively barren central plateau, some of which had dimly remembered ethnic Visigothic origins, though these were overlaid with Berber, Arabic, and, increasingly, Islamic culture. This opposition persisted even during the tenth-century imposition of central government over the peripheries, and would break out again dramatically in the eleventh-century civil wars, after which Arab Spanish unity disintegrated.

England and Norway

What linked aristocratic social development in the western and eastern provinces of the former Roman empire was thus the militarization of practice and ideology; what differentiated the two was the survival of taxation in the east (and its reintroduction in Arab Spain), and the resultant maintenance of a powerful centre of gravity in the political capitals, Constantinople and Córdoba, and, outside Europe, Damascus and Baghdad. The politics of land thus had relatively little role in Byzantine or Arab society. Aristocrats got as much land as they could in each, as in the west; but this process was much less dangerous to rulers.

The societies to the north of the Frankish world shared some of these similarities, while maintaining numerous differences from the Romano-Germanic societies of the west until the ninth century and often later. It is necessary to stress at the outset that these societies were even more heterogeneous than those discussed up to now, for they had largely independent origins. The Celtic societies of Ireland and Scotland diverged in many significant ways from the 'Romano-Celtic' societies of Wales or Brittany; Anglo-Saxon England developed in clearly different ways from Saxony, Denmark, or northern Scandinavia, whence its rulers had come; the Slav lands were different again, with Poland and Bohemia developing as states in the tenth century, and some of their western neighbours, for example the Liutizi, consciously rejecting statehood. They did have common features, notably clearly defined warrior elites devoted to small-scale fighting and the gift-exchange of treasure, and substantial free peasantries, but any attempt to generalize across all of them risks banality. I shall here, therefore, discuss only two of these societies, England and Norway.

Anglo-Saxon England shows the clearest development, thanks to a convergence of narrative sources, documents, and archaeology. Its conversion to Christianity in the seventh century furthermore opened it up to influence from Francia; as noted in Chapter 1, it has claims to being the most successful Carolingian-style polity in Europe by the tenth century. It had to come a long way, however. Three centuries earlier, it would be hard to argue that the Anglo-Saxon kingdoms had much political coherence at all, and a century earlier than that even social classes are barely visible. The Anglo-Saxons took over Roman agricultural territories, but if there is one Roman province with a complete social and political break between the empire and the Germanic polities it is the Anglo-Saxon, that is English, sections of Britain. The sixth-century Anglo-Saxon communities seem to have operated on a tiny scale, with dozens of autonomous units scattered across the island. Cemetery archaeology and, increasingly, settlement archaeology allow one to argue with a fair degree of conviction that, although there were certainly relatively rich people in the English lands at the start of the sixth century, only at the end of that century do they stand out as a separate economic group, whose status and wealth must have derived from exploiting others. It is in the same period that the county-sized kingdoms, Kent or Sussex or East Anglia, seem to have crystallized; and in the seventh century slightly larger polities, Wessex or Mercia or Northumbria begin to appear as the product of conquest. Even these were still very small indeed and, for that matter, poor by continental standards.[17]

Seventh-century Anglo-Saxon England was thus pretty small-scale. But it did have an aristocracy. In the first laws we have, from Æthelberht of Kent around 605, they were legally recognized in a way that Frankish aristocrats still were not; and in eighth-century accounts of the same period—notably that of Bede, written in the 720s—that aristocracy is highly warlike, kept in royal households only by grants of land, gifts of treasure and by generous feasting, and capable of moving from one king to a more successful one with great ease. It is interesting that this well-defined and self-conscious aristocracy—identifiable even by its style of speaking, as Bede tells us in a story about a noble called Imma who tried to escape in disguise from a lost battle in 678 but was recognized—was at the same time so restricted in material terms that archaeologists can still only with difficulty distinguish it from the more prosperous end of the peasantry.[18] It may be that the status of an aristocrat was fenced off by essentially ritual, rather than economic, distinctions from the free peasants or *ceorls* who were his neighbours. It may just be, however, that the seventh century was a period of very rapid social change, and that Bede's account tells us more about eighth-century aristocratic identity than that of the seventh. Either way, it is at least clear that what one might refer to as an aristocratic calling became steadily more explicitly defined. In the seventh century, even landownership is barely documented; kings, notables, churches, on the one side, and peasants, on

---

[17] These assertions summarize much recent archaeological work: see the syntheses in S. R. Bassett (ed.), *The Origins of Anglo-Saxon Kingdoms* (Leicester, 1989); C. J. Scull, 'Archaeology, early Anglo-Saxon society and the origins of Anglo-Saxon kingdoms', *Anglo-Saxon Studies in Archaeology and History*, 6 (1993), pp. 65–82.

[18] Bede, *Historia ecclesiastica*, 4. 22, ed. and trans. B. Colgrave and R. A. B. Mynors, *Bede's Ecclesiastical History of the English People* (Oxford, 1969), pp. 402–3.

the other, had competing rights to take surplus from tracts of land, without the latter being for the most part in any clear sense tenants of the former. By the end of the eighth century, this was changing, and land tenure on a Roman, or Frankish, model became increasingly normal. The free peasantry still had a political role in English communities, however, as participants in court assemblies, and as liable to military service and construction work for kings. It was this public service that Offa could draw from when he built his dyke against the Welsh in the late eighth century, and that Alfred could draw from when he built fortified towns and fought off the Vikings in the late ninth. By then, aristocrats could certainly be dominant—and domineering—in England, but they had not cancelled the public role of the free.

The image of the aristocratic retinue feasting with the king is one we have seen in Francia; in England, too, it carried with it obligations of mutual support and loyalty. This was not because both societies were Germanic; it can be found in Wales and Ireland as well. The image of the warrior bound to fight for his lord by feasting obligations was general in the early middle ages: *The Gododdin*, a Welsh poem which some believe may contain a core originally composed in Scotland in the sixth century, may put it best when it says such things as 'like a wolf in fury, . . . Gwefrfawr was invaluable in return for wine from the drinking-horn', or, more sharply still, 'The men went to Catraeth, swift was their host; pale mead was their feast, and it was their poison'.[19] Feasting could kill you (even if not by the sword, by the cholesterol, given the meat consumed), but it was part of being a warrior, and a noble.

Where the societies of northern Europe differed was in the rigidity of their social structures. England was here at a mid-point; Ireland was much more rigid, and the Scandinavian societies, as it seems, rather less. In Scandinavia, it seems that even hierarchies took a long time to establish themselves, except probably in Denmark. Our sources tend to be fairly late, but for Norway we have a handful of tenth-century poems, and twelfth-century laws that have analogies with the twelfth-century laws in its colony Iceland, which separated itself off politically in the late ninth and tenth century. We can at least

---

[19] *Gododdin*, stanzas iv, viii, ed. I. Williams, *Canu Aneirin* (Cardiff, 1938), trans. K. H. Jackson, *The Gododdin* (Edinburgh, 1969), pp. 117, 118–19.

make hypotheses, therefore, about this latter period. In Norway, it would be hard to say there was a defined aristocracy at all. Here and in Iceland, communities of free peasants, rich or poor, looked to independent and highly ritualized public assemblies or *things* as their major political focus. From the late ninth century onwards, *jarls* (regional rulers) and kings sought to establish hegemony over these *things*, but it was a slow and intermittent process, barely complete in the twelfth century. It is not that such communities were havens of equality; there were certainly richer men of higher status, called *goðar* in Iceland or *hauldar* or *hersar* in Norway, who had the right to lead or represent their lesser neighbours, whether in the *thing* or at war. But this status brought little permanent power over these neighbours, and not even all that much relative wealth. Norway was a violent place; all men were quick to anger, and keen to feud. Distrust was only sensible; as the tenth-century *Hávamál* proverbs said, 'before making your way up the hall you should observe and note all the doorways, for you can never be certain when you will find enemies present'; or 'he is a foolish man who thinks that all who smile at him are his friends; he will discover when he comes into the *thing* that he has but few supporters'; or 'a man ought to be a friend to his friend and repay gift with gift. People should meet smiles with smiles and lies with treachery.'[20] The Norwegians evidently knew that their social world was hard to negotiate. But the absence of fixed power relations meant that it was at least possible, indeed even normal, to negotiate one's social and political position, as was impractical in England after 600 at the latest: not only was one dealing with neighbours who, whether richer or poorer, were in a comparable economic bracket, but even status distinctions were relatively fluid, except for the sharp difference between slavery and freedom. Norwegians fought wars and recognized military leadership—they were of course active Vikings in the ninth century—and indeed recognized feasting and gift-exchange obligations with *jarls* and kings, just as did every society we have looked at. At the local level, too, there were structural distinctions between the powerful and the weak. But social skills could overcome them. Norwegians (and still more Icelanders, who had no kingship) were in these respects about as far

[20] *Hávamál*, stanzas 1, 25, 42, ed. and trans. D. E. M. Clarke, *The Hávamál, with Selections from Other Poems of the Edda* (Cambridge, 1923), pp. 45, 51 and 55.

away from the civilian Roman world we started with as one could possibly get.

The peasantry

This brings us on to peasant society, for in northern Scandinavia even 'aristocrats' were usually direct cultivators or stockraisers. Peasant societies in our period, however, cannot be divided up and described in groups in precisely the way aristocracies can. As noted earlier, they are far less visible in our sources, so we can simply say less about them; furthermore, what we can say is generally about very external matters, such as how kings in their legislation thought they ought to behave, or what landowners reckoned their rents were. Peasant societies were also multifarious. Peasants are subsistence cultivators, and their socio-economic practices therefore vary with every change in the local ecology, which in Europe is frequently; their social relationships were also closely associated with patterns of landownership, which were equally, but differently, changeable. I cannot therefore present a broad set of types of peasantry as I did for aristocracies, for the problems of typicality are that much greater. I shall offer a set of very brief empirical sketches of three of the better-documented peasant societies of early medieval Europe, without any pretension to completeness, before offering some broad-brush generalizations.

Let us begin with the tenants of the monastery of Saint-Germain-des-Prés in the suburbs of Paris in the early ninth century, recorded for us in remarkable detail, down to the names of children, in an estate-register or polyptych from the early years of the ninth century. The economic aspects of this famous text are discussed further in Chapter 3; here, the picture of local society is the key question. Saint-Germain owned a large set of estates to the south and west of Paris, sometimes making up what seem to be contiguous blocks of land of considerable size. Most of these estates were certainly royal gifts, though sometimes aristocrats had given them, and very occasionally the polyptych refers to peasant properties that had been swallowed up by them. By 800, however, it is clear that entire villages in what has become the Paris conurbation, such as Palaiseau and Villeneuve, were wholly owned by the monastery. Peasant society was thus tenant society. The social divisions were those between different types of tenant, free (*ingenuus*) and unfree (*servus*), living on monastic holdings called *mansi*. The free–unfree divide was the basic division, but it was partially undermined by the detailed terms of the leases, which are recorded in the polyptych, with the possibility of unfree tenants holding 'free' *mansi* and reduced services, or free tenants holding 'unfree' *mansi*, and so on. Furthermore, intermarriage was possible, which probably brought social advancement to unfree husbands of free wives, and certainly brought freedom for their children. One must assume, then, that there was quite a complex pecking-order in each village, inside a frame of generalized subjection to detailed monastic control, which extended to instructions about cutting roof-tiles out of logs, feeding chickens, and weaving cloth.

Saint-Germain's estates used to be considered typical of western Europe in this period; this is not now widely believed. As said earlier, most landowning was far more fragmented than these great village-sized estates, which indeed only seem common at all in parts of north-west Francia, and subsequently also in parts of England, particularly Mercia and Wessex. In the Rhineland, central and southern France, northern Spain, and Italy we find scattered estates, and, as a result, villages with a very large variety of landowners. In any given village, indeed, one could find lands belonging to a larger or smaller set of absentee owners, farmed by tenants (free or servile), and also village-based owners, who could themselves vary in wealth and status from small aristocrats to subsistence cultivators, and who could have property focused in one village or else scattered across several. Around Lucca, for example, which certainly fully belonged to this pattern, and which is well documented for the eighth and ninth centuries, concentrations of surviving land-transactions even allow us to draw distinctions between villages. Lunata, a village on a main road 5 kilometres east of the city, had a number of prosperous local owners with several tenants each, of which the best known, Crispinus (documented 742–764), was a merchant and may have had a city house as well. This stratum of owners seems to have dominated the village; but they also were clients of the bishop of Lucca, and gave land to his churches, hence also ensuring the survival of their charters. Contrast neighbouring Pieve San Paolo, to the south of Lunata but not on the road, where there seems to have been only one leading local family in the eighth century, more peasant proprietors, and little outside landowning before the end of the century. The free owners of the village sold land to each other, and not to outsiders, thus maintaining a tight, relatively inward-looking local society. This suddenly changed in 793 when the main local landowner, Saximund, gave much of his land, including portions of two private churches—and the charters of the previous two generations of land dealers—to the cathedral; the village must have opened up as a result, and probably became less tight and stable.[21]

Fragmented landownership patterns of this type give more social role to the village as a micro-political unit. St Germain could have divided and redivided its estates as it chose, and maybe even moved peasants physically to fit. Crispinus and Saximund, however, had to deal with neighbours, who, however less rich and influential, could not be commanded in the same way, except in the case of their own direct dependants. They therefore had to be dealt with politically, maybe in the framework of public village-level decision making. Not that Lucchese settlements ever had very powerful village institutions; even village identities were often uncertain, for settlement patterns were very fragmented in the area, with no real village nuclei. The city held a lot of power and authority in its hinterland; its duke or count dominated local justice, for example. Local political foci were probably, increasingly, village churches, of which there were many—Lunata had two by 800, Pieve S. Paolo had three—some private, some episcopal; their priests were themselves landowners and rural dealers, attracting pious donations. As a result of such gifts, priestly families in the ninth century were often the central families in villages.

For clearer patterns of village decision making, we have to look to regions where there were even fewer substantial local owners, and maybe more nucleated settlement. One such is eastern Brittany, which is documented in the ninth-century charters of the monastery of Redon. These charters depict a society with few outside owners (until Redon began to expand), and with a relatively restricted stratum of wealthy locals, called *machtierns*. These men had some local authority, for example as presidents of courts and assemblies, but very little power to coerce—certainly nothing like as much as a count. Village territories (here called *plebes*) more or less ran themselves:

---

[21] See C. Wickham, 'Aristocratic power in eighth-century Lombard Italy', in A. C. Murray (ed.), *After Rome's Fall* (Toronto, 1998), pp. 153–70, at p. 168.

free villagers (or the richer among them) guaranteed land transactions, acted as sureties in disputes, and indeed judged court cases in village courts. The existence of the latter (they are called *placitum* or *mallus*, standard Frankish words for judicial assemblies) shows that a Breton *plebs* had far more organizational coherence than a village near Lucca; a *plebs* was something one could seek to dominate, and indeed fight over. It is equally notable that these Breton peasantries did not accumulate land to the same extent that one can find in, for example, Italy; their competitiveness seems to have been political rather than economic. This, like the power of their local assemblies, has closer analogies in the *thing* societies of Norway than in most of the rest of Carolingian Europe.[22]

This is as far as we can go here in setting out differences; these anyway have to be set against what peasants had in common. First, they were, as already noted, subsistence cultivators, with a sprinkling of full-time or part-time artisans: their first concern had to be their crops. Bad weather marked even surer ruin than wicked lords. Weather magic was common; Agobard of Lyon in the late 810s wrote a tract against the widespread belief in storm-makers (*tempestarii*), who could bring or avert rain and hail; and a spell involving St Christopher survives in an early eighth-century text written on slate, from the Asturias in northern Spain: 'let the village where the monk Auriolus and his brothers and neighbours live, and all its properties . . . not be harmed on trees, fields, vineyards, and fruit-trees . . . let the hail turn to rain.'[23] Secondly, in nearly every part of Europe, they lived in geographically defined communities, whether nucleated or dispersed, which meant something to them emotionally or politically, or, increasingly, in religious terms, as rural churches or monasteries and their attached ritual steadily became more widespread across the eighth to tenth centuries. Thirdly, they had to deal with lords, royal, aristocratic, or ecclesiastical, who either owned their land and took their surplus, or else perhaps owned land nearby and sought to

[22] See in general Wendy Davies, *Small Worlds: The Village Community in Early Medieval Brittany* (London, 1988).

[23] Agobard of Lyons, *De grandine et tonitriis*, ed. L. van Acker, *Agobardi Lugdunensis opera omnia* (Turnhout, 1981), pp. 3–15; partially trans. P. E. Dutton, *Carolingian Civilization* (Peterborough, Ontario, 1993), pp. 189–91; cf. *Vie de Théodore de Sykéon*, c. 52, ed. and trans. A. Festugière (Brussels, 1970), p. 45; partial English trans. by E. Davies and N. H. Baynes, *Three Byzantine Saints* (London, 1948), p. 126; I. Velázquez Soriano, *Las pizarras visigodas* (Murcia, 1989), no. 104, pp. 312–14.

extend their own properties at the peasants' expense, often in violent ways. Peasants could be the clients or followers of lords too: they could seek to exploit lordly power, not just resist it or evade it. Lords 'protected' their weaker neighbours, after all. The word 'protection' is used in our sources, and if its meaning is today sometimes ambiguous, thanks to its association with the Mafia of Italy or the USA, that ambiguity would have been well understood by any early medieval lord or peasant too. But the relationship between lordly oppression and rapaciousness and peasant resistance was essentially one of conflict: and this was so across the whole of early medieval Europe, as in all the peasant societies of history.

We can be a little more precise in characterizing these continuities. I want to look, at least briefly, at four aspects of this: peasant hierarchies, village collectivities, peasant family structures, and peasants and lords. Peasants were not all equal, as we have already seen, but the way they were unequal needs to be brought out more. The basic distinction in every early medieval village society was between free and unfree. Free men (I shall return to women in a moment) had public rights, to own, to sell, to participate in courts and decision making; the unfree did not. The manumission, that is, the freeing, of the unfree was a common pious act, particularly in the wills of landowners, but it was not always easy (the Visigothic church banned the manumission of *servi* on church lands, for example). In many European societies freedmen remained permanently under the legal patronage of their former owners; manumission was not a way of evening out social status. Solidarity between the free and the unfree was hard to achieve as a result, and not infrequently we can find court records in which a *servus* claims that he is really free, but his free neighbours witness against him and he loses. But the distinction was, all the same, not an absolute one. As we shall see in Chapter 3, free and unfree tenants did the same sort of services for and paid the same sort of rents to their landlords, for example; although unfree tenants were more subject, it was a relative difference only. It is for this reason that I have avoided translating *servus* as 'slave'. Essentially, in village society there was a more articulated hierarchy than simply that between free and unfree, stretching from substantial local landowners with their own tenants, through peasant proprietors, free tenants, and down to unfree tenants. The division between owners and tenants was in practice almost as important as that between free and unfree, although it was more easily bridgeable; many peasants owned some land plots and rented others as well. In this grey area, status may have been as flexible and negotiated as in Norway. Where villages differed was, as we have seen, in where the balance lay between these social strata: whether there were many owner-cultivators, or any owners at all, or any unfree tenants.

The free–unfree division undermined village solidarity; but so also did the behaviour of local elites. In the early middle ages, village politics was seldom so absorbing that the richest local owners would dedicate themselves to it alone; they generally looked outwards, and upwards: to the most accessible aristocrats, and to the public arena. Free peasants had military responsibilities in all early medieval polities; in Visigothic Spain, so even did the unfree. Although these were never called on in full (no early medieval state, even Byzantium, had the logistics to feed an army of hundreds of thousands of peasants, who anyway would have had little training or equipment), a peasant who could afford a sword and a horse and had an aptitude for military service could undoubtedly find a chance to perform it, either for a private lord/patron or for the king/count, or for both. The slow extension of links of military dependence to the lower levels of the clienteles of aristocrats in the Carolingian period included many members of village elites. In the tenth century, not just in the ex-Carolingian lands but in England and Castile as well, these lesser *milites* came to see themselves as a small-scale local aristocracy, and the division between them and their unmilitary neighbours became steadily sharper. One of the features of the decades around 1000 in much of the west was indeed, as we shall see, that this latter division closed access to the aristocracy and the king for the majority of the peasantry.

This slow trend was also the underpinning for some of the more dramatic examples of social mobility of the period, the low-born plucked from the dust and made counts, like Leudast of Tours in the 570s, or bishops, like Ebbo of Reims in the 820s, or even Byzantine emperors, like Basil I (867–886). Such 'upstarts' were regularly sneered at by commentators—except Basil, at least, whose dynasty lasted over a century, thus making criticism unprofitable. Famously, Ebbo was attacked by the historian Thegan: Louis the Pious 'made you free, not noble, which is impossible'. Thegan was Ebbo's opponent in the sharp Carolingian factional struggles of the 830s; the latter's allies might have been less harsh, for Ebbo was undoubtedly a powerful man. But his fragile political position was shown when he was deprived of episcopal office in 835, the most severely punished of his faction.[24] Such rapid social mobility was always likely to be risky. It was also, of course, pretty rare. But it was possible because the peasantry were still part of the public sphere, at least in theory.

I have stressed that villages were not always as yet coherent collectivities: either because they were too internally divided or because, as near Lucca, village identity was still relatively inchoate. But they did exist as concepts, and sometimes they had a certain organizational force. There are signs that early Frankish villages—or groups of villages—had local courts, run by local judicial experts called *rachimburgi*, who knew an oral version of Salic law, and could be instructed to 'speak' it by litigants. Such courts would clearly have parallels to the Breton *plebs* and the Norwegian *thing*, and versions of them (possibly less formal) must have existed elsewhere to resolve local-level disputes. Another law shows that Frankish villages were also clearly enough constituted for free males to have a right of veto on new settlers. Although this veto is sufficiently hedged around in the text to make it clear that one man could not exercise it on his own, the law at least shows that a migrant could not settle against the will of a sector of a village. Furthermore, not only in Francia, but in most other places, even Lombard Italy, villages were ascribed collective responsibilities in law codes, for catching thieves or fugitive *servi* for example, which presuppose at least a minimum common identity. In Byzantium, too, the 'Farmer's Law', a mysterious set of enactments which might come from almost any of the empire's Greek-speaking territories and date to almost any period between the sixth and the ninth century, shows free villagers regulating the common lands of the village territory, and also underwriting the taxes of fellow-villagers.[25] It has to be admitted that, taken as a whole, these activities are not that surprising, and probably could be found in every society divided

[24] Thegan, *Gesta Hludowici imperatoris*, cc. 44, 56, ed. E. Tremp, *MGH, Scriptores rerum germanicarum* 64 (Hanover, 1995), pp. 232–8 and 252; trans. Dutton, *Carolingian Civilization*, pp. 151–2 and 155.

[25] *Pactus legis salicae*, cc. 57, 45 (on migrants), ed. K. A. Eckhardt, *MGH, Leges nationum germanicarum*, 4.1 (Hanover, 1962), pp. 214–17 and 173–6; trans. K. F. Drew, *The Laws of the Salian Franks* (Philadelphia, 1991), pp. 120–1 and 109–10; W. Ashburner (ed. and trans.), 'The Farmer's Law', *Journal of Hellenic Studies*, 30 (1910), pp. 85–108 and 32 (1912), pp. 68–95.

into village territories that has ever existed. (The most surprising is the Frankish law on new settlers, which as a result has a large historiography.) But they at least bring to our attention the dimensions of local cooperation, and some differences in its intensity. Broadly, villages were stronger where there was more collective economic activity—pasturing, woodland use—and weaker where there were strong outside landowners to dominate local political practice.

Most peasant families were nuclear: that is to say, they consisted of a married couple and children, not any wider grouping such as grandparents or brothers'/sisters' families. The fact is very clear in the polyptychs, but is supported by more scattered evidence elsewhere as well. Maybe this is just because peasant houses were fairly simple, and also because people died at a relatively young age: certainly wider family loyalties were felt, for example in inter-family feuding. But there was a clear emphasis on the nuclear family unit. Inside this unit, there was a life cycle, focused on the moment of marriage and a subsequent period of childraising as the height of social relevance for any married couple; after that, their children slowly replaced them. Guy Halsall's recent archaeological study of the cemeteries of the territory of Metz in the sixth and seventh centuries shows how the highest quantity of female gravegoods was associated with women in their late teens and early twenties, presumably the marriageable age, although the highpoint for men was both later and longer, roughly in their twenties and thirties. One could reasonably conclude that women married around or before the age of 20 and men at around the age of 30, perhaps after a period of warfare or other public service. After that, both men and women were steadily buried with fewer gravegoods: they appear to have lost relevance, women sooner than men, but after their forties both of them. Society around Metz gave no particular public prerogatives to the old.[26] This seems a plausible picture; elsewhere, it will have varied, but maybe only in detail.

It must be added that as soon as one considers the archaeological evidence for gender differences, which tends to emphasize female display in the cemeteries of most of western Europe between 500 and 700, one is struck once again by how little this is paralleled in any written sources, in which women (particularly non-aristocratic women)

[26] G. Halsall, *Settlement and Social Organization: The Merovingian Region of Metz* (Cambridge, 1995), pp. 75–109, 254–7.

hardly appear at all. At most, in land documents, the consent of wives to the legal actions of husbands is required (as often in Italy), and even this is not universal. One must conclude that, even more than at the aristocratic level, women were restricted to the private arena: to life inside the small and uncomfortable houses of the peasantry. Women were expected to marry, and to remain under their husbands' control. Except in Francia and Byzantium, they seem only to have inherited land from their parents if they had no brothers. Apart from movables, they got at most a parental dowry. Even this was fairly small, for brides got most marriage-gifts from their husbands, who kept effective control of these gifts until their deaths. In Italy, in particular, women never had any period of legal independence: they were under the guardianship of their father or brothers, then their husband, then their sons. Elsewhere, a relative independence was only available at widowhood. And yet, to repeat, women were an important shop window for their blood families, as the wealth of ornaments associated with the graves of pre-eighth-century teenage women attests. In public, they were physically visible but ideologically invisible at the same moment.

Peasants also had to live alongside aristocrats, who were either landlords, lords, patrons, dangerous neighbours, or all of these simultaneously. Aristocrats were indeed intrinsically dangerous, as has already been stressed. As the Greek historian Procopius said of the Ostrogothic aristocrat Theodahad in the Italy of the early 520s: 'to have a neighbour seemed to him a kind of misfortune';[27] Theodahad was far from unique in this. It is possible nonetheless that, in the west, the period in the last two millennia in which aristocrats were least dominant was the period c.500–800; in the Byzantine east, the dates might be 650–850. Roman aristocracies in the west survived the Germanic conquests, but not necessarily unscathed; Germanic aristocracies took some time to develop. In the east, the seventh-century crisis similarly undermined aristocratic hegemony. It is not that the rich did not survive, but they could not necessarily dominate their peasant neighbours, unless the latter were their immediate dependants. Only in the eighth century in Francia and Italy, the ninth in England, the tenth in Castile and Byzantium, later still in Scandinavia, did fully-

---

[27] Prokopios, *History of the Wars*, 5. 3. 2, ed. and trans. H. B. Dewing (Cambridge, Mass., 1919), p. 25.

fledged aristocratic hegemonies begin to develop again. The evidence for this development is mostly very poor, it should be admitted. In Francia and in particular Italy one sign is a set of ninth-century court cases in which peasants protest to public powers about aristocratic domineering. In Castile, these tensions appear closer to 1000. In England, a sign that aristocrats may have become structurally dominant is the archaeological evidence for market exchange, which is confined to East Anglia in the eighth century but takes off elsewhere from the late ninth. What we lack is much evidence for full-scale peasant revolts, in other words systematic resistance to these shifts. Saxony had one, the great Stellinga uprising, in 841–842; the Asturias in northern Spain had one in about 770. On a smaller scale, a set of court documents show a valley in the high central Italian Apennines, the Valle Trita, holding off a monastic landowner for over a century, between the 770s and the 870s. All three of these cases seem to have been examples of relatively marginal and coherent, largely peasant, societies facing an unusually rapid advance in lordship, and, on these occasions, fighting back. Peasants fighting back are also attested in Francia, south of Paris, where in 859 a sworn association of peasants was created to oppose the Vikings; significantly, it was the Frankish aristocracy who destroyed it—it was too dangerous a precedent.[28] But it has to be said that there could have been more such examples: ninth-century England is a particularly interesting absentee, for it must have been undergoing sharp social changes to the detriment of peasants, given the wealth and prominence of aristocrats that is visible in our richer tenth-century evidence. The encroachment of the powerful, when it became serious, was anyway not successfully resisted, in this epoch. By 1000 aristocratic power was dominant again everywhere, almost as much as it had been under the Roman empire.

---

[28] Ninth-century Frankish court cases: see J. L. Nelson, 'Dispute settlement in Carolingian West Francia', in W. Davies and P. Fouracre, *The Settlement of Disputes in Early Medieval Europe* (Cambridge, 1986), pp. 45–64, at pp. 51–2; for Italy (esp. the Valle Trita), see C. Wickham, *Studi sulla società degli Appennini nell'alto medioevo* (Bologna, 1982), pp. 18–28; for the Stellinga, E. J. Goldberg, 'Popular revolt, dynastic politics and aristocratic factionalism in the early middle ages', *Speculum*, 70 (1995), pp. 467–501; for the Asturias, A. Barbero and M. Vigil, *La formación del feudalismo en la península ibérica* (Barcelona, 1978), p. 261; for 859, *Annales Bertiniani*, ed. R. Rau, *Quellen zur karolingischen Reichsgeschichte* 2 (Darmstadt, 1972), p. 98; trans. J. L. Nelson, *The Annals of St Bertin* (Manchester, 1991), p. 89.

Peasant societies were less militarized than aristocratic ones, and of course less rich and powerful. But they lived by some of the same rules: males in both were quick to take offence, and to react violently; males and females in both associated binding obligations with the exchange of gifts; status was associated above all with wealth, legal independence, and military prowess. There was, furthermore, a continuum between the poorest free peasant and the richest aristocrat, a continuum composed of tiny gradations of social status, which could only with difficulty be climbed, but which placed the whole of free society under the same sort of legal obligations. This would continue for some time in Byzantium and in Scandinavia, in polities of strong public power or weak aristocracies. It would change in the tenth century in the Latin west, however, that is, in the post-Carolingian world and its English and Spanish neighbours and imitators. I shall end this chapter by describing that process of change.

The year 1000

Aristocratic clienteles were a feature of the whole of the early middle ages, as indeed before and after. They were based on exchanges of gifts and favours, both upwards and downwards: lords gave protection, land, treasure, or feasts, and expected political and military loyalty in return. This was normal and praiseworthy. A Frankish king in the seventh century, for example, provided that if an aristocrat were sent away by the king to fulfil a royal function, that 'all his court-cases, and those of his friends, sworn dependants, or those in his legitimate sphere of influence' would be suspended until he returned. The aristocrat's role was to support his followers, and they needed him to be there.[29] In the Carolingian period, the rituals surrounding this dependence became slightly more articulated, as the oath of fidelity became more elaborate, and as it became commoner for lords to give lands to dependants with more explicit reference to the fact that they could take the land back if the dependant was disloyal (such 'conditional tenures' were sometimes called *beneficia*, or *feuda*, fiefs,

---

[29] *Marculfi formulae*, 1. 23, ed. K. Zeumer, *MGH, Formulae merowingici et karolini aevi* (Hanover, 1882–6), p. 57.

though the terminology remained vague for a long time). But Merovingian lords had been able to take back such lands before, in practice, and this operation, a military one, was not rendered any easier later just because the terminology of gift-giving had changed. More significant as a change was that under the Carolingians it became ever clearer that royal and comital armies were made up of these clienteles alone (including those of kings and counts themselves). Military service and military identity thus became regarded as aspects of aristocratic service, not simply the public obligations of free men; and, as noted earlier, they came more and more to be seen as a privilege, marking out *milites* as different from the non-military members of society. This pattern began already in the mid-ninth century; by the late tenth, families of *milites* could often be seen as lesser aristocrats, seeking their own local powers over the peasantry. By the early eleventh century, the structural difference between military aristocrats and peasants had become crystallized in the theory of the three orders: those who pray, those who fight, and those who work; this theory had ninth-century, if not earlier, roots, but its full elaboration only began after 1000. It had a long future in front of it: in France, the separation between these three 'estates' would only end in 1789.

Nonetheless, in all periods, the local dominance of aristocrats was a fact of life, and was one of the main reasons why elites wanted royal support and patronage. The Carolingian period, indeed, was in much of the west, as already noted, the period when aristocratic local hegemony became in practice complete. This power in theory conflicted with the local judicial power of the count, but not so much in practice: even excluding the frequent situation where the local lord was the count himself, *placita* were assemblies of aristocrats, and a peasant who wanted to contest the local domination of his own lord was not likely to win there. The life of Count Gerald of Aurillac in southern France (d. 909), who was so virtuous an aristocrat that he was regarded as a saint, gives us a clear idea of what such unusual virtue was in the late ninth and early tenth century: it included sexual abstinence to be sure, but also the refusal to let his men live by plunder when they were short of food in local wars, the insistence indeed that they paid the proper price for things as they went along, and the insistence that all such wars should only be defensive. Gerald's *placita* were also remarkable, not only because he let criminals off lightly but also that he had them at all, and judged according to law.

Gerald was further saintly in that in the civil wars of the 890s he continued to be a vassal of the king, who was nowhere to be seen, rather than transferring his loyalty to other dukes or counts. Needless to say, other aristocrats did relatively few of these things. Most significant, though, is that, in a time when royal and, on a local level, comital power still existed, at least in theory, even as saintly a man as Gerald was in practice beholden to no one, and, both in the *placitum* and outside it, did exactly what he thought fit.[30]

On one level, then, between 850 and 1100, and indeed before and after, aristocrats dominated without a break. They stayed with kings if they could and defied them if they had to, hoping to get away with it (which sometimes they did); at the local level they used their personal military clienteles to throw their weight around with little fear of reprisal, except from rival aristocrats. This was equally true of the ninth century, when kings were powerful, the tenth century, when local dukes and counts were more important points of reference, and the eleventh, when all lords had established their own judicial tribunals and in many parts of Europe the *placitum* either fell into disuse or simply became the personal tribunal of the count as a hereditary local lord. In French historiography in particular, either the collapse of royal power in the tenth century or the collapse of that of counts in the late tenth and early eleventh has for long been seen as a watershed in historical development; but viewed from the standpoint of the aristocratic dominance of *local* society, it could be argued that nothing really changed. Such an argument has been quite strongly put in recent years.[31]

The arguments for continuity are striking, but they are, all the same, not wholly conclusive. The elements I have just characterized, military clienteles and local power, had roots far back in the past, but in the tenth century, the later tenth century in particular, they began to mesh in different ways, and elements of discontinuity began to appear as well. One is the *placitum*. However much such assemblies were in practice dominated by aristocratic interests in the Carolingian period, they did represent a public legal system,

---

[30] Odo of Cluny, *De Vita sancti Geraldi Auriliacensis*, cc. 1. 8, 11, 17, 20, 23, 32, 33, 35; *PL* 133, cols. 641–3, 646–7, 649–50, 653–4, 655, 656, 660–4; trans. G. Sitwell, *St Odo of Cluny* (London, 1958), pp. 99–101, 104–5, 111–12, 113–14, 115, 122–5.

[31] See in English, but referring also to the French debates, the discussions in *Past and Present*, 142 (1994), pp. 6–42; 152 (1996), pp. 196–223; 155 (1997), pp. 177–225.

with a kingdom-wide authority, where royal legislation was at least sometimes recognized and put into practice. It represented legality; the private measures of lords, though unchecked in practice, were illegal if they were in conflict with the *placitum*. In those parts of eleventh-century Europe where the *placitum* vanished, these private measures instead crystallized into fully-fledged tribunals, with their own territorial remits, in what the French call the *seigneurie banale*. This was a real change: what had been illegal now constituted legality. There was no more give and take between two kinds of local power, either; the *seigneurie* was all there was. Similarly, when aristocrats stopped looking to kings or dukes/counts for status and patronage, and based their position solely on their own local powers, even if these local powers were essentially unchanged, the political system had shifted. Here, too, a give and take between centre and locality had gone, and local power was all there was left. These shifts simplified political structures very notably, and they were widespread in western Europe. Between roughly 1000 and 1050 they occurred in most of what is now France, except in the most coherent counties such as Normandy and Flanders; in the parts of the German kingdom that now make up the Low Countries; in northern Italy (where even the developing city states behaved a lot like collective lordships); in Catalonia. Even in England, where kings were strong, this was the period where the military aristocracy, by now clearly distinguished from the peasantry, began to build the fortified residences that would soon become castles. These are signs that England might have matched the Continent even without the Norman Conquest.

If all power became locally based in much of Europe in the eleventh century, that power could no longer be informal and de facto. Even the most chaotic *seigneurie banale* began to generate its own rules—on the basis of older local customs, but by now much more explicitly characterized. Local legalities thus began to be more clearly defined. So did the parameters of local power, seigneurial territories; so did its power-centres, which were increasingly focused on castles. So did social divisions, as military activity ever more clearly defined the boundaries of the aristocracy, and legitimated the establishment of seigneurial powers by each military family. All territories became more clearly characterized, not only seigneurie, but village and parish as well. These local building-blocks were by the twelfth century sufficiently clearly characterized for them to be the basis on which reviving central government would be built. This would be a renewed public power that, for the first time, owed nothing to the Roman past.

Figure 6 Palace of Santa Maria de Naranco, Oviedo, built during the reign of King Ramiro I, 842–850

3

The economy

Jean-Pierre Devroey

Between 400 and 1000 more than nine men out of ten lived and worked in the countryside, primarily in the context of a subsistence agriculture. At least as great a proportion of the total agricultural production must have been consumed on the spot, by farmers and their immediate neighbours (craftsmen, priests, magnates). The nature of the economy and the proportion of rural inhabitants were not fundamentally different from that of the Roman empire. But ancient society is perceived by all to have been an urban civilization. A Roman town concentrated and consumed an important share of the agricultural surpluses for the benefit of its elites. There is nothing comparable with this organization and lifestyle in any of the 'towns' of north-western Europe before the year 1000. Many historians, indeed, speak in terms of 'proto-urbanization' for this period. In about 1020 it was inconceivable for bishop Gerard of Cambrai to divide mankind in any other way than between 'people who prayed, peasants, and warriors'. A century later, the cleric Galbert of Bruges expressed his sense of belonging to a group when he called the inhabitants of Bruges 'our citizens'. For the historian, *the* essential question is whether the early medieval economy is synonymous with 'rural economy'? What are the forms of urban civilization before the year 1000?

Apart from the attempt by Marc Bloch in 1939 to give some coherence to the notions of a 'first' and a 'second' feudal age,[1] the majority of historians have been reluctant to consider the years before and after 1000 as a whole. Rather, they have considered the medieval economy and society from the eleventh to the fourteenth century as a phenomenon *sui generis*, to be explained by an acceleration of the

---

[1] Marc Bloch, *La Société féodale* (Paris, 1939); trans. L. Manyon, *Feudal Society* (London, 1961).

effect of one or more factors of growth (demographic, technological, social, . . .), that they measure in decades rather than centuries. Misunderstandings of developments both before and after the year 1000 are a consequence of this foreshortening of chronology.

The traditional interpretations

Since the emergence of economic history as a discipline in the nineteenth century, its methods and concepts have been deployed to explain what were perceived as 'two key moments of western history', namely, 'the end of ancient civilisation' and 'the birth of Europe'. First of all, the question of the true nature of the medieval economy also involved the denial or pursuit of the idea of medieval capitalism. Most historians have agreed that the 'end of antiquity' coincided with the 'end of slavery'. This question has been reopened recently. For Bonnassie and Bois, slavery *stricto sensu* (with the assumption that human beings are legal and economic objects) was maintained until the end of the tenth century, whereafter a few decades of social upheaval resulted in the 'feudal revolution'.[2] If it is indeed the case that slavery never completely disappeared from wealthier households in the middle ages in the west, then slaves can have played no more than the kind of modest complementary role in the workforce that can be documented in sixth-century Byzantium. In the west, it is possible that the emergence of the great classical estates from the seventh century onwards was everywhere accompanied by the installation of former slaves in hereditary tenures. With the integration of unfree people in the community of Christians, which left intact the social and legal discrimination against them, we have the general traits of what Marc Bloch called the 'first serfdom'.

There is a rather broad consensus concerning the idea of an early medieval 'interlude' marked by a general 'ruralization' of the economy.

[2] P. Bonnassie, *From Slavery to Feudalism in South-Western Europe* (Cambridge, 1991); G. Bois, *La Mutation de l'an mil* (Paris, 1989); trans. J. Birrell from French original of 1989. *The Transformation of the Year One Thousand: The Village of Lournand from Antiquity to Feudalism* (Manchester, 1991). Criticism by A. Verhulst, 'The decline of slavery and the economic expansion of the early middle ages', *Past and Present*, 133 (1991), pp. 195–203.

Its most characteristic expression is regarded as the Carolingian estate (perhaps because it is the best documented), with its granary, its tools and farm equipment, its craftsmen, and specialized workshops. Such an estate is thought to witness to the domination of a closed and self-sufficient economy without a real need for money or trade. According to this view, therefore, the early medieval economy is equivalent to a domestic economy. It is a *non-commercial* society.

An alternative interpretation, not necessarily mutually exclusive, was proposed by Henri Pirenne and might be called the 'Belgian paradigm'. For Pirenne, a substantial continuity of culture and civilization was apparent in the west until the end of the sixth century. It was interrupted by the Arabic conquest of the Mediterranean which eventually separated the two parts of the old Roman empire, plunged the west into economic depression and political disorder and inaugurated a steady shift of the gravity of Europe to the north-west, both politically with the emergence of the Carolingians and, in the economic sphere, with the 'reawakening' of urban life from the eleventh century onwards.[3]

'Little Belgium', therefore, was for Pirenne a paradigm of western history. It was a 'microcosm', which was destined to be not only the 'battlefield of Europe', but also would offer a forum for the exchange of ideas between the Latin and Germanic worlds and hatch the 'ancient democracies of the Low Countries'. These views were in line with Pirenne's personality as a 'historian *engagé*, son of his time, nationalistic, liberal, bourgeois, optimistic . . .: who saw history as a record of progress driven by urbanisation, trade and capitalism'.[4] Perhaps because of the dominant role played by the Mediterranean in Pirenne's arguments, few historians have emphasized the excessive concentration of his thesis on the Carolingian world and the meagre attention devoted to events in the western Mediterranean after the seventh century.

How can the extraordinary flourishing of economy and urban society in the twelfth century be explained? What were the starting points and rhythms of this growth: the seventh century, with the reawakening of new commercial flows in north-western Europe; the

[3] H. Pirenne, *Mahomet and Charlemagne* (London, 1968); trans. Bernard Miall from the posthumously published French edition of 1937.
[4] A. Verhulst, 'L'Actualité de Pirenne', in G. Despy and A. Verhulst (eds.), *La Fortune historiographique des thèses d'Henri Pirenne* (Brussels, 1986), pp. 149–53.

ninth century and the Carolingian Renaissance; the eleventh century with the rebirth of towns? Was it a response to external stimulus, stemming from the rebirth of trade in the tenth and eleventh centuries? Or was it self-generated, sustained by the dynamism of the countryside, and the production and control of the agricultural surplus necessary to urban life and to castles by groups of nonproducers? Who helped to create this growth: the great merchant venturers, the Carolingian kings, or their monks who controlled the great estates or the peasants who cleared new land?

Current research emphasizes the dynamics of the relationships between town and countryside from the early middle ages onwards, and the role of religious and political agents in economic development. The accumulation of capital was made possible by the siphoning off of surplus from source to centres of control, that is, from the countryside to the towns and from the peasant producer to the noble or bourgeois consumer. The countryside and its economy, in short, are fundamental for the development of Europe.

Facts and key issues

Thanks to archaeology, phenomena documented by written sources, such as war and politics, have been integrated into a broader vision of the relationship between man and his environment. From the third century onwards, the climate deteriorated steadily, becoming colder and wetter. The lowest point was probably in the sixth century, with an average diminution of temperature of 1.5°C. The impact of climatic change should be assessed at the regional level, though the lack of precise information makes this difficult. During the early middle ages, winters were probably less severe in Asia Minor than in the west, but generally both the landscape and the climate of the Byzantine world were harsh. In the west most of the information about the weather, epidemics, floods, or famine is drawn from dramatic accounts in the *Decem Libri Historiae* and the hagiographical writings of Gregory of Tours. Yet Gregory's descriptions cannot necessarily be extrapolated to provide an account of weather patterns in western Europe as a whole in the sixth century, let alone elsewhere. Physical anthropology and palaeopathology are also yielding an increasing quantity of data. A recent synthesis based on 5,000 tombs in Germany from the sixth and seventh centuries shows that 60 to 75 per cent of the adults died aged between 36 and 38 years old, and that the overall health of the population was poor. They suffered from poliomyelitis, rickets, and other diseases associated with vitamin deficiencies. Most of this information, however, is without any precise social or economic context. Indeed, it is virtually impossible to link any excavated burial site found in open country with a known settlement. Recent analysis of the urban sites of Marseilles, dated from the fourth to the sixth century and Maastricht, dated to the seventh and eighth centuries, on the other hand, suggests considerable social mobility and relatively favourable living conditions in an urban milieu, where one might have expected a stronger indication of problems with the food supply. With such exiguous evidence, however, generalizations are simply not possible. In Byzantium, the mobility of the rural population was a permanent feature. Cultivable lands could be abandoned and then later revert to agricultural use once more. Part of the exodus from the countryside can be attributed to the attraction of towns. But in part, too, the move to towns and desertion of the land was due to the excessive burden of the land tax. In the Balkans, the vulnerability of the peasantry was exploited by the magnates, who seized their lands, cattle, or slaves and reduced them to a state of dependence. In 535, Justinian declared this 'calamity' to be commensurate with 'a barbarian invasion'.[5] In other areas, the abandonment of the land was due to external factors, such as war, crop failure, and plague. The plague of 541–542 was part of a series of natural calamities: drought (from 516 to 521 in Palestine), earthquake (in Antioch in 529), locust invasion (in 516 and 517 around Jerusalem), and just before 541, eighteen months of insufficient sunshine prevented fruit from ripening. The epidemic of 541–542 was a bubonic plague of exceptional scale, probably comparable in its ravages with the Black Death of 1348–1350, which wiped out a quarter to a third of the population of western Europe. As in the fourteenth century, moreover, the plague was succeeded by a golden age of agricultural and industrial wages. Justinian's legislation confirms that the craftsmen and the land workers took advantage of the shortage of labour to demand prices and wages two or three times higher than usual.

[5] *Iustiniani Novellae*, ed. R. Schoell and G. Kroll, *Corpus Iuris Civilis* 3, 6th edn. (1954), pp. 1–2.

In the west, it is tempting to explain the contrast between the economies of the north and south of France in terms of supposed differences in the duration and intensity of the plague. But there is little justification for such a sweeping explanation. The 'elasticity' of the bio-geographical milieu confronted with demographic crisis was probably an essential factor at local level.

During antiquity and the beginning of the middle ages, Asia Minor had been an area of permanent crop cultivation and domestic animal breeding. The wars of the tenth century, and destruction that they wrought made a part of the land unusable for more than itinerant animal breeding, before the settlement, during the Turkish period, of new, previously nomadic, peoples. In the fragile areas of *terra rossa* of the Mediterranean basin, the extensive abandonment of the cultivation of semi-arid terrain and the desertion of the land contributed greatly to the erosion of the soil, which made any reclamation more difficult and accounts for the appearance of scrubland. In Italy, pollen analysis in temperate areas records a general advance of forest and of forms of secondary vegetation. But a new balance was established between men and the environment which allied sylvo-pastoral uses with the intensification of agricultural practices in farming plots close to where people lived, resulting in a more balanced diet.

In northern Gaul and the Rhineland, the encroachment of forest and heath are attributed to the weakening (which started in the third century) of the extensive agricultural system of late antiquity and to a fall in population. The importance of population movements is reflected in the shifting of the linguistic boundary between 'Romance' and 'German'. In the most densely populated areas, the continuity in the occupation of the land is very marked. From the third century onwards, the large 'colonial' Roman villae, aimed at the supply of towns and the army, were abandoned and there was a shift of the settlements from the plateaux to the valleys. At the same time, small family farms grew in number and cultivated areas shrank. These lands were retained for agricultural use, but the peripheral areas and the poorest or the heaviest were left to lie fallow, often until the assarting from the waste in the eleventh and twelfth centuries. The characteristic landscape of Merovingian villages is a settlement composed of scattered little hamlets, with a multitude of little fields separated by uncultivated lands. The relatively small size of these human settlements matches those of the excavated burial sites rather well.

From the seventh century onwards, the growth of population resulted in the expansion of land under cultivation and the creation of new areas of settlement by both peasants and lords. One should not, however, overestimate this expansion of arable land, for it was but the beginning of a very long drawn out process which culminated in the twelfth and thirteen centuries. After the phase of the scattering of farms, a regrouping in regions like Rhenania or Burgundy becomes apparent in the tenth century, accompanied by large-scale abandonment of hamlets. In other places, where animal breeding dominated, settlements installed in clearings maintained a semi-permanent character throughout the early middle ages.

The decline of the Roman villae was gradual. New archaeological methods of excavation have uncovered not only stone buildings but also constructions in lighter material or wood, which characterize late Roman rural settlements. In many places, there was a more or less makeshift of existing structures, with an increasing use of wood construction techniques. The documentation allows us to follow this development from the third century onwards. By the end of the fourth century, these new types of building are to be found all over the north-western empire though they do not appear for another century in southern Gaul or Italy. In the centre of France, where corresponding signs of the persistence of the ancient Roman aristocracy have been found, the laying of very late Roman mosaics at the end of the fifth century and at the beginning of the sixth, suggests a longer material and social survival of the villa. Part of the wooden constructions which become more frequent from the fourth century onwards are an inheritance or an adaptation of Gallo-Roman techniques. On the other hand, post holes, indicating wooden buildings, seem to reappear in Roman Gaul during the third century after an absence of three centuries.

A new type of settlement became common in north-western Gaul from the sixth century onwards. It comprised a cluster of independent farms, connected by a network of paths, with each farm enclosed by a palisade or a ditch and surrounded by granaries on poles, huts, silos, and workshops. This form of settlement coincides with the appearance of a new word: *mansus*. Simply denoting 'house' in the sixth century, *mansus* came to mean the house and its surrounding enclosure before being applied in the eighth century to the hereditary farm of a family of tenants.

The awakening of the eighth century

From the eighth century onwards, the climate became progressively warmer to reach an optimum in the eleventh century with 1.5 to 2°C more than the average (4° into subarctic areas at the time when the melting of the ice field enabled Scandinavian navigators to reach America). At the turn of the seventh and eighth century, the study of human remains seems to indicate everywhere, in the north, as much as in the south, a significant decrease in malnutrition. Paradoxically, famines are more frequently mentioned (there are references to sixty-four famines between the eighth and the eleventh centuries, which makes an average of one every six or seven years). However, the interpretation of these data is delicate. Once the distinction has been made between 'great hungers' of cyclic character, that is, the food shortage which happens in the gap between two harvests, and local famine, it can be seen that the number of universal famines diminished in the tenth century to increase again during the eleventh. Must we then attribute the recurrence of general famine to the (unexpected) growth of the population and regard it as the hard price which the peasantry had to pay for expansion to begin?[6]

Signs of recovery are seen more often from the seventh century onwards. Demographic growth, therefore, seems to be at work as much in the north as in the south. Studies of demographic data from some Carolingian polyptychs of the ninth century in Italy (Farfa, San Vincenzo al Volturno), in the Provençal south (Saint-Victor of Marseilles), and in their favoured region, namely, between the Seine and the Rhine (Saint-Germain-des-Prés, Saint-Remi of Rheims) create an image of a pioneer population, relatively young and mobile, sensitive to peaks of mortality, but able to respond to them with a swift increase in the birth rate. Crisis and food shortage did not have any lasting effect on the long-term trend. According to the polyptychs, the population was able to double in a time span of 50 to 150 years.[7] Swift

---

[6] P. Bonnassie, 'La Croissance agricole du haut moyen âge dans la Gaule du Midi et le nord-est de la péninsule', in *La Croissance agricole du haut moyen âge*, Flaran 10 (Auch, 1990), pp. 13–35.

[6] J.-P. Devroey, 'Courant et réseaux d'échange dans l'économie franque entre Loire et Rhin', in *Mercati e Mercanti nell'alto medioevo: l'area euroasiatica e l'area*

and widespread increase probably did not take place before the demographic surge of the eleventh century. But a growth in the number of people in the agricultural areas where the inhabitants had been established for the longest period of time had begun at the end of the eighth century. A density of population of 20 to 30 inhabitants per square kilometre was possibly reached in the Paris area or on the estates of the abbey of Saint-Bertin as early as in the middle of the ninth century. In the Abruzzese mountains, whose agricultural potential certainly did not equal that of the Île de France, Wickham has proposed the figure of 18 inhabitants per square kilometre in the Val Trita. The practice of allocating plots to tenants, and marked peasant mobility made possible both the local intensification of agriculture recorded in ancient cultivated areas and the development of new areas, though the scale is not comparable with that reached by assarting in the eleventh century. Thus, until the end of the first millennium, the landscapes of the north-west of Europe were sharply divided between areas densely populated for a long period of time and areas more sparsely populated and used perhaps only on a semi-permanent basis. One has, however, to be cautious of the bias introduced by the origins, ecclesiastical or royal, of most of the sources. In Auvergne, the local nobility established its landed wealth, on the one hand, with properties received *in commendam* from the magnates or by the usurpation of richer lands and, on the other hand, by the colonization of rougher terrain, sometimes virtually deserted. This part of their patrimony does not show up in the sources before the tenth century, when these families started to found religious settlements or were drawn into the great movement of endowment which accompanied the expansion of Cluny.

The late antique city

The Roman state was based on a network of two thousand cities supported by taxes on agricultural production. Each city would normally contain a forum, a theatre, and an amphitheatre, baths, and,

mediterranea, Settimane di studio del Centro Italiano di studi sull'alto medioevo 40 (Spoleto, 1993), pp. 327–89 and P. Toubert, 'The Carolingian momentum', in A. Borguière (ed.), *A History of the Family* (Cambridge, Mass., 1996, from French original of 1986).

from the fourth century onwards, a cathedral. The city was also the principal place of residence of the governing elite who were also responsible for the collection of taxes. Around two capitals, Rome and Constantinople, the cities constituted the network of a *world economy*—or more precisely of a *world state* centred on the Mediterranean. This state was able simultaneously to gather and to distribute basic foodstuffs, to feed the urban masses, and to provision the frontier garrisons. The permanent army consisted of about 600,000 to 650,000 men. The range of fossilized seeds discovered in the silos of the Rheinland military sites testifies to the extent of the trading networks within the Roman world of the fifth century: the troops of the Rhine *limes* (and their horses) consumed einkorn, Polish wheat, durum, spelt, wheat, barley, rye, oats, millet, and rice (this last, a clear import!). Local villae, on the other hand, produced only two or three varieties of cereal. Rome was able to use for its service a system for the distribution of foodstuffs at world-state level. This system was based on tax and on the income of huge imperial estates. The pancake or the porridge of the legionary was a true product of the synthesis of the Roman world.

Justinian and Charlemagne

Since the death of Pirenne, the question of the end of ancient civilization has mostly been considered in the chronological and geographical areas that he had privileged, namely Merovingian Gaul. Recent archaeological excavations have made neighbouring Italy, divided after the reconquest of Justinian between the eastern empire and the succeeding Germanic states, a fundamental area for the analysis of the end of the system of production and distribution in the Mediterranean world.[8]

Urban decline is an important theme of historiography. It is assumed that one-third of the 372 ancient cities of peninsular Italy, enumerated by Pliny in his *Natural History*, decayed. In the areas reconquered by the Byzantines, the survival of cities nearly reaches

---

[8] The following remarks are mostly based on E. Zanini, *Le Italie bizantine: Territorio, insediamenti ed economia nella provincia bizantina d'Italia (VI–VIII secolo)* (San Spirito, 1998).

100 per cent and examples of serious decline are rather rare. Why was there this respite compared with the rest of the western empire? It can be explained by the persistence in the Byzantine empire of the communications network of road, river, and sea, of which the ancient centres constituted the structural hubs. Of course, the Italian urban landscape was affected by general phenomena such as the Christianization of space and public monuments and the abandonment of suburban areas. But the cities of Byzantine Italy differ from other Italian cities in three ways. First, the city imposed itself definitely as an essential centre of the defence system of the Byzantine territories. Secondly, it was 'maintained' thanks to the revitalization of the institution in charge of the upkeep of the buildings and of urban public services. Lastly, urban space there avoided for a while at least the breakdown of urban structures and ruralization which are characteristic of the fate of ancient cities elsewhere.

Rome provides a good example of the difficulties of determining the exact process of change. Around 400, the city had probably half a million inhabitants. It had probably less than one-tenth of this in the seventh century. Some have seen in Rome's transformation the birth of a polynuclear city, comprising a small nexus of grouped settlements, separated by non-built-up areas.[9] It seems that a real town centre more extensive than the river bank area may have survived.[10] Rome remained a major centre of consumption and trade in Italy. The imperial *annona*, with its free distribution of cereals was possibly maintained until the end of the sixth century. In the seventh and eighth centuries, the city drew its food supply from the public, papal, and ecclesiastical patrimony in the Latium countryside and the latifundia of Sicily. The ceramic finds of the Crypta Balbi chart the fluctuations of commercial exchanges between Rome and the rest of the Byzantine empire. Until around 650, North Africa was prominent. In the last third of the seventh century, when Byzantium definitively lost its African possessions, ceramics and amphorae from the Aegean and from the east become predominant. From the mid-eighth century, new local pottery dominates. It was probably stylistically influenced by the glazed ware of Constantinople, but it is certainly a local production. This change coincides with the crisis in the religious,

[9] R. Krautheimer, *Rome: Profile of a City, 312–1308* (Princeton, 1980, 2nd edn. 2000).
[10] Zanini, *Le Italie bizantine*.

political, and economic relationship between the papacy and the Byzantine imperial administration. Nevertheless, the Crypta Balbi evidence suggests a still very active trade but one oriented towards the elite and luxury goods. On the other hand, international trade apparently did not extend into rural areas. This does not necessarily indicate a dichotomy between cosmopolitan papal and Byzantine Italy, on the one hand, and Lombard Italy, on the other, especially if the different regions be taken into account. In the south of Italy, the great majority of episcopal sees did not survive the Byzantine retreat. Out of one hundred bishoprics in the duchies of Spoleto and Benevento, hardly ten survived in 700, but all these dioceses were certainly very small, centred on little towns, and were mostly in hill country. They would in any case barely have counted as villages in northern Italy. Archaeology has multiplied the examples of urban crisis in northern Italy, with discoveries of areas which had returned to agricultural use, the abandonment of road networks, and wooded buildings in the heart of ancient Roman public spaces. However, landowners never abandoned the city, as they appear to have done in north-western Europe. Southern Gaul remained urban; so did much of Spain. The Lombard kings established their permanent capital at Pavia, and their dukes certainly resided in cities, with all that that implied in terms of population. A city like Lucca in Tuscany kept most of its Roman plan and perhaps the same density of occupation. Fifty-seven new places of worship are mentioned between 700 and 900. One-third of the churches and half of the houses mentioned in the sources before 1000 were already situated outside the Roman town walls, like the duke's palace. By the eighth century the inhabitants included merchants, luxury craftsmen, goldsmiths, members of the professions, cauldron makers, doctors, tailors, builders, and minters. Some indeed were land-owners. The cathedral and urban church estates as well as those of the secular rulers were generally managed from the city, so that the land controlled by urban inhabitants and institutions must already— or still—have formed a good proportion of the entire Lucchesia. Lucca was clearly socially and economically dominant in its territory by any criterion, in ways that had not substantially changed from the Roman world, and would not greatly change henceforth.[11]

[11] C. Wickham, *The Mountains and the City: The Tuscan Appennines in the Early Middle Ages* (Oxford, 1988).

The reconquest of Justinian temporarily restored Byzantine Italy's place in the Mediterranean economy. Italy was again part of the distribution and trade network, characterized by exchanges of local raw materials (as is proven by the continuity in production of containers in the vicinity of towns like Milan and Ravenna) and of foodstuffs and manufactured goods in North Africa and in the Syrian–Palestinian area. During the sixth century, statistics on shipwrecks found in the Mediterranean illustrate the continuity of commercial activity in the central Mediterranean (Sicily and Malta), where the finds datable to the fifth century represent slightly more than half the number of finds from the fourth century, in contrast to the western Mediterranean where the finds for the fifth, sixth, and seventh centuries are extremely scarce. While the ceramic (and monetary) profile of Byzantine and Lombard Italy are totally different and suggest the existence of virtually impenetrable barriers between these two rival states, the overall profile of the ceramic finds is comparable in Genoa and Marseilles. The Byzantine distribution network reached the ports of the western Mediterranean, Gaul, and Spain through Liguria. Like the political alliances and the intense religious exchange between the Franks and Constantinople in the sixth and seventh centuries, the prosperity and sudden interruption of the supply of African and eastern wares to Gallic markets in the middle of the seventh century could be explained by the end of Byzantine control over Liguria rather than by a general crisis of exchange all over the Mediterranean world. From 650 onwards, trade in the Adriatic attracted eastern wares and the salt of Comacchio, in an exchange that Venice managed to dominate and expand as early as the beginning of the ninth century.

In Gaul, the centre of political gravity and the exchange networks were definitely oriented towards the north-west. It would not be until the fourteenth and fifteenth centuries that another great sea, the North Sea, would become the focus of a new world economy, with the internationalization of the grain trade. The 'regionalization' of the Roman economy had been underway since the crisis of the third century and was a fundamental component of medieval Europe.

The western city

In the west, many cities lack a continuous history. They broke up into nexuses of small settlements, separated by ruins and spaces converted to use as market gardens and vineyards. They were populated by a few hundred or few thousand inhabitants. An important political and religious centre like Tours seems to have been reduced to two small religious complexes during the Merovingian period. One is beside the cathedral, in the ruined area within the Roman town walls; the other is outside the walls, around the abbey which housed the relics of Saint Martin. Even Aachen, the centre of Charlemagne's empire, was not impressive by the standards of Roman cities such as Ravenna, Milan, Arles, or Trier, by those of the contemporary Byzantine oriental towns or even by those of medieval Rome and Naples. In the Frankish world, power was not exhibited in the city, but at the spring assembly (see Chapter 1) (and to a lesser extent the palace) where the magnates gathered, to confirm bonds of fidelity and exchange gifts and tribute offerings. Neither the assembly nor the palace corresponds to the notion of a permanent capital or even, from the sixth century onwards, to a location in a town. It was radically different for the Lombard or Visigothic kings, who had capital cities with a court and permanent administration at Pavia and Toledo.

After 400, Christianity was a city-based religion, with communities grouped around bishops who were leaders of their *civitas* (see Chapter 4). The western *civitas* (that is, the city and its surrounding district) remained essentially a place of worship until the end of the tenth century. It is in this sense that one can speak of continuity in the ancient urban network, including the cities of north-western Europe. Indeed, the excavations of the last decade have uncovered remains of Roman buildings which had been built there many years previously. This is primarily a functional continuity, which expresses itself in a striking way in the permanence of religious geography. Between 400 and 600, it was the presence or absence of a bishop which determined the survival or death of a Roman city. Secondary settlements also survived during the early middle ages, they continued to have a social, political, administrative, and religious function in the heart of a small region.

The overall architectural picture of the early medieval city remains fairly sombre: dismantled town walls, public infrastructures progressively abandoned, plundered buildings, increasing use of wood in the building of houses. The one area which is an exception to this is the intense activity of church building: forty in Merovingian Metz, twenty-nine in Paris, eighteen in Lyons, and twelve in Bordeaux. From the seventh century onwards, construction work began for the most part to be concentrated on the abbeys which were being founded in the countryside. The Frankish kings preferred to live in rural palaces nearby rather than in the ancient cities themselves. At a lower level, the lay and ecclesiastical magnates favoured a variety of residences, and occupied a network of centres of power in palaces and *castella* and on rural estates, in abbeys, and at ancient *vici*.

Another exchange system was born during the same period, at the boundaries of the Frankish world. At the end of the seventh century, the abbeys of north-western Gaul had stopped organizing caravans to fetch olive oil and other Mediterranean products brought from Fos and Marseilles. Between the Loire and the Rhine, the estuaries of the great rivers became points of entry for travellers, diplomats, merchants, pilgrims, and missionaries from across the Irish sea, the Channel, and the North Sea. Few Franks used these routes. Anglo-Saxon and Frisian sailors activated trade and created new harbour settlements.[12] Two of these emporia are especially important for seventh-century Francia, namely, Quentovic (on the Canche, in Neustria) and Dorestad (on the former course of the Rhine, south of Utrecht, on the border between Austrasia and Frisia). On the other side of the sea, Lundenwich, next to the site of Roman London, Hamwic, on the site of the future Southampton, and Ipswich in East Anglia were established. These emporia or 'wiks' were centres of international trade. Others, such as Dublin, Birka, Hedeby, or Kiev, witness to the trade stimulated by the Danes, Norwegians, and Swedes. It is not clear whether these 'wiks' were spontaneous creations or royal foundations. Nevertheless, the kings took advantage of their existence, by making them compulsory entry points for the merchants, where customs dues were collected and the exchange and recasting of foreign currencies took place. Next to the harbour was an industrial area, where people, as in other inner urban sites worked with bone, horn, leather, and metals.

[12] S. Lebecq, *Marchands et navigateurs frisons au haut moyen âge* (Lille, 1983).

There was also an agricultural or market gardening zone. The dispersal of finds (except for the production of pottery which is very concentrated) hints at domestic production. The role of artisans in the rural economy is often insufficiently acknowledged: woodwork, the extraction and processing of iron ore, the manufacture of weapons and tools are all mentioned in the polyptychs (the detailed descriptions of estates drawn up from the ninth century onwards). Textile production merits special consideration. Flax and hemp are demanding and labour-intensive crops, and were produced chiefly by peasant farmers. Cloth was in part produced by collective workshops (*gynecea*), where specialist female workers or tenants' wives gathered to spin, weave, and make clothes. Nonetheless, the bulk of textile production was within the family, as is shown by the distribution of finds of archaeological artefacts linked with textile activity.[13]

The concentration of commercial activities in the new wiks or in annual fairs contrasts very strongly with the situation in Italy and southern Gaul where the role of 'ports of trade' was played by cities such as Comacchio, Venice, Naples, or Marseilles. In the Frankish kingdom the decline of the wiks had begun by the 820s and 830s, before the first Viking incursions. From 850 onwards, it is possible, though this may be a false impression created by gaps in the evidence, that sites on either side of the North Sea were destroyed or abandoned. In Dorestad's case, for example, the estuary silted up. At the beginning of the tenth century there was what may be a resumption of commercial activities in settlements of Roman origin or a move to new sites (Lundenwich to London, Quentovic to Montreuil-sur-Mer, Dorestad to Tiel and Utrecht). There may have been a hiatus in the trade of north-western Europe between c.870 and c.920, but with the continued flourishing of other centres such as Dublin, York, Birka, Novgorod, and Kiev, this is unlikely.

The 'ruralization' of Frankish elites (from the seventh century onwards and not, as it has been said for too long, from 500) has as consequences a real dispersal of places of power to which southern Europe can be clearly opposed, where there are convincing signs of the persistence of an elite and an urban lifestyle. This can explain the earlier appearance (or the permanence) in Italy of a 'domination' of

[13] J.-P. Devroey, 'On men and women in early medieval serfdom', *Past and Present* (2000).

towns in the countryside and the rise of a community of interest and of forms of organization of collective life amongst urban population in Milan, Pisa, or Lucca at the end of the ninth and in the tenth century. In the north-west there is indeed some functional continuity in the ancient urban network. But the breaking up has been total between the seventh and the ninth century in the economical function of the city, the mode of residence of consumption of the elite and the concentration of agricultural surpluses. One has to wait until the eleventh century to witness the offspring of a new urban civilization in the west.

The Roman villa

The evolution of the countryside must be considered in the long term. In Provence from the first century AD, there was a concentration of property in units of various sizes and a progressive specialization in the production of oil and wine and in sheep rearing. In two generations between the middle of the third and the beginning of the fourth century, these activities ceased or were greatly reduced in scale. The production of wine amphorae diminished in the third century and stopped in the fourth. It was in the fourth century that great northern vineyards came into their own. Generally, agricultural production became more regional at the expense of exporting activities.

While the presshouses and wine storehouses of Provençal *villae* were progressively abandoned, classical social and cultural values persisted. Profits were now diverted towards the building of churches, and great rural fortunes still existed among those property owners who had overcome the crisis and embellished their *villae* with new buildings and rich mosaics. The *villae* seem to have changed during the fourth century from acting as the centres of production and processing of agricultural products to serving the function of collection centres of rents and taxes in kind. In speaking of the great landed estates between *c.*400 and *c.*1000, historians use the term 'great estate' (French, *grand domaine*) which goes back to the Latin *latifundium*. In German, the word *Grundherrschaft* is applied to the whole of the medieval period. In French, one hesitates to speak of *seigneurie* before the tenth or the eleventh century. *Villa* (the ancestor of our 'village'), which designated the dwelling of the master in classical Latin, was used from the sixth century onwards to designate territories whose size may range from one hundred to several thousand hectares. In the sixth and seventh centuries there were still those who owned very considerable areas of land, especially in Francia (see Chapter 2), but these are more rent(i)ers than entrepreneurs. 'He who, before, ploughed the land with one hundred ploughs, now longs in vain for a pair of oxen': Remembering the 'good old times' before the Vandal invasions, Prosper of Aquitaine speaks not of the disappearance of great estates, but of the farming by the owner. Everywhere, direct exploitation was replaced by rent. The same property was sometimes called *villa* (master's house) and sometimes *vicus* (rural settlement). This apparent confusion evokes the mechanism of the patronate which brings villages of free peasants to place themselves under the protection and the 'fiscal umbrella' of *potentes* (powerful men). Thus, a village is progressively incorporated to an estate. At the beginning of the third century the owner of a large Provençal estate derived most of his income from the sale of the produce of his olive trees and grape vines. In order to increase his fortune, he could try, as indeed he did, to enlarge his property at the expense of smaller or less dynamic neighbours. From the fourth century onwards, to be a great land-owner was no longer to exploit a farm after the manner of Columella, the famous first century AD agronomer, but rather to be the patron of a network of dependants and protégés, of sharecroppers and tenants. Henceforward, to increase one's wealth meant to dominate (be the *dominus* . . .), and to force one's neighbour to sell or surrender his property rights to become a dependant or tenant. The growing confusion in the vocabulary of agricultural contracts between 'rent' and 'tax' illustrates well a change of activity of the great landowner from gentleman farmer to patron of a territory in which immunity has granted him the mediation of all the requests of the state. The magnates no longer count their fortune in thousands of *iugera* of land, but in *villae* and in hundreds of *colonicae* or *mansi*. It was no longer a matter of cultivating the land but of extracting a rent from the group of men of which one had become, metaphorically, the *paterfamilias*, the *senior*. The taxation in kind taken by the master of the *villa* does not seem to have exceeded one-tenth of the income of the peasant farms during the Merovingian period, which is substantially less than the former land tax.

Rural transformations, 400–1000

New archaeological techniques have identified encroachment of the forest, clearing of vegetation, and qualitative variations of the landscape. A prime example of new understanding is that drawn from the study of animal bones. In Gaul, the Roman conquest favoured the dominance of large cattle at the expense of the indigenous species, smaller by 20 to 30 centimetres. The same trend affected other domestic species. From the fifth century onwards, the species of large animals, whether cattle, sheep, swine, or even poultry, disappear and were replaced everywhere, until the end of the middle ages, by the smaller breeds of the pre-classical period. The decrease in the size of horses is much less marked. This is enough to rule out the idea that animal husbandry no longer had the capacity to manage selection techniques. One may surmise that the decrease in the size of the other animals is an indication of the predominance of smallholdings throughout the middle ages. The place of the horse in medieval society probably explains the care which was taken to select animals of sufficient size for travel and combat. Horses were bred and reared by specialist horse breeders. The horse's harnessing to the plough, with the shoulder collar, and its more general use as a farm animal were widespread in north-western Europe only from the twelfth century onwards.

There was also a slow but profound change in the importance and the geographical distribution of cultivated cereals.[14] Around 400 in the west two or three indigenous species (barley, spelt, wheat) predominated. The diffusion of rye and oats, mainly reserved for animal feedstuffs in antiquity, was slow at first, accelerated from the seventh century onwards, and expanded dramatically in the tenth century. Up to the ninth century spelt predominated in the north-west of the Frankish kingdoms. In the tenth century, spelt gave way to wheat and barley. Rye and oats, because they are so much hardier, played an important role in the growth of cereal culture in north-western Europe. Suited to poorer soils and to harsher climates, planting oats could prepare ground, winning to agriculture neglected or

---

[14] J.-P. Devroey, *Études sur le grand domaine carolingien* (Aldershot, 1993).

temporarily cultivated land and allowing a second possibility of harvest between the biennial alternation of winter wheat and fallow.

The history of food in Italy, evidenced by clauses in rent contracts, suggests a much richer and more varied diet. In addition to cultivated products, the farmer gathered other food from the wild such as fruits, fish, and game. In the *curtes* of Santa Giulia di Brescia in northern Italy at the beginning of the tenth century, for example, the range of cultivated cereals was much wider and dominated by rye (39%), wheat (20%), and millet (16%). For historians like Duby or White, antiquity and the early middle ages were characterized by technological stagnation and a rudimentary economy; the eleventh century brought a series of innovations—triennial crop rotation, the plough, and especially the shoulder collar—that released the constraints on modes of production and inaugurated a period of uninterrupted growth until the Black Death.[15] Delatouche was one of the first to break with this idea of a medieval 'agricultural revolution'. He argued that pre-industrial societies all practised a millennia-old traditional form of agriculture, with its crop yields, plants, and animals, which lasted until the nineteenth century when there really was an agricultural revolution. Tools or agricultural techniques like the plough with a mould board to turn heavy clods of earth or triennial crop rotation were already known and locally used in antiquity. Ancient horse harness was no more and no less efficient than the famous horse collar of the eleventh century. There was never any real rupture in technological knowledge between antiquity and the middle ages.[16]

What really changed between 400 and 1000 are the levels of distribution and the economic and social relationships within which these tools were used. Let us discard first of all the idea of the absolute 'superiority' of the heavy plough (with mould board) in relation to the swing plough, for the use of the one or the other depended on soil type and the local climate. The Mediterranean soils of *terra rossa* on a limestone bedrock are suited to extensive cereal culture and to dry

[15] G. Duby, *Rural Economy and Country Life in the Medieval West*, trans. C. Postan (Los Angeles, 1968, from French edn. of 1966); L. White, Jr, *Medieval Technology and Social Change* (Oxford, 1962).

[16] R. Delatouche, 'Regards sur l'agriculture aux temps carolingiens', *Journal des Savants* (1977), pp. 73–100. See also G. Comet, *Le Paysan et son outil: Essai d'histoire technique des céréales (France VIII–XV siècles)* (Rome, 1992).

arboriculture. These conditions imposed a system of low productivity, based upon biennial crop rotation and the work of the swing plough, which ventilates the soil without provoking excessive evaporation and the rising to the surface of mineral salts that would be the result of deeper ploughing. In the medieval countryside, the fertility of the soil and diversity of agrarian life was the direct outcome of man and his labour. In 893, in the harsher conditions of the Ardennes, the *culturae* of the *villae* of Tavigny or of Villance grew only oats. At the same time, the two mills of the village ground *maslin* (a mixture of wheat and rye) and extracted malt. The peasants paid rent in rye and spread dung to fertilize their lord's fields. The distinction between intensive and extensive agriculture is therefore between family holdings and the extensive cereal culture of the great estates.

The evolution of the great estates

Compared with the estate of the Carolingian period, the Merovingian *villa* was far smaller, with less arable land and less cleared for tillage. The tenures were generally less numerous and their association with the estate was very loose. The main income came from the cultivation of the lord's land and the taxes paid by tributary peasants. During the seventh century the elements of the 'great classical estate' began to appear, with its twofold organization, under which the demesne land (farmed directly by the landlord), enlarged and redistributed, is developed through the services imposed on the *manses*. A study of the vocabulary applied to rural institutions highlights the appearance of new terms and new realities. The appearance of a new term, *mansus* and its semantic evolution take on special significance. Hypotheses concerning the origin of the *mansus*—a holding created to normalize the situation of *servi casati*; a royal institution—have yet to be confirmed. On the other hand, it is well established that the *mansus* created, from the seventh century onwards, a very strong link between the dwelling, its inhabitants, and the farmlands, forming a farming unit within the framework of the manor. The tenants enjoyed extensive rights to the forest and wasteland and could transmit the possession of their tenure to their children. In exchange they were liable to taxes and services fixed by the customs of the estate.

The *riga* or piece-work appeared around the year 600 as a system of small strips of land on the estate which were the responsibility of different manses, from the first ploughing to the bringing in of the harvest. The strip shape of these plots suggests that they were ploughed with a heavy plough with a fixed mould board. They were probably cultivated from year to year by the same family, which facilitated the supervision of the labour. In the tenth and eleventh centuries, many of these plots became the possession of the farmer who cultivated them in exchange for a minimal rent.

During the seventh century, the relationship between the lord and his peasants has been expressed in the edicts of the Merovingian rulers, preserved in the *Lex Baiwariorum* and the *Lex Alamannorum*. These laws present, from a theoretical point of view, two types of tenures or manses associated respectively with freedom (albeit from late antiquity, a *colonus* no longer enjoyed full freedom of movement) and servitude. Typically, a 'free manse' (*mansus ingenuus*) was subjected to a certain number of 'public' taxes, linked with military service, mixed with 'private' taxes, in kind (agricultural and animal products; wood or wooden utensils, metal work, or textiles; manufactured goods) and/or in money and labour services. The last named would mostly entail the cultivation of the lord's demesne land, local cartages, and long-distance transportation (*angaria*). To the *riga* were added *corvées* of ploughing (*opera corrogata*) accomplished several times a year by the tenants with the ox team from the manse on the large fields (*culturae*) of the estate. The overall tax in kind may have represented between 10 and 15 per cent of the income of the farm. The efficiency of this system and its success in drawing out new resources for the master and the tenant is illustrated by the fact that Charlemagne was able to insist upon compulsory payment of the tithe (a supplementary charge of 10 per cent on all the revenues of the land and of animal breeding) to the benefit of the parish churches.[17]

The typical charges of the servile manse (*mansus servilis*) added to some taxes in kind the obligation to provide the master with a certain number of work days, usually three, per week. West of the Rhine, an increasing number of servile manses also had to do ploughing

---

[17] *Capitulary of Herstal,* 779, c. 7, ed. A Boretius, *MGH, Capitularia regum francorum* I (Hanover, 1883), no. 20, p. 48; trans. P. D. King, *Charlemagne: Translated Sources* (Kendal, 1987), p. 203.

corvées, and the service of three days of work per week was often required from free manses, which had been exempted from it hitherto. The difference between free and servile tenures remained more marked east of the Rhine.[18]

A legal decision of Charlemagne during the summer of 800, made at the request of peasants from the Le Mans region, shows the existence of a very strong link (stronger than the legal status of the dependant) between the productivity of the work on the tenure and its duration.[19] The service accomplished by the tenant with his plough, freed him from the obligation to offer two other days of manual work per week to his lord. The king forbade lords to demand more than the rules required with respect to *opera*. The description of the burdens of the manse, at the time of the redaction of the polyptychs, thus created a legal relationship between the landlord and his tenants through granting heritable tenure of a farm saddled with a specific set of levies and services.

During the ninth century, there was no longer a correspondence between the status of the tenant and that of his tenure. A free man settled on a servile manse owed 'servile' work. A serf occupying a free manse fulfilled the same obligations as a free tenant. From an economic point of view, there was thus a strict equality (absent in theory from social and legal relationships) between free and non-free people within the manse. For resident serfs, the allocation of tenure meant the chance to create a home and to transmit tenure to their children. This constituted a radical step forward. Even the non-resident serfs benefited from a better status in the context of the great ecclesiastical estate. A charter of St Gallen of 817 shows *ancillae* (women attached to the estate) dividing their week between three days of work for their master and three others for themselves.[20] On the estates of Saint-Remi of Rheims, there was on average a ratio of one free man to one serf among the dependants. Around 850, freedmen and serfs amounted to less than a quarter of the total population.

The evolution of a servile population and of work services tell the

---

[18] A. Verhulst, *Rural and Urban Aspects of Early Medieval Northwest Europe* (Aldershot, 1992).

[19] *Capitulum in pago cenomannico datum*, ed. Boretius, MGH, *Capitularia regum francorum* I, no. 31, pp. 81–2.

[20] H. Wartmann (ed.), *Urkundenbuch der Abtei St Gallen I (700–840)* (Zürich, 1863), no. 228, p. 220.

same story, namely, the quest by a lord for a specialized and well-equipped workforce for the development of the estate and a relative indifference to manual labour. There was a ready supply of brute strength on which an estate manager could draw at will and at the peak times of the agricultural year, such as haymaking, harvest, and the grape-picking season. *Corvées* of ploughing and long-distance cartage were the most durable elements of the manorial system and were the services most wanted by the lord. Charlemagne's decision of 800 is exemplified in the lands of the abbey of Saint-Germain-des-Prés located south of the Seine. It is the basis for a 'virtuous circle' by which a tenant who possessed draught animals was busy only one day per week, in exchange for the work that his plough team carried out on the arable lands of the estate. Ploughing with a team of from four to eight oxen is a striking feature both of the Carolingian countryside of the north-west of Francia and of the manor in England from the tenth century onwards.

The installation of the 'classic manorial system' between the seventh and the ninth centuries between the Loire and the Rhine, testifies to the will of the Frankish sovereign and of the magnates (lay and ecclesiastical) in that region to produce cereals on a grand scale without resorting to slave labour. The creation of hereditary *manses*, the reception of tenant farmers, and the supply of cattle to be raised and maintained all testify to the will of the lord to secure the services of a group of men, specialized farmers, farm labourers, or cowherds, who could handle the plough. Similarly, the wives and daughters of these men reared families and were responsible for textile production. Whether this system was 'efficient' is largely irrelevant, for it was so widespread and lasted for a century at least in the central part of the Frankish world. It is much more important to seek to understand why it was set up; for what it was used; why it was not set up elsewhere, particularly in the south. The scarcity of written sources leaves the southern societies of the ninth century in obscurity. But much can be drawn from comparisons with the situation elsewhere.

Rural society and the state

In Byzantium, tenant smallholdings quickly became the most widespread mode of cultivation, with the decrease in the number of large estates and a near total eclipse of farming by the owners until the eleventh century. The needs of the state were fulfilled through a direct relationship with the peasantry (see Chapter 1). Provided that he paid his dues and taxes, the Byzantine peasant was accountable to no one.[21] The state tolerated this situation, for it enabled it to recruit the army and raise taxes directly from the peasantry, without intermediaries. The re-emergence of the great estates at the turn of the eighth and ninth centuries, and resumption of the role of the magnates as middlemen for the collection of taxes did not alter the essentially 'rentier' nature of the relationship between masters and peasants in Byzantium.

Another aspect of peasant obligations recorded in the Frankish polyptychs was the transport of goods. In the ninth century, networks, based on *corvées* of transportation, around and to domanial centres, can be documented in the heartland of Francia and northern Italy. The surpluses of the estates were collected and, according to the needs of the great secular and ecclesiastical landowners redistributed, to central places, namely abbeys, palaces, or ports of trade, like Quentovic. A portion of this produce was put to commercial use. Some of it also contributed to the services in kind due to the state, such as the supply of soldiers or the provisioning of the army. Up to the tenth century in Italy, this network for the transport of agricultural products was linked to urban centres, supplied from the warehouses of the great ecclesiastical landowners in Pavia, Milan, Mantua, Parma, Piacenza, and others. The domanial agents who travelled these routes were gradually supplanted by professional free merchants, notably those from Venice. Exchange based on the domain thus gradually merged into new and larger commercial networks.[22]

---

[21] M. Kaplan, *Les Hommes et la terre à Byzance du VIe au XIe siècle* (Paris, 1992).

[22] P. Toubert , 'Il sistema curtense: La produzione e lo scambio interno in Italia nei secoli VIII, IX et X', *Storia d'Italia. Annali 6: Economia naturale, economia monetaria* (Turin, 1983), pp. 3–63 and A. Verhulst, 'Marchés, marchands et commerce au haut moyen âge dans l'historiographie récente', in *Mercate e Mercanti* (Spoleto, 1993), pp. 23–43.

Charlemagne's *Capitulare de villis* (*c.*800) was the expression of the king's desire to exploit the production of the fisc lands (royal estates) and great ecclesiastical estates for the support of the administration and his military campaigns.[23] The geography of the polyptychs and the great classical estates is thus a 'political geography'. All this system of direct production of cereals, of transportation and concentration of the surpluses was set up at the core of the kingdom, as well as in the newly conquered regions such as Lombardy and Saxony. The king resided for the most part in the different palaces of the heartlands where his own lands and followers were concentrated. There he raised the army and there too he took the great abbeys under royal protection. These abbeys participated threefold in the *functiones publicae*, namely, military service, gifts, and prayers for the royal family.

In central Francia in the ninth century, moreover, the Frankish king did not hesitate to remove benefices from church lands to give them to his vassi, or to force the church to maintain mounted soldiers at its own expense. These *milites* lived on the income of the taxes of the *manses* which had been assigned to them. A letter of Lupus of Ferrières, in 840, paints a vivid picture of the misfortunes of *milites* of the abbey, who, overwhelmed by the cost of ceaseless campaigns, had spent all the rent paid by the peasants.[24] The *mansus* was also used as a means of measuring the contribution of free people and of nobles when raising exceptional taxes, like the tributes paid to the Vikings in the second half of the ninth century, or the size and nature of the military contingent: a foot soldier for four *manses*, a mounted soldier for twelve. A system in which dependants paid rent in money and kind to the aristocracy probably applied to most southern areas of the Carolingian empire as well. South of the Loire, for example, where bipartite *villae*, *corvées*, and polyptychs are practically unknown, the king was a remote element of the rural world and the big property owners are the military and ecclesiastical elites. In areas such as Brittany, Iceland, Catalonia, or central Germany, however, rural societies

---

[23] *Capitulare de villis*, ed. Boretius, *MGH, Capitularia regum francorum* I, no. 32, pp. 82–91; trans. H. Loyn and J. Percival, *The Reign of Charlemagne* (London, 1975), no. 15, pp. 64–73.

[24] Lupus of Ferrières, Ep. 16, ed. L. Levillain, *Loup de Ferrières: Correspondance* (Paris, 1964), pp. 94–7; trans. G. W. Regenos, *The Letters of Lupus of Ferrières* (The Hague, 1970), no. 16, p. 32.

were prosperous and independent, controlled mainly by the logic of subsistence economy. Such social groups excluded neither slavery (within the context of work on the family property), nor the existence of some social stratification, but their essential axis lay in the preponderance of a peasantry, which controlled its own lands, with more or less autonomy and in rather loose hierarchies of dependence. The leading men were rooted in the village community.[25]

The problem of rural growth

One cannot therefore link the rural growth of the early middle ages to any specific form—great estate, small property and peasant autonomy—of social organization for agricultural production. The reduction of public and private obligations, which had fallen most heavily on the peasantry, created greater prosperity which was a prerequisite for a demographic growth and a general increase in the volume of the production. This initially resulted, in the west at least, in an extension of land under cultivation. In Byzantium, soil and weather conditions were not so conducive to expansion.

The 'progress' recorded in the countryside is not sudden or 'revolutionary', but is the slow increase produced by an intensification of agricultural practices. The diffusion of new techniques went hand in hand with institutional and social innovations. The condition of the non-free segment of the population was definitively differentiated from slavery, when their master provided them with an inheritable tenure and allowed them to set up their own families and households. With the clearance of land, free landlords could establish new *manses*, while free peasants chose to bring their lands to a magnate in exchange for tenure, in order to escape the responsibilities of the free man, namely, taxes and military service, and to benefit from the immunity and the protection of their new master. All these transformations made the peasant and his family, with his expertise, his animals, and his agricultural tools, the essential actor of rural life.

---

[25] Bonnassie, 'La Croissance agricole du moyen âge' and C. J. Wickham, 'Problems of comparing rural societies in early medieval western Europe', *Transactions of the Royal Historical Society*, 6th series, 2 (1992), pp. 221–46.

The year 1000 and beyond

There are few historians who have not adopted the caesura of the tenth century as an end or beginning of a period. But the most serious difficulty to overcome is of a heuristic nature. The excavations of rural sites of the eleventh century are rare and offer few points of comparison with the previous period, where the remains of abandoned settlements abound. As for the written sources, quite apart from their scarcity, they often differ in nature and interpretation is difficult. Many institutions in the eleventh century, moreover, made particular decisions about what they wished to be remembered about the past, and selected from their historical records and archives accordingly.[26] Other types of sources simply cease to be produced as the systems they described were superseded. The polyptychs are a case in point. For sources as detailed as the Carolingian polyptychs concerning the rights and obligations of peasants, it is not until the twelfth century with the charters of rural franchises, regulations, and custumals that we again have sources offering comparable detail. It is thus essential to take a long view in investigating medieval institutions. Take the example of the fate of the *corvée* of ploughing and labour services recorded in the late polyptychs of the end of the tenth and early eleventh century. The rough work, long insisted upon, is now hardly mentioned. On the other hand, the former owners of the great estates had devised an effective and durable system of *corvées* to ensure the ploughing of the arable lands of the estates. In Romerée, in the south of present-day Belgium, about the year 1000, the *corvée* was still required in its 'Carolingian' form, namely, nine days of harnessed ploughing; two shared-*corvées* of a *bonnier* (approximately two hectares), but only twenty-four days of manual labour, concentrated during the most intense period of the agrarian cycle, namely, the haymaking and the grain harvest. In Thiais, at the beginning of the thirteenth century, the descendants of the tenants of the *manses* listed in the polyptych of Saint-Germain-des-Prés, continued to perform nine days of ploughing. Instead of three days of work per week,

---

[26] P. Geary, *Phantoms of Remembrance: Memory and Oblivion at the End of the First Millennium* (Princeton, 1996).

manual work was reduced to one day for mowing. Between the Sambre and the Meuse in the twelfth century, the former tenants of the *manses* were a minority among the villagers, with charges and privileges inherited from the past, the *masuirs* (old French, from the Latin *mansionarii*). The structures of the old *manses*, gradually sub-divided, are still identifiable from references to the quarter lands (*manses* divided into four) or to old rented *corvées* allotments. The mass of the peasantry was obliged to pay a rent which was a propor-tion of the harvest or of the land under cultivation. This land com-prised dismembered lands of the old *manses* or lands won from the former or by assarting from the waste. At the same time, all were subjected to new charges, raised per head or for the use of common facilities, such as the oven or the mill. This means that little remained of the manorial system where once it had flourished. Thus any con-cept of growth in the middle ages cannot depend on the model of the Carolingian villa in order to understand the eleventh century. Never-theless, the dynamism of the great estate is a crucial indication of long-term rural and demographic expansion.

In the ninth century, Flanders, the great area of urban development of north-western Europe, was still an area where the manorial system was underdeveloped or marginal. Pirenne's central idea of a *birth* of the medieval city in the eleventh century precipitated by the reawakening of international trade and industrial production must now be completely revised. For Pirenne, the *castrum* (fortified settle-ment) was not only not a city, but had no urban characteristics. Its population did not produce anything by itself, and, from an eco-nomic point of view, its role was that of a simple consumer. Yet the definition of the medieval city should also take account of the importance of consumption in urban growth in both Flanders and Italy. The city was a centre of consumption, production, and trade. Alongside the merchants, it is necessary to make room for the other components of urban population, namely, the ecclesiastical and lay elites, the administrators, town garrison, servants, and craftsmen, and to acknowledge their role as consumers or sellers of farm surpluses. All things considered, it is a question of applying to the eleventh and twelfth centuries a wider understanding of what an exchange econ-omy means, just as the cartages of a Carolingian monastery played a vital role in early medieval trade. Nor should we forget the activities of the landlords: in 1095, the count of Hesdin's men went down the valley of Canche to the sea (where Quentovic had been) with corn and wine and brought back salt and fish!

The long slow rise of the western European economies

A glance at the history of the regional economies in the southern Netherlands between the seventh and twelfth centuries underlines the importance of long-term developments. The extent of the inter-regional exchanges between the Frankish, Anglo-Saxon, and Scandinavian worlds between the seventh and the ninth century is well known. From such a perspective it is clear that communication and exchange, in their multiplicity of forms (trade, migration, plunder, war, gifts, and tribute) were not stopped by the invasions or short-term political crises. Flemish merchants frequented the port of London shortly after the year 1000. In 1127, the death of the count Charles the Good was reported in London the next morning. At the end of the eleventh century, the world of Godric of Finchale, the archetypal merchant venturer and 'animated with the spirit of capitalism', as Pirenne put it, encompassed the shores of the North Sea, namely, England, Scotland, Denmark, and Flanders.

Anglo-Flemish marriages show the strength of these cross-Channel contacts in the ninth and tenth centuries. Count Baldwin I of Flanders eloped with Judith, daughter of King Charles the Bald of the west Franks, who was by the age of 16 the widow of two kings of Wessex. Baldwin's son married Elftrude, the daughter of King Alfred the Great. There was also intellectual commerce: the English monks Dunstan and Æthelwold were in contact with Ghent, where Gerard de Brogne had just revived the abbey of Mont-Blandin. The Danes in about 1030 and the Normans in 1066 set about establishing states which straddled the trading circuits of the eighth, ninth, and tenth centuries. At the beginning of the eighth century, Anglo-Saxon and Frisian merchants had sailed up the Seine to Paris, carrying the wine to be sold at the fairs of Saint-Denis. It was with a cargo of wine that men of Rouen went to the port of London in 1000.

The notion of a continuum is also helpful in considering the historical conditions for a gradual growth of the medieval economy.

Thus, the Frisian 'crossroad' (seventh to ninth centuries), Carolingian agricultural growth, the vitality of the English monetary economy
(seventh to twelfth centuries), the diversification of the Flemish rural
economy (tenth to thirteenth centuries), the industrialization and
urban concentration of cloth production (eleventh to twelfth centuries), the creation of broader systems of circulation and new continental gateways, connecting the north-west to the south such as
the Flemish and Champagne fairs, Ghent, Bruges, and Cologne (late
tenth to thirteenth centuries). The long agricultural growth started in
the eighth century. As explained above, the small family farm also
seems to have been a key element in the intensification of agriculture
by means of the adoption of the draught horse for ploughing, the
diversification of production, a better balance between agriculture
and breeding, and the establishment of new crops and industries.
From the early eleventh century onwards, the exchange of goods and
networks of secular power are increasingly focused on towns. It is still
difficult to gauge the attractiveness of the city for a rural population.
Nevertheless, from the end of the eleventh century, the growth of the
urban population was fast and uninterrupted. The appearance of a
wage-earning class and the masculinization of the textile workforce
during the eleventh century certainly constituted a crucial element in
this transformation. It contributed to the shaping of the two aspects
of medieval society: the countryside and the real city, conscious of
itself, eager to govern itself, able to retain the elites and to attract the
poor.

Generally, it is necessary to view the medieval city as a social reality,
a human landscape, and to raise the question of the emergence of a
distinctively urban society. Many roads led to the city. The city was a
great city if it were simultaneously the political or administrative,
economic, religious and cultural centre of a large area. Trade, merchants, and industry alone could not make a city great. From the
eleventh century onwards, the city differs from the countryside in the
nature, culture, and dynamism of its elites. These *meliores* were not
foreigners and adventurers, but a mixture of nobles, knights, lay and
ecclesiastical administrators. Henceforth, agricultural surpluses were
concentrated (whether as goods in warehouses or in the form of
taxes) and consumed in the city. The wealth was used for public and
private buildings, fine clothes, and the patronage of the arts. It kept
tradesmen in business, paid the wages of the craftsmen and servants,

and supported charitable institutions. There the princes lived, the clerics gathered, and the architects, sculptors, and goldsmiths worked. Trade was a consequence of urban society, not a cause. The new elites played a leading role in the birth of 'the city as city', with its own regulations, administration, justice, and the freedom of the citizens. Cities in northern Europe were self-governing, though they never became urban republics and acquired independence like the Italian communes. All inhabitants of the city benefited from the 'freedom of the city'. Nevertheless, the *meliores* were in charge and thus secured the exclusive control of finance and commerce until the great social revolts at the beginning of the fourteenth century. The industrialization of cloth making in the cities explains the precocity and the importance of the Flemish towns. Their exceptional size stimulated the demand for foodstuffs and raw materials in the countryside. It accounts in turn for the intensification and the advance of Flemish agriculture in the thirteenth and fourteenth centuries.

Urban consumption was also crucial for early medieval Italy. There, the continued residence in town of the social elites and the importance of urban landowning in the countryside ensured the domination of the city over the countryside at a very early stage. In the north of Italy, in cities such as Milan, Lucca, Pisa, and Genoa in the tenth century, the concentration of commercial and artisanal activities sustained the emergence of new classes, who soon struggled for power with the traditional elites of the city, namely, the bishop, counts, or public representatives, and powerful landowners. Here, as in Flanders and in the north of France, the outcome of these conflicts in the twelfth and the thirteenth centuries led to the institution of communes. In northern Italy cities had acted as collectivities, at least informally, from the late seventh century onwards. In Byzantium, the upsurge of new urban sites and the probable expansion of older cities from the tenth century onwards was made possible only by a substantial increase in agricultural production. But, there was one very significant difference between Byzantine towns and their counterparts in Flanders and northern Italy. In Byzantium, towns were so dominated by the landowning elite that the other groups (merchants, entrepreneurs, and craftsmen) were never able to gain control of the towns.[27]

---

[27] A. Harvey, *Economic Expansion in the Byzantine Empire, 900–1200* (Cambridge, 1989).

The hypotheses developed in these pages make the case for an extended process of economic expansion on either side of the year 1000. One should not regard this long development as a synchronous, progressive, and continuous movement. We still lack detailed studies of the economy of particular regions. An economic perspective alone is not enough for a balanced picture of the cities and the countryside. To understand the birth of the 'urban landscape' in terms of both space and time necessitates an integrated approach, attentive to social and cultural factors and to the production and the consumption of material goods.[28]

[28] The remarks on the evolution of Flanders after year 1000 are mostly drawn from J.-P. Devroey, ''Twixt Meuse and Scheldt: Town and country in the medieval economy of the southern Netherlands from the sixth to the twelfth century', in P. Vandenbroek (ed.), *The Fascinating Faces of Flanders: Through Art and Society* (Lisbon, 1998 and Antwerp, 1999), pp. 48–76.

Figure 7 Franks Casket

4

Religion

Mayke de Jong

'Real Christianity'

Early medieval Christianity has a bad odour in modern historiography. Wedged in between the golden age of the Church Fathers and that of the Gregorian reform, early medieval varieties of Christianity have long been considered as a deviation from the 'real thing': Christianity became a religion at the service of secular powers, in which public ritual prevailed over personal belief. This modern disparagement of early medieval Christianity focuses upon a salient feature of the period we are dealing with here: the integration of religious and secular authority, and the importance attached to the public cult of God in the context of the well-being of kingdoms and empires. Hence, exploring the nature of Christianity as a public religion, upon which the salvation of kings, kingdoms, and peoples depended, will be the central aim of this chapter.

When Bishop Jonas of Orleans (d. 840) evoked a golden age of the 'ancient fathers', he attempted to underscore the huge decline of proper penitential rituals in his own dreadful day and age. Jonas had a pristine early Christianity in mind, an authoritative source of wisdom to draw upon in view of reforming religious and social practice in his own society. Yet the texts that in Jonas's view embodied ancient Roman ritual were in fact the product of a more recent liturgical creativity in the early medieval kingdoms of the west; the appeal to old and therefore venerable tradition consolidated the results of innovation.

The notion of an original and therefore 'real' Christianity belongs to a long and still unbroken tradition that perceives Christian values as essentially timeless and superseding change. This unchanging substance of Christianity is embodied in canonical texts—not only in Scripture, but also in the writings of the Fathers. Throughout the centuries, this 'sacred page' (*sacra pagina*) has served as a model for the present. The one permanent feature of Christianity is the fact that change was—and still is—conceived of in terms of a return to an authoritative past. Modern historians of Christianity therefore tend to experience a powerful sense of continuity, as well as the temptation to become engaged, in their turn, in a centuries-old debate about which version of Christianity might be more 'real' than others. But from a historian's point of view, this question is irrelevant. It is the self-definitions of Christians in the past and their shifting parameters that should be investigated, as well as patterns of change obscured by a rhetoric of continuity.

New Christendoms

In 312, before going into the battle at the Milvian bridge near Rome, 'about noon, when the day was already beginning to decline, he [Constantine] saw with his own eyes the trophy of a cross of light in the heavens, above the sun, and bearing the inscription, WIN [THE BATTLE] BY THIS. At this sight he himself was struck with amazement, and his whole army also, which followed him on this expedition, and witnessed the miracle.' This is a story of the Emperor Constantine's conversion on the eve of a battle that was to give him the imperial crown, as told by Bishop Eusebius of Caesarea: a sudden revelation, comparable with Saint Paul's experience on the road to Damascus (Acts 9: 1–9), persuaded the emperor to commit himself to the God who brought victory. In subsequent centuries, Eusebius' narrative was to become the model *par excellence* for a ruler's conversion; to turn from paganism to Christianity was to become a 'New Constantine', and also, to gain entry into the seductive world of the economic and cultural riches within the confines of *Romanitas*. At first glance, Eusebius' depiction of Constantine's conversion seems fundamentally different from subsequent early medieval representations of barbarian kings opting for Christianity. Whereas Constantine's conversion was supposedly an individual experience, the barbarian rulers' decision in favour of the new God was usually depicted as a collective one, requiring consultation with the leading men. Yet Eusebius furnished a revealing detail: before going into battle, Constantine's entire army witnessed the sign in heaven. Eusebius's model—an emperor and his army witnessing a divine revelation—became the cornerstone of early medieval standard narratives of royal conversion. These had some recurrent features: an already Christian queen urging her husband to convert; hesitation on the part of a king weighing ancient loyalties to the ancestral gods against the superior powers of the Christian God; the promise to convert if the new God would give a clear sign of these powers, usually victory in a battle; and then, the baptism of the ruler followed by his warriors. The ideal conversion of a barbarian king was both a collective and an entirely voluntary act, leaving the honour and freedom of the ruler and his people unimpaired. In his *Ten Books of History*, Bishop Gregory of Tours (d. 594) inserted the Franks into a biblical and Roman past. He portrayed the conversion of King Clovis (d. 511) as a prolonged process of joint decision making, at the court and in the army. A victorious battle clinched the matter for the king, and he was followed to the baptismal font by more than 3,000 of his warriors. *The Ecclesiastical History of the English People* written by the Northumbrian monk Bede (d. 735) propagated this model of rational conversion to an even greater extent. Bede's triumphant tale of the Christianization of the English begins in 597, featuring Æthelberht of Kent, the first English king to take the plunge. But Bede's tale of the conversion of Edwin of Northumbria, towards the very end of a string of conversions of English kings, is as good an example as any of the ideal this author had in mind when he reflected on the past of the English people, bound together by a process of Christianization. The king and his 'wise men' debated the merits of the new and unfamiliar faith at great length in the royal hall. Coifi, the chief pagan priest, admitted that his gods had insufficiently rewarded him, and volunteered to lead the destruction of his own shrines. King Edwin was baptized in York on Easter Day 627, 'with all the nobility of his kingdom and a large number of humbler folk'.[1]

Conversion of the type favoured by Bede and other narrators of

[1] Bede, *Historia ecclesiastica gentis anglorum*, II, c. 14, ed. and trans. B. Colgrave and R. A. B. Mynors, *Bede's Ecclesiastical History of the English People* (Oxford, 1969), pp. 186–9.

barbarian history entailed the emergence of a new Christian people (*gens*). Political identity was largely defined by religious boundaries. This was no barbarian peculiarity, for a similar quest for religious unity—at least in the domain of the public cult—had gained momentum in the Christian Roman empire of the late fourth century. Hence, barbarian kings and their peoples converted once they had entered the Roman orbit. When the Visigoths settled within imperial territory in 376, they were allowed in on condition that the entire people would adopt the faith of the empire. Accidentally, the Visigoths embraced the then dominant doctrine stressing the human nature of Christ, which would subsequently be condemned as the heresy called Arianism. The Visigoths played a key role in the conversion of other Germanic peoples, so Arianism initially became the religion of the ruling elite in a number of post-Roman kingdoms, while the indigenous population—and their powerful bishops— adhered to 'Catholic' Christianity. This religious divide temporarily frustrated the aim of creating one Christian people, but not for long. The Burgundians abandoned Arianism in 516, the Visigoths in 589; only the Lombards in Italy wavered between Arianism and Catholicism until the mid-seventh century. Thanks to Bishop Gregory of Tours, King Clovis has the reputation of having converted immediately from primeval paganism to Catholicism, but recent research has revealed that this ruler had also explored the merits of the Arian competition.[2] To Gregory, Arianism represented all that was vile and insidious, a heresy posing a potential threat to the newfound Christian unity of the Franks.

England had also been part of the Roman empire, but here Roman culture had been less firmly implanted than in Gaul or Spain. Had the Anglo-Saxon peoples that settled in England after the mid-fifth century encountered anything like the well-organized church of the Romanized Continent, with its powerful bishops who were also leaders of their communities, they might well have followed the usual pattern of accepting Christianity upon entering former Roman territory. Instead, Anglo-Saxon rulers initially remained pagan. This is not to say that Christianity was completely eradicated in England, for communities of British Christians still existed in the 590s, and

---

[2] Danuta Shanzer, 'Dating the baptism of Clovis: The bishop of Vienne vs the bishop of Tours', *Early Medieval Europe*, 7 (1998), pp. 29–57.

King Ethelbert of Kent had married a Frankish princess, Bertha, who brought her Christian entourage with her, including a bishop. Christians in Kent presumably requested missionary assistance from Rome; we do not know for certain from which circles this call for help came, for Bede's portrayal of the victorious growth of English Christendom left no room for a varied religious landscape.

The conversion of England became the personal project of Pope Gregory the Great; he responded to the call for help, and in 597 sent his missionary Augustine to Kent. To Æthelberht, the Pope wrote that he should be 'like Constantine [who] transcended in renown the reputation of former princes'; Gregory compared Ethelbert's Christian wife Bertha with Helena, Constantine's mother. This was no less than an invitation to Ethelbert to adopt a Roman past, and to look upon Constantine as a predecessor in whose power and renown he might now share. In Ireland—never part of the empire—Christianization also meant the forging of a closer link with the Roman world. Already in 431 Palladius, a member of the Gallo-Roman aristocracy, was sent to Ireland to minister as a bishop 'to the Irish believing in Christ'. Palladius' mission has been overshadowed by Patrick, Ireland's celebrated missionary. For all his fame, very little is known of Patrick and his activities in Ireland. In the eighth century, the church of Armagh harnessed the saint to its bid for primacy, and legends began to flourish. According to Patrick's own *Confession*, this British Christian was carried off as a slave to Ireland; after having escaped, he returned to Ireland to preach the faith, inspired by a vision. This may have happened around c.450, but no contemporary source confirms this traditionally accepted date.

The monastic nature of the Irish Christianity, with abbots ruling the church, has often been contrasted with the 'episcopal' organization of the continental churches. These differences have been exaggerated, however, and moreover, it was not a matter of an authentic Irish church created out of nothing by Patrick. By c.700 Ireland indeed knew large monastic federations led by abbots wielding great religious and secular authority, but this was the result of a gradual process also occurring in England and on the Continent: there as well monastic life had become integrated in the structures of religious and political power. Monasticism originated in the late third century in Egypt as a movement of lay men and women who radically renounced 'the world', which included secular as well as ecclesiastical power. By the early seventh century, however, monks and nuns enjoyed the patronage of the great and good, inhabiting a network of sacred communities upon which 'the world' relied for prayer. This is the history of monasticism in a nutshell. Tension between abbots and bishops is part of it, but so is episcopal support of the monastic movement. In areas without a strong episcopal organization based on the Roman *civitas*—the basic civil administrative unit—monastic communities provided an alternative type of ecclesiastical organiza-tion, serving as important religious centres supported by royal and aristocratic power. This was the case in northern Gaul and England, and even more so in Ireland, but this was a matter of degree, rather than a fundamental deviation from a general pattern.

But there were also real differences. Irish Christianity was more open to native traditions, which were not rejected as 'pagan' but incorporated into the new religion. Furthermore, a rigorously ascetic Irish monasticism cherished the ideal of 'pilgrimage' (*peregrinatio*); to follow Christ meant a radical break with the security of the monas-tic confines at home. Irish monks were to wander the face of the earth throughout the early middle ages, offering their services as scholars and missionaries to rulers across the sea. One of the most famous wandering Irishmen was Columbanus, who came to the Frankish realm in 590 and founded the monastery of Luxeuil on land belonging to the royal fisc, with royal support. He was in the vanguard of a drove of Irish *peregrini* flocking to the continental courts between the late sixth and ninth century—missionaries, but also scholars attracted by the patronage of Carolingian rulers. Of course the Irish also 'peregrinated' to their neighbours in England, for this was the first port of call. Hence, the English kingdoms were converted by two Christian traditions that had grown apart, having developed different liturgical customs over time, especially with regard to the date when Easter was to be celebrated. In Whitby in 664, at a meeting chaired by King Oswy of Northumbria, matters came to a head. The king opened by 'observing that all who served the One God should observe one rule of life, and since they all hoped for one kingdom in heaven, they should not differ in celebrat-ing the sacraments of heaven'.[3] This is Bede's celebrated account,

---

[3] Bede, *Historia ecclesiastica*, III, c. 25, ed. and trans. Colgrave and Mynors, *Bede*, pp. 294–309.

and the outcome of the meeting is well known: Roman tradition prevailed.

Yet this famous story should not be taken as an indication of the existence of a 'universal Roman Church' in control of an expanding early medieval *Christianitas*. The new Christian realms might invoke Roman authority, but these polities primarily defined themselves by drawing strict liturgical boundaries coinciding with their respective 'peoples' (*gentes*). The quest for a truly uniform Christian cult was a crucial element that defined the identity of a king and the leading men of his *gens*, who were accountable to God for their 'people'. This is why King Oswy chaired and arbitrated the discussions in Whitby, just as continental rulers habitually convoked and presided over ecclesiastical councils. Such gatherings usually brought together the bishops of a particular kingdom.

There was nothing particularly barbarian about this arrangement; after all, the Emperor Constantine had presided over the ecumenical council of Nicaea (325), the foundation of Catholic orthodoxy. In the post-Roman west, Constantine and Nicaea remained influential precedents for the conduct of kings during such eminently public and highly ritualized conciliar meetings. Church councils both expressed and enforced the unity of the polity. This was particularly true of Visigothic Spain after King Reccared's conversion from Arianism to Catholicism in 589. From then on, the fight against insidious heretics and other outsiders was one of the means of strengthening the cohesion of a kingdom full of strife; so was the unity of the cult. As the king and his bishops expressed it at the fourth council of Toledo in 633, 'let there be no more diverse ecclesiastical custom among us, who are contained within one faith and one realm; for this is also what the ancient canons have decided: that one and the same province should keep to the same custom of singing the Psalms and celebrating the Office and Mass'.[4] One faith and one realm, these were the key words. The argument that clinched the debate, both in Whitby and in Toledo, was the 'Roman-ness' and universality of an authoritative tradition. Yet this very notion of universality became an important element in the self-definition of Christian polities claiming the 'ancient canons' as their exclusive heritage.

[4] Fourth Council of Toledo, c. 2, ed. G. Martínez Díez and F. Rodríguez, *La Coleccíon canónica hispana 5. Concilios Hispanos: segunda parte*, Monumenta Hispaniae Sacra, Serie Canónica 5 (Madrid, 1992), pp. 183–4.

How 'universal' was papal Rome by c.700? Since the days of Pope Leo I (440–461), the bishops of Rome had claimed to be the direct successors of Saint Peter and the leaders of a universal church. This crux of papal identity was still cherished in Rome in the seventh century, in spite of the fact that from the late sixth century onwards the Roman clerical hierarchy increasingly became the province of Roman aristocrats. Gregory the Great had a universal and expansive Christianity on his mind, but his active support of the conversion of the English has become so famous that it is easy to forget how exceptional such papal commitment was. Gregory's successors left the missionary initiative to the kings and churchmen from the north who cherished an ideal of Rome as a source of authentic Christianity, as the constant stream of pilgrims from northern Europe to Italy's sacred places testifies. The papacy depended for its continued existence on its memories of past glory, and its identity as the successors of St Peter, but even more on the 'Rome in the mind' of northern men like Bede, Willibrord, and Boniface. Would papal authority as we know it have survived without these great expectations in England, and without successive emperors pacifying Rome and protecting the papacy, in order to preserve a source of authentic Christianity uncontaminated by in-fighting and scandal? Before Charlemagne was crowned emperor in Rome in 800, he had to rush to the aid of Pope Leo III, who had been captured and tortured by Roman aristocrats. Subsequent emperors, be they Carolingian or Ottonian, worked hard to keep the vital font of authority as pure as it could possibly be. When Otto I became emperor in 962, it was after having reimposed order on papal Rome; purifying Rome had become the hallmark of the true emperor.

In 800, a confident new Christian empire emerged, emphatically endorsed by papal authority. Yet initially the Carolingian polity had conceived of itself as a competitive New Israel of the Franks, with as strong a sense of its superiority as other competing Christian polities. By the 820s, this notion of the 'New Israel' was superseded by a conception more suitable to what had become a huge Christian empire encompassing many peoples: the *ecclesia gentium*. This concept was the Carolingian version of Saint Paul's 'Church of the Peoples', a church that was no longer restricted to the Jews who had been the first followers of Christ, but invited all the gentiles who wished to join, and share in the hope of salvation. The political ideology of this vast Carolingian empire/*ecclesia* still retained much of its flavour of a 'New Israel', held together by the mortar of religious and cultic unity. Whereas the church of late antiquity had been a part of the Roman empire, without being entirely identical with the structures of political power, in Carolingian ideology this relation was reversed. The empire itself derived its coherence from the fact that it was an *ecclesia gentium*, a world defined by correct Christianity, as opposed to false versions thereof.

Charlemagne's long and bloody campaigns against Saxony in the 770s and 780s represented the ugly face of conversion. Baptism was forced upon all Saxons; any public pagan practice merited a death penalty. This type of Christianization was reminiscent of late Roman imperial might throwing its weight behind Christianity, but it was at odds with the ideal of voluntary and honourable royal conversion with which Carolingian ecclesiastical leadership was familiar. Charlemagne's most influential counsel in the years of the Saxon campaigns, Alcuin of York, surely knew Bede's *History* by heart; against this background, the forcible conversion of Saxony was a shocking deviation from the authoritative models of the past, and Alcuin did not hesitate to make his criticism heard in high quarters. Yet this violence was also the ultimate consequence of a more general principle to which Alcuin subscribed as well: a 'correct' Christian cult was the crucial ingredient of the identity and cohesion of early medieval polities. If salvation in the wake of expansion met with resistance, it was imposed by force.

Behind all this loomed the demanding God of the Pentateuch, the stern and unrelenting judge of kings and the peoples in their charge. In the post-Roman kingdoms, the Old Testament served as a source of 'old law' upon which new kingdoms might be built. Of course the New Testament held pride of place, for it had superseded the Old, and the church had now supplanted the synagogue—all were agreed on that. But when all was said and done, the New Testament yielded precious little in the way of 'good old law'. Wherever strong new polities emerged, it was with constant reference to an authoritative Old Testament past. A vengeful God demanding unswerving loyalty from the people of Israel and its kings: this was the image that was foremost in the minds of early medieval rulers. In the *Admonitio generalis* (789) Charlemagne compared himself with the biblical King Josiah finding and implementing the Book of Law; this is only the most famous instance of a ruler harnessing the Old Testament to the identity of a recently established polity. Christian rulers of the early middle ages were aided and advised by bishops and abbots, but this did not detract from their eminently royal role: to supervise the correctness of the Christian cult, just as their Old Testament predecessors had been responsible for good worship in the Old Israel. Old Testament legal precepts infused early medieval law. In 603, the strict and legalistic observance of the Lord's Day in Rome had provoked Gregory the Great's displeasure; he accused his flock of 'judaizing', and explained to them that real Christianity was not a matter of such rigorous formality. Three centuries later, a detailed and formal observance of Sunday had become part of Charlemagne's legislation, along with tithes and a whole host of other legal precepts inspired by the Old Testament. In 797 Charlemagne clearly stated his views on the division of God-given tasks (*ministeria*) between the Pope and himself: the latter was to raise his pure and priestly hands in prayer to God, like Moses, while Charlemagne got on with the task of defending Christianity, ensuring the safety of those who prayed.

At first glance, this reads as a typically western statement affirming the dualism of church and state, as opposed to a Byzantine tradition of 'caesaropapism'—that is, emperors laying down the religious law to all, and supposedly keeping trembling bishops in their place. It is gradually becoming clear, however, that the differences between east and west have been exaggerated.[5] Carolingian bishops were not averse to casting themselves in the role of a contemporary Nathan, that is, as prophets chastising their more or less penitent David, but their eastern colleagues were equally capable of claiming the moral high ground in confrontations with the emperor. And the Byzantine emperors were not the only ones to make religious policy their business; their western colleagues also viewed themselves as the guardians of the correct cult, and therefore as the moral leaders of their people—bishops included. The royal and episcopal offices were not identical; each had their own 'ministry', a God-given task. Yet as the Emperor Louis the Pious explained in 825, all the different 'ministries' within the empire/*ecclesia* were derived from the supreme imperial *ministerium*.

---

[5] Gilbert Dagron, *Empereur et prêtre: Étude sur le 'césaropapisme byzantin'* (Paris, 1996).

In the political strife of the 830s, a group of Frankish bishops challenged this view, calling themselves the 'vicars of Christ', and claiming superiority for the episcopal ministry on the grounds that only bishops were capable of 'binding' (imposing a public penance on) and absolving sinners; the keys to Heaven were in their hands. This was a minority point of view, however; the majority of the Carolingian ecclesiastical leadership accepted that the ruler bore the ultimate responsibility to God for the sins of the people of whom he was in charge. If kings neglected the duty of 'correcting' their subjects, God would punish the people by sending plagues, pestilence, crop failures, and military defeat. Whenever such disasters occurred, the first question asked at the court in Aachen (and elsewhere) was: 'What have we done to offend God?', to be followed by the second one: 'How can we atone for our sins and avert God's wrath?' The answer was, by doing penance, either collectively—by fasting, prayer, and litanies—or individually, in aid of the 'stability of the realm'. Already during Charlemagne's reign, public atonement gained ground as a vitally important safeguard to the survival of polity; under his son Louis, it became the predominant frame of reference for political action.

Similar patterns can be found in the eastern empire. The humiliating loss of Syria, Palestine and Egypt to Muslim conquerers from the 630s onwards, an onslaught that was only halted by the Emperor Leo III in 717, caused a profound ideological turmoil. An embattled eastern Roman empire also perceiving itself as a New Israel asked the fundamental question. How have we sinned? Why has God punished us so severely, deserting his Chosen People? One possible answer was: because we have fallen into idolatry, confusing the worship of the one God with that of images. Between 730 and 843, the so-called Iconoclast controversy transformed the eastern Roman empire. The iconoclasts ('icon-smashers') held that the worship of images of Christ, the Virgin Mary, or the saints violated the Second Commandment: 'Thou shalt not make unto thee any graven image, or any likeness of anything that is in the heaven above . . . Thou shalt not bow down to them, for I the Lord thy God am a jealous God, visiting the iniquity of the fathers upon the children . . .' (Ex. 20: 4–5). Within the eastern empire, this was a minority stance. Images were omnipresent in the churches of the east, as a focus of intense popular devotion: this was the most conspicuous difference between the Christian east and the encroaching Islam. Yet the minority point of view held sway at the court in Constantinople; the conviction that idolatry had indeed been the sin so grievously punished by God as to send the Arabs led to Emperor Leo's celebrated decree against image worship (726). The devotion of the Sacred Cross became the only accepted alternative: 'in this sign' Constantine had gained his victory, and so had the Emperor Leo in 717 when he halted the advancing Arab armies. The view of the court—which owed a lot to people who read their Old Testament better than most—deeply offended rural popular devotion, and especially monastic piety. To the icon-worshipping party, God had been offended precisely because of insufficient veneration for the traditional sacred images.

In the course of more than 150 years of Iconoclast controversy, loyalties predictably varied, at the court and elsewhere, and the context of the debate changed profoundly. By the mid-ninth century a Byzantium emerged with the worship of icons firmly in place as an enduring and crucial element of its identity, a very different world compared with the eastern Roman state of 650. The heated dissension over image worship in broad strata of society was a typically eastern phenomenon; the western response to the debate about images remained restricted to a few court intellectuals and their emperor, Charlemagne, who took a lively interest in the matter.

Yet these differences are less important than a profound similarity. In both east and west the struggle over 'real Christianity' transformed the Roman Christian empire into the very different religious and political landscape of the early middle ages. The new polities were 'post-Roman', in the sense that the Christian Roman past remained an authoritative source of authentic Christianity; after all, this had been the Age of the Fathers. But it was an even older and more sacred past that shaped the early medieval world, in west and east, namely, the biblical past of the Old Testament, and the notion of the Chosen People guided by its ruler to salvation.

Elusive others: Jews, heretics, and pagans

The identities of the post-Roman New Israels were defined in contrast to negative 'others': Jews, heretics, schismatics, and, of course, pagans. The dangers posed by these 'enemies of the Christian people' were mostly in the eye of the beholder: these were useful enemies, strengthening a sense of coherence and unity. When it came to identifying and classifying 'others', early medieval authors derived their categories of thought primarily from Scripture. The real heir to the Roman empire, in terms of political strength, economic wealth, and geographic expanse, was the Ummayad Caliphate of Damascus, and its Abbasid successor in Baghdad. Yet little was known of Islam in the west, except the incongruous notion that these pagans—a strictly monotheistic faith—worshipped 'idols'. Likewise, the Jews were perceived within a biblical frame of reference that often remained a theoretical perspective. In the early medieval west, Jewish communities were minute islands in a big Christian sea. There were some sporadic attempts at converting Jews harshly in Merovingian Gaul, and a more consistent policy in the Visigothic kingdom to prevent Jewish converts to Christianity from returning to their original faith. It is difficult to assess whether the laws issued in Toledo actually led to a fierce and programmatic persecution, but there is no doubt that the Visigothic Christian polity increasingly came to depend on an ideology revolving around the dangers of a Jewish contamination of a Gothic and Christian purity. Still, the real effects of this strident anti-Judaism are not known, and the Visigothic legislation remained an exception in the early middle ages; the Carolingian emperors consistently and actively protected Jewish merchants in royal service.

In the north, where Jewish communities were even less numerous, Jews were an enemy primarily known from Scripture. Above all, the Jews were the 'prior people' of the Old Testament; those who had forfeited their right to be God's Chosen People by not recognizing Christ as the Messiah. This notion of the New Israel taking over from the Old was at the heart of early medieval biblical commentary; the model was provided by the Fathers, but their early medieval successors elaborated on this theme to their heart's delight. This held true of Bede in his Northumbrian monastery, way up north, who had never encountered a Jew in his life. But other Old Testament scholars such as Hraban Maur (d. 856), the abbot of Fulda and archbishop of Mainz, turned to Jewish experts in order to discuss the finer points of 'historical' exegesis, that is, the elucidation of Old Testament history and geography. The domain of spiritual exegesis, which brought out the true meaning of all these facts, was strictly a

Christian affair. Hraban and his fellow biblical commentators were fully engaged in appropriating Old Testament history and translating it into an allegorical Christian truth, an operation to which the presence or absence of 'real' Jews was immaterial. The 'truth of the Jews' was something from which Christians should distance themselves, because it was literal-minded and erroneous; on the other hand, the Old Testament past with its models and heroes was the new past adopted by the New Christendoms.

In real life, heretics were even thinner on the ground than Jews. One of the curious features of the early medieval west is the absence of the popular heresies so characteristic of the second half of the western middle ages, as well as the typical focus of popular heresy: the self-styled holy men roaming the countryside so familiar in the eastern Roman empire and Byzantium; in the east, heresy was a matter of vociferous public discussion. Only rarely did such uncontrolled religious charisma leave a trace in the written sources of the west. In the 740s a certain Aldebert gained a large following, including bishops, in the region of Soissons; the man claimed to possess a Letter from Heaven and had a saint's Life written for himself, contrary to all accepted principles of saintly humility. His adamant adversary was Boniface (d. 754), the English missionary who became a prime agent of ecclesiastical reform within the Frankish polity. At Boniface's behest, Aldebert was condemned at a synod in Rome (745), and turned into a heretic of truly heroic proportions in a way that far exceeded his actual importance.[6] But Aldebert and others of his ilk were useful enemies, embodying a negative image of sanctity that helped to define the proper channels of the sacred.

Real heretics, equally rare, tended to come from learned circles. As far as can be determined, the waves they caused remained limited to the learned echelons of society. By the late eighth century, these included the court. At the Council of Frankfurt (794) Charlemagne presided over discussions about adoptionism, a doctrine that claimed that Christ was God's adopted son. A chorus of Frankish and Italian bishops appealed to Charlemagne, who listened to contentious

---

[6] Nicole Zeddies, 'Bonifatius und zwei nützliche Rebellen: Die Häretiker Aldebert und Clemens', in M. T. Fögen (ed.), *Ordnung und Aufruhr: Historische und juristische Studien zur Rebellion*, Ius Commune, Sonderhefte 70 (Frankfurt am Main, 1995), pp. 217–63.

theological debates, as Constantine had. This was a clear sign of new imperial authority about to manifest itself, but nonetheless, adoptionism did not spread beyond the happy few who had mastered the intricacies of the Trinity. The same held true for the heresy of the learned monk Gottschalk in the 850s. His strict Augustinian reading of predestination frightened bishops, who worried that the faithful might become utterly fatalistic if they learned that they were predestined to salvation or damnation, regardless of their efforts during life on earth. Gottschalk's ideas were hotly debated in monasteries and at the court of Charles the Bald, but there is no sign that the views of this Saxon monk of aristocratic birth held a wide appeal. His sympathizers and opponents were other cognoscenti: learned monks, bishops, courtiers, and kings. Yet 'heretics and schismatics' assumed momentous importance in Carolingian biblical commentary; they served as a powerful metaphor for any disruptive force that might pose a threat to the politico-religious order.

The third possible guise of 'the other' was paganism. The insurmountable divide between Christians and pagans was part and parcel of the self-definition of the new Christendoms in the west, whose career as so many New Israels had begun with kings abandoning their pagan gods. But the Christian authors who depicted paganism did not do so as ethnographers, but as men trying to explain the falsehoods of the 'old religion' to the Christian elites for whom they wrote. They built paganism into something comprehensible to their Christian audiences, complete with temples where idols were worshipped under the aegis of powerful priests. Bede's portrait of the pagan priest Coifi was influenced by Christian ideas about proper priestly conduct. When Coifi set off to destroy his own temples, he mounted the king's stallion, bearing arms. As Bede commented, all this had been forbidden to Coifi when he was still a pagan priest, a thought that would easily occur to a monk familiar with Christian notions of the incompatibility between shedding blood and serving at the altar.[7] Another example of such theoretical notions of paganism is the letter Bishop Daniel of Winchester sent to his pupil Boniface in 723–724, when the latter was a missionary

---

[7] Bede, *Historia ecclesiastica*, II, 13, ed. and trans. Colgrave and Mynors, *Bede*, pp. 184–5.

in Thuringia. Daniel explained how one should argue with the heathens in order to convince them of the truth. Daniel's advice was not to argue back, but to let the pagans fall into the trap they set for themselves by boasting of the genealogy of their gods. Then difficult questions should be asked: do you really think that gods who are born and not eternal are powerful? When were these gods born? Why have they given up procreation? Who reigned before them? What about eternity and creation? Why do the Christians inhabit the warm and fruitful areas producing wine and oil, whereas the pagans have been left with the cold regions of the north?[8]

This essentially Christian and learned image of pristine paganism can hardly have been a real support to Daniel's pupil in the missionary field. What kind of pagans did Boniface encounter in Hesse and Thuringia, where he was active when Daniel wrote his letter of advice? 'Real paganism' only emerges in Willibald's Life of Boniface, where the saint is depicted as triumphantly felling the sacred oak in Geismar.[9] Yet the felling of sacred trees had a long literary pedigree going back to Sulpicius Severus' Life of Saint Martin (c.397), one of the most influential hagiographical texts of the early middle ages. Boniface's collection of letters yields a very different picture. He devoted most of his energy to stamping out the deviant varieties of Christianity that had flourished in the wake of earlier missionary campaigns. Significantly, Boniface's most explicit attack on 'real paganism' concerns Rome and the celebration of the Lupercalia, about whose festivities for the new year Boniface had heard upsetting rumours.[10] Otherwise, his many queries to assorted popes and English colleagues dealt with 'errant Christianity', a more powerful enemy than the pristine heathens with their orderly pantheon conjured up by his teacher Daniel.

To a considerable extent, the paganism as represented by Christian authors was a literary one, a 'paganism in the mind'. The laws

---

[8] Boniface, *Epistolae*, no. 23, ed. M. Tangl, *Die Briefe des Heiligen Bonifatius und Lullus, MGH Epistolae Selectae* 1 (Berlin, 1916), p. 40; trans. E. Emerton, *The Letters of Saint Boniface*, 2nd edn. (New York, 2000), p. 28.

[9] Willibald, c. 6, ed. R. Rau, *Briefe des Bonifatius: Willibalds Leben des Bonifatius* (Darmstadt, 1968), p. 494; trans. C. H. Talbot, *The Anglo-Saxon Missionaries in Germany* (London, 1954), p. 45.

[10] Boniface, *Epistolae*, no. 50, ed. Tangl, pp. 90–1; trans. Emerton, pp. 59–60.

of the Frisians speak of child sacrifice on the beaches of the bleak north, and of high tide claiming the sacrificial victims. All this was 'paganism', but not necessarily in the sense of an organized religion with an elaborate doctrine about gods and their respective powers. Pagan cult sites seem to have been connected with sacred trees, mountains, fountains, valleys, and islands, rather than with particular deities; pagan practice included auguries, divinations, and sacrifice. This was the kind of practical religious devotion that might easily be integrated into any new religion, including Christianity. Conversion was, first of all, a matter of behaviour and practice, and of refraining from activities identified as non-Christian. The adoption of a different world-view and a set of beliefs would follow in due course, but it was not what Boniface and his colleagues initially worried about. Baptismal formulas were drawn up in Old High German, so the new converts might publicly declare that they abjured 'Donar, Wodan and all their pomp'. These definitions of paganism came from missionaries, not from the pagans themselves. A neutral category of secular culture with its own traditions and festivities no longer existed; social practice was either Christian or pagan, and the latter included anything that appeared remotely 'superstitious'. Auguries, amulets, incantations, and other forms of magic represented the kind of practical device to which anyone, baptized or not, may have resorted. In the so-called Corrector, a compendium of illicit practices drawn up by Bishop Burchard of Worms (d. 1025), one mostly finds magic practised by people who probably considered themselves to be Christian. The frequent theft of chrism from churches for magical purposes is a case in point; surely this was not a clear indicator of persistent paganism. The early medieval texts supporting the counter-offensive against errant Christianity are a mine of information about the ways in which real Christianity was defined: in opposition to broad and varied spectra of magico-religious practices classified as a single category, namely 'superstition and paganism', to be eradicated whenever such phenomena were encountered in real life.

Archaeology does not yield reliable information about paganism either. If someone was buried with grave goods, including a cross, did this make him or her a pagan, because of the presence of grave goods, or a Christian, because of the cross? Paganism began where Christianity ended. It was the frontier separating 'them' from 'us', within the Christian polities as well as in the vast and dangerous world outside. This frontier was there to be crossed by the preachers of the faith, either followed or preceded by the armies that supported their conquest.

Sacred domains and strategies of distinction

'God that made the world and all things therein, seeing that he is Lord of heaven and earth, dwelleth not in temples made with hands' (Acts 17: 24). In opposition to a Roman world full of sacred places and spaces, Christianity was initially a religion without shrines; wherever the faithful gathered for worship, God would be present. This ideal was to be embraced once more by Protestantism, but it was alien to late antiquity and the middle ages. Throughout this entire period, Christianity was very much a religion based on sacred places and spaces—above all, on the 'places of the saints' (*loci sanctorum*). From the early fourth century onwards, a competing Christian topography emerged within the sacred landscape of classical antiquity, rapidly supplanting its rival. Pilgrimage integrated the Holy Land and its sacred sites into this new Christian landscape, but its real landmarks were the corporeal remains of the martyrs within the boundaries of the Christian empire. The cult of the martyrs connected the newly established church to its heroic history of suppression; the martyrs only became the focus of an intensely local and competitive devotion once the actual persecutions were a thing of the past. Roman custom dictated that the dead be kept well away from the living, so the martyrs had been buried outside the precincts of the city, together with their persecutors. Here they remained, until 'a tide of relics flowed into the cities', as Robert Markus expressed it: martyrs became fellow-citizens.[11] By 386, when Bishop Ambrose of Milan founded a great new church outside the walls of his town, it was unthinkable that this edifice could be consecrated without dedicating it to martyrs who would be corporeally present. Ambrose responded to popular demand, orchestrated or not, and 'found' the remains of the martyrs Gervasius and Protasius. The discovery

---

[11] Robert Markus, *The End of Ancient Christianity* (Cambridge, 1990), p. 148.

(*inventio*) of the two martyrs and their triumphant transfer (*translatio*) to the new basilica created a momentous ritual event, enabling the bishop to repair his temporarily strained relations with the imperial court.

The translation of Gervasius and Protasius was to become a model of the episcopal control of sanctity, and of the ability of the powerful—initially bishops and abbots, but in due course also kings and aristocrats—to turn the remains of the saints into localized resources of sanctity, and to harness them to the cause of their own authority and legitimacy. Hagiography was an indispensable instrument in this process. Hundreds of saints' lives (*vitae*) were produced from late antiquity onwards, as well as miracle collections and reports on the miraculous *inventio* and *translatio* of relics. Martyrs did not entirely disappear, but they were different from their late antique predecessors; they might be bishops killed in political strife, missionaries killed by pagans, or confessors being 'living dead'. Most of the early medieval saints were bishops, abbots, and abbesses with an impeccable social pedigree. As Bishop Isidore of Seville (d. 636) expressed it: 'They could have been martyrs, had it been in the time of the persecutions.'[12] Hagiographers adapted themselves to the literary models of their predecessors, and, moreover, to the high expectations of those who commissioned them to 'write up' a particular saint. Like Ambrose's Life of his two martyred protagonists, most hagiography was intended to lead the forces of the sacred into well-defined channels connected with political power, be it episcopal, royal, or both. To say that hagiography was mere propaganda for the saint in question is missing an important point. The question should be: who controlled a saint's cult, and could therefore tap into these sacred resources?

The answer for most of early medieval Europe is: bishops, to begin with, and then, increasingly, kings, who came to depend on monastic prayer for the 'stability of the realm' and their own welfare. Sanctity developed into a powerful focus around which political and social support might be mobilized. In 704, in a charter freeing the monasteries in his realm from secular services, the Anglo-Saxon King Ine said that such communities 'should be worthy to pour out prayers for

---

[12] Isidore of Seville, *Etymologiarum sive originum libri XX*, 7. xi , ed. W. M. Lindsay (Oxford, 1911), Lib. VII. xi. 4, lines 23–4.

the state and prosperity of our kingdom, and for the forgiveness of committed sins before the face of the divine majesty . . .'.[13] This is just one example of a more general pattern. Increasingly, early medieval rulers had a vested interest in safeguarding the purity of the *claustrum*, for monastic prayer offered 'satisfaction' to God for the sins of the polity, and thus supported the stability of the realm. In the Frankish kingdoms, this cultural revolution started in the seventh century; it is in this period that those exercising political power—kings as well as aristocrats—came to depend on the prayer of monastic communities and on the intercession of resident saints. Merovingian rulers developed a peculiar system to gain access to these sacred resources. They granted 'immunities' to their favoured monasteries, guaranteeing that no royal servant would have access to sacred space; they also persuaded bishops to grant exemptions of various kinds, by which the bishop voluntarily gave up his right to interfere with the internal life in the monastic communities within his jurisdiction. By granting immunities and exemptions, kings and bishops—often in unison—created sacred spaces that would be undisturbed and therefore all the more effective in their prayer for the powerful that had guaranteed their liberty. From 751 onwards, the new Carolingian rulers continued to rely on monastic prayer and property. They also needed to shield their sacred spaces from contamination and disturbance, but did so in ways different from those of their predecessors. The more heavy-handed Carolingian 'protection' (*tuitio*) of monastic communities created an even closer alliance between the royal court and its monastic dependencies.

Within the topography of royal power such sacred spaces were of crucial importance, so rulers interfered directly in the internal ordering of life in the cloister, demanding that the prayer supporting stability to the realm would be conducted along similar lines, and according to an authoritative model. It was within this context that the *Rule* of Benedict of Nursia emerged as the dominant form for monastic life and prayer—in the Frankish empire from 800 onwards, but subsequently throughout northern Europe, a predominance that remained until the mid-eleventh century. Initially, this sixth-century

---

[13] W. de G. Birch, *Cartularium Saxonicum: A Collection of Charters Relating to Anglo-Saxon History* (London, 1885), no. 108, I, p. 157. And see Catherine Cubitt, *Anglo-Saxon Church Councils c.650–c.850* (London and New York, 1995), p. 112.

Italian text was no more than one of the many directives by which abbots tried to regulate life within their communities; many of such 'texts' were only transmitted orally. Benedict's *Rule* gradually gained authority north of the Alps because Pope Gregory the Great—the initiator of the Christianization of England—had included a Life of Benedict in his *Dialogues*. Benedict became the 'Roman abbot', another example of the canonical authority men in the north looked for in an Italy full of sacred resources. Well before 774, when the Carolingian armies incorporated these sacred treasures into the growing empire, high-status English and Frankish 'monastic observers' had travelled south to find and investigate the type of monastic life they considered to be the 'real thing'. As in the case of the papacy and canonical texts sent Frankish rulers, the high expectations of the men and women from the north went a long way towards upholding the identity of Italy as the promised land of monastic authenticity.

Within the Frankish empire—including Italy—Benedict's *Rule* became something its author could never have envisaged: the 'law' of a monastic life upon which the stability of the Carolingian realm depended. But the *monasteria* of this period were very different from the small and intimate community for which Benedict wrote. Ninth-century commentators on the *Rule* had huge royal abbeys in mind, full of children to be educated, guests to be received, and estates to be managed. The *claustrum*, the secluded inner space only accessible to members of the community and a few privileged 'neighbours', became the architectural and mental safeguard of an essential measure of sanctity and peace. Not only monks and nuns were 'cloistered', the same went for canons (*clerici canonici*), though the latter had more freedom of movement. Reform councils in Aachen in 816/817 attempted to create a clear divide between monasticism proper (monks and nuns who followed Benedict's *Rule*), on the one hand, and canons who lived a communal life devoted to prayer and pastoral work, on the other.

This new strategy of distinction had only a limited success, and mostly reveals the extent to which these two groups had become conflated; it also became a source of confusion to historians, who have perceived the Anglo-Saxon and Celtic 'minsters' (*monasteria*) in charge of pastoral duties as a deviation from the supposed norm: a 'Roman' ecclesiastical organization based on bishops and local priests. Yet until the tenth century at least, it was religious communities, not the familiar parishes centred upon villages, that remained the pillars of ecclesiastical organization. Monks and canons, and anything in between, met the demands of the laity for votive Masses, and furnished the pastoral care later associated with parish priests. No wonder such communities became difficult to distinguish from one another.

The celebration of votive Masses became the primary duty of all these powerhouses of prayer. The very concept of Mass had changed drastically. From a communal ritual commemorating Christ's death and resurrection, Mass itself became a sacrifice, a gift to God accompanied by special prayers indicating the purpose for which this particular Mass was offered. There were Masses for every eventuality: good weather, a rich harvest, the fertility of women, safe journeys, the victory of the royal army, and, above all, for the commemoration and salvation of the dead. At the council of Attigny (762), a group of bishops and abbots created a network of mutual prayer linking their religious communities, promising to read fixed amounts of Masses and Psalters on behalf of each other's dead. Soon, this movement blossomed into the great 'Books of commemoration' (*libri memoriales*) of the ninth century, containing thousands of names of the dead and the living from religious houses, but also those of the upper echelons of lay society, with members of the ruling dynasty heading the list. At first glance it would seem that religious women were put at a severe disadvantage by this increasing emphasis on votive Masses, a demand that could only be fulfilled by ordained monks and canons. To some extent this is true; yet ascetic women represented a particularly desirable type of virginity, more family-bound than that of their male counterparts, but also more pure, because these women were further removed from the corridors of court and power. Still, major female communities were not entirely cut off from the political fracas, as appears from the nuns of Remiremont pointedly refusing to pray for a king—Lothar II—who had rejected his legitimate spouse.[14] A royal nunnery going on a prayer-strike must have had some sense of the importance of its Psalters read for the ruler, even if Masses could only be taken care of by male priests attached to the community.

---

[14] Stuart Airlie, 'Private bodies and the body politic in the divorce case of Lothar II', *Past and Present*, 161 (1998), pp. 3–38 at p. 37.

Figure 8 Gelasian Sacramentary, produced probably at Chelles, or Jouarre, in the first half of the eighth century

This intense prayer activity was fuelled by changing attitudes towards death and what awaited humankind, once it passed this final threshold. The Last Judgement and the Resurrection at the end of times were still perceived as the final reckoning, but this ultimate judgement had come to be preceded by an earlier one, immediately after death. Sinners who had not managed to redress the balance of sin by due penance in their lifetime were expected to have to endure the torments of an intermediary and purgatorial limbo, from which only pure prayer could release them. To a large extent, monastic prayer served the needs of the dead, and of their surviving kinsmen who gave lavish gifts to religious communities in order to save the souls of the departed. A visionary literature developed which charted the geography of the hereafter, but also served as a warning voice within the corridors of power. By depicting kings and emperors suffering torments in purgatory, thinly-veiled criticisms were levelled at rulers who did not live up to the model of Christian kingship.

On the one hand, there were monks, nuns, canons, and their female counterparts who prayed with pure hands in ascetic communities; on the other, there were the ordinary priests ministering to rural communities from which they could hardly be distinguished. The gulf between the institutionalized and the rural clergy was also a social one, for most of the inhabitants of the powerful *monasteria* came from the upper echelons of society. The majority of these men and women had entered religious life in childhood, often as a gift 'to God in the monastery' (as the *Rule* of St Benedict expressed it) by their parents; this was a social and religious privilege, which also entailed a substantial donation of land, usually comprising the child's inheritance. In theory, status differences within the community were superseded by an order of seniority and merit, but in practice, the social hierarchy in the world outside persisted within the cloister. A vast social distance separated the institutionalized clergy from their *familia*, the dependant servants, and peasants who enabled the members of the community to devote themselves to their extensive duties of prayer. The same held true for nunneries and communities of canons. Bishops keeping hunting dogs were a traditional—and symbolic—bone of contention: these animals were liable to bite the poor who came to the bishop's residence, begging for sustenance.

Many 'ordinary priests', ministering to rural communities far removed from the episcopal and monastic centres, must have suffered as many hardships as the members of their flock. It is not easy to get a clear picture of this particular group, for the bulk of the written sources we now depend on were produced in the religious communities sufficiently wealthy to become centres of literacy and learning; hence, their membership is in the limelight, whereas rural priests remain largely in the dark. What we do know is that the early medieval rural priesthood was of a bewildering variety that still awaits further exploration. A well-defined parish structure, with the village priest at the bottom end of a hierarchical chain of command headed by the bishop, only fully materialized after *c.*1000. Earlier attempts by Carolingian bishops to take the rural priesthood in hand reveal that such priests came in very different shapes and sizes. They might be monks in orders, in charge of a small monastic establishment (usually called a *cella*) ministering to 'the people', under the authority of the abbot or abbess, or priests who were the rural representatives of canonical communities led by bishops. Such priests might live in great isolation, but they were still the rural vanguard of the *monasteria*, rather than part of an established network of parishes. But then there were also priests in charge of churches established by secular or ecclesiastical lords on their private lands. These lords, founders of their own churches, remained in control of their foundation and its proceeds—the obligatory tithes and the voluntary gifts of the faithful—using this income as a tool of lordship; sometimes only a small portion was reserved for the sustenance of the priest himself. Such priests might very well be freed serfs, recruited from the very peasantry they baptized and buried; the social distance between their flock and themselves was minimal, if any existed at all.

Some of the ensuing problems become clear from the so-called *capitula episcoporum*, directives issued by Carolingian bishops attempting to discipline and 'correct' the clergy in their diocese, and also from the surviving manuscript evidence of handbooks for priests. Two interconnected issues were involved. Rural priests became the object of *correctio*, a programme of reform intensified after Charlemagne's imperial coronation; significantly, the first episcopal directives appeared shortly after 800. The Christian empire should have a priesthood worthy of its exalted role as God's *ecclesia*—that is, priests who ministered at the altar with 'pure' hands, unsoiled by sex and blood; moreover, all priests should be literate and have adequate books to support them in their duties. First and foremost, however, bishops were adamant that rural priests should rise above their flock, becoming part of a clergy with its own privileges and solidarities, the lowest rank of an ecclesiastical hierarchy headed by episcopal authority. Hence, priests who were economically dependent upon lay lords should be brought back within the fold of episcopal and canonical jurisdiction. Throughout the ninth century, kings and bishops cooperated in this venture; some of their instructions for reform cast a bleak light on the predicament of 'ordinary' priests. As a capitulary issued in 857 by Charles the Bald expressed it: 'Priests and their servants are not to be dishonoured, and they are not to be flogged, and they are not to be thrown out of their church without the agreement of their bishop.'[15] But there were also priests who did well for themselves, developing into local power brokers who caused their bishops a lot of headaches. Archbishop Hincmar of Rheims (840–882) had to contend with a priest who, after having attracted malicious gossip from his flock on account of his illicit sexual relations, got involved in a drunken brawl, wounding a fellow-villager; when Hincmar suspended the culprit, pending his deposition at a provincial synod, the man disappeared to Rome, returning triumphantly with a papal letter calling Hincmar to task for supposed uncanonical procedures.

Sexual purity was the cutting edge of the strategies of distinction elevating the rural priesthood above the laity around them. In Hincmar's day and age, the ideal of priestly celibacy already had a long history, which gives the impression that for centuries, ecclesiastical leaders fought a battle lost at the outset. If in the mid-eleventh century 'Gregorian' reform still needed to fight clerical marriage, priests in preceding ages must surely have misbehaved collectively. This linear view of the history of celibacy should be discarded. Predictably, zeal for reform fluctuated, but the incredible persistence of the ideal of clerical celibacy, up to the present day, is more significant. Similar arguments in favour of celibacy were employed in very different situations. In 384/385 Pope Siricius explained to Bishop Himerius of Tarragona that, unlike their Old Testament predecessors who only

---

[15] *Allocutio missi cuiusdam Divionensis* (857), c. 1, A. Boretius and V. Krause (eds.), *MGH Capitularia* II (Hanover, 1897), no. 267, p. 292.

sacrificed intermittently, Christian priests should be celibate, for their obligation to celebrate the Eucharist on a daily basis prevented them from purifying themselves properly before touching the body and blood of Christ. Pope Siricius had bishops in mind, married men who had entered episcopal office after a secular career; to live chastely under the scrutiny of their inquisitive household, with their wife—the *episcopa*—secluded at the other end of the episcopal palace, would endow such secular men with an instant authority and charisma. This model of the married bishop vowing himself to celibacy without dissolving his marriage persisted well into the sixth century. Theodulf of Orléans (d. 802) repeated Pope Siricius' basic argument, but he envisaged a different clerical landscape, in which the *monasteria* had become the real bastions of celibacy and purity; here, all priests, deacons, and subdeacons who might be 'in touch' with the sacred altar precincts could be expected to have clean hands. By the early ninth century, Augustine's fear of the emergence of a first class of Christians, ascetics lording it over the ordinary faithful, had come true, even at the level of the clergy. With regard to celibacy, the west followed a trajectory different from that of Byzantium. In the east, the upper ecclesiastical echelons—patriarchs in particular—were recruited from monasteries and therefore were celibate, but ordinary priests were allowed to marry.

The divergent attitudes in east and west are intriguing, and make one wonder about the varying demands and expectations of those who remain most in the darkness of the sources: the laity. In our period, this was not the clearly defined category it would become after c.1050, when *clerici* claimed the monopoly of the sacred and its written tradition, and increasingly denied the laity direct access to these resources. From the beginning, it was baptism that made someone a member of Christendom. Baptism remained a public affair, though the intricate rituals surrounding adults converting to the faith—veritable and prolonged 'rites of passage'—were increasingly supplanted by infant baptism. In its wake, another enduring institution entered upon the scene: spiritual parenthood. Godparents became the ones to pronounce the baptismal vows for the infants they were to receive from the font, assuming responsibility for the welfare and religious education of their godchildren. Godparenthood also created and supported powerful networks of social and political solidarity that were as important as the much better studied 'feudal' relations.

Predictably, it is within the very upper echelons of society, and mostly in the loquacious ninth century, that we can get an idea of what religious life for 'the laity' may have entailed. This was a laity mesmerized by the *claustrum* and its promise of quiet, sanctity, and salvation. Kings, queens, and powerful aristocrats 'withdrew' to monasteries, either at moments of political embarrassment, or on the eve of death. To die in a monastic habit was surely a safer route to Heaven than to make the dangerous journey directly from the turmoil of the world. This was the elitist way of preparing for death—even a royal one, as appears from aristocrats following the royal example. Meanwhile, in the lower reaches of society, a long process of 'Christianizing death' continued. The tremendous importance of the intercession for the dead shows that the long-term solicitude of kinsmen concentrated first of all on the care of their deceased in the hereafter; Christian burial rites followed in the wake of the prayer for the dead. Given that bishops and abbots took care of the burial of the poor as an act of charity, a Christian burial remained an expensive affair. By 900, this was probably within reach of most people, which also meant that the exclusion of those who had died as grievous and unrepentant sinners began to make sense. The happy few were buried *ad sanctos*, near the saints they had supported during their lifetime, and within the confines of the 'monastery'—of whatever variety—that most successfully mediated between God and mankind. *Monasteria* were not only powerhouses of prayer, but also vast burial sites, harbouring those wishing to be close to the saints when Resurrection was at hand. Regardless of the first judgement directly after death, fears and hopes of the Last Judgement remained intense. Some people despaired of salvation, or simply disbelieved it. In the missionary country of East Saxony, Bishop Thietmar of Merseburg (d. 1018) told a string of horrific stories about the dead who wandered at night, even attacking hapless priests in their own churches, in order to convince the 'illiterate' that the Resurrection of the dead at the end of times was by no means an outrageous idea. With his flock, the learned bishop shared a nightmare: the dead might return in the dark, to haunt the living.[16]

Between baptism and death, Christian time impinged on people's lives. Christian feast days defined the course of a week, a month, or a

[16] Thietmar, *Chronicon* I, cc. 11–13, ed. W. Trillmich, *Thietmar von Merseburg, Chronik* (Darmstadt, 1974), pp. 14–19.

year: Sundays, days of fasting, the feast of the saints. Interpretations
of proper festivities might vary. Some clerics objected to Rogations—
a communal and penitential plea for the support of the saints—being
turned into a display of gorgeous clothes on the part of the powerful,
but then again, pious laymen may have had similar qualms; 'correctness' was not the prerogative of the clergy. Laymen were not required
to make regular appearances in church, and neither did they have to
take frequent Communion. From the sixth century onwards, Christmas, Easter, and Pentecost were the only appropriate times for
Communion, and of these three momentous occasions, only Easter
remained. Just like the clergy, the laity needed to cleanse themselves
from the pollution of sexuality before venturing to have physical
contact with the 'terrible sacraments' (*terribilia sacramenta*), so
Communion was an important occasion demanding a lengthy preparation. Lent therefore became a period of collective purification, a
preparation for Easter, the principal Christian feast. Stories ran rife
about laymen who had 'lapsed' during this crucial period, indulging
in marital sex, but who still managed to make it to Easter Communion after due contrition and a miraculously brief penance
granted by a saint. Such tales expressed the hopes of people falling
short of an ideal that was nonetheless very much alive. Lent was also
the season for confessing one's sins and doing penance. From the late
seventh century onwards, an originally monastic practice—regular
confession and penance, as a way to cleanse oneself from the stain of
sin—gradually entered lay society. This engendered an extensive
literature of 'penitentials', handbooks for confessors, containing
detailed lists of sins and ways to make amends. Such texts are by no
means a straightforward reflection of the actual behaviour of ordinary sinners, but they do reveal a lot about the aims and perceptions of
those trying to build a Christian society. These regular penances—
usually fasting and alms-giving—were supervised by priests; scandal-
ous sins that had offended God and society merited a public penance,
however, administered by the bishop. Public penance was not an
everyday affair; it was an exceptional punishment, primarily aimed at
those with sufficient standing in society to create a real 'scandal', such
as aristocrats guilty of flagrant sexual sins or outrageous violence.
The humiliating ritual of public penance included a deposition of
arms on the altar; the actual penance entailed a long period of semi-
monastic existence. This struck at the core of an aristocratic code of

honour hinging upon military glory and the control of one's family and household.

To glean information about the religious universe of the laity from texts predominantly produced by clerics is obviously hazardous. But this delicate operation is bound to fail if modern sensibilities about the divide between laymen and clerics are projected upon the distant past. Some of the lost voices of ordinary priests and ordinary laymen may be heard, underneath the dominant discourse, but if we want to listen, the opposition between clergy and laymen should be exchanged for a more important one prevalent at the time: the powerful (*potentes*) and the vulnerable (*pauperes*). Neither should late medieval religious practice be taken as some kind of an end station to a linear process starting in the early middle ages. The slow emergence of the Christian marriage ceremony is a case in point. Christian marriage rites did exist in the early middle ages, in the shape of a blessing of the couple and their marital bed. Yet most of the nuptial rituals, from the betrothal and property arrangements to the cheerful crowds seeing the couple to their marital chamber, remained a lay affair—the business of the two families who created a lasting alliance through the strategic pairing off of members of the younger generation. Marital blessings, like sumptuous burials, were something for the happy few. Clerics were well advised to keep out of marriage rituals, unless the couple were a particularly pious one, guaranteed to enter marriage as virgins, and of impeccable aristocratic descent. Pope Nicholas (d. 867) supplied the newly converted Bulgars with a long and detailed list of good Christian practice, but according to this pope a Christian marriage ceremony was not what distinguished a Christian from a pagan. There were more important things: a Christian marriage should be indissoluble, and all kinsmen were out of bounds as marriage partners, including those acquired by godparenthood. This was indeed the agenda that had crystallized in early medieval Europe, including papal Rome. From the sixth century onwards, a mind-boggling array of kinsmen became forbidden marriage partners. This wide-ranging anti-incest legislation is a typical post-Roman development, and a primary concern of the rulers of the early medieval New Israels: the first ramifications of forbidden kin are found in barbarian law codes and royal decrees. By the time Pope Nicholas instructed the Bulgars, a highly impractical consensus forbidding marriage until the 'seventh degree' (read: no blood relations, affines or spiritual kin of whatever kind) had been reached. Like public penance, which disarmed the fighting men, this taboo on kin-marriage cut deep into the life of the aristocracy. Much as incest avoidance was occasionally manipulated to serve ulterior aims, such as a legitimate separation from an unwanted partner, exogamic marriages were the norm among early medieval aristocrats.

Was early medieval Christianity 'top-down'? Yes, if one means by this that kings and aristocrats vied for control of sacred resources, and turned them into bases for building legitimate power. No, if one discards the familiar perspective of clerics pitted against 'the laity', and listens to discordant voices claiming their own kind of real Christianity. Pope Gregory the Great enjoyed tremendous authority in the early medieval west, but his lenient pronouncements on ritual purity went unheeded, along with his view that in liturgical matters 'unity might exist in diversity', as long as Christian communities were one in their love of Christ and their neighbours. Christians demanding correct ritual won the day, and literal interpretations of the Old Testament became part of mainstream Christian thinking among clerics and laymen alike. Could the ideal of clerical celibacy in the west have endured, without those dependent upon the purity of prayer clamouring for reform, for the sake of their salvation?

Changing legacies

After the mid-eleventh century, the so-called Gregorian Reform deeply affected the churches and kingdoms of the west, with far-reaching political consequences known as the Investiture Controversy. A much more self-confident papacy and clergy set about redrawing the boundaries between the secular and the sacred, claiming the latter as the exclusive domain of the clergy. Yet the river of eleventh-century reform was fed by many tributaries reaching into the distant past. 'Simony', the sale of ecclesiastical office, was one of these; priestly purity was another. These were old issues rephrased in a new context of heightened anxiety about the limits of the sacred, so new strategies of distinction were developed. Some of the background to eleventh-century change has been outlined above, and it yields fundamental questions about change and continuity yet to be addressed. Most historians have treated the eleventh century as a profound watershed. Early medieval conceptions of real Christianity became a major victim of this, for pre-1000 versions of Christianity became defined as the dark and primitive predecessors of the real thing erupting on the scene in the eleventh century. But as we have seen, Christianity in the earlier period was a complicated phenomenon with its own claim to 'reality'.

When it comes to the transformation of religious belief and practice, the year 1000 is a particularly useless landmark. Change occurred slowly and almost imperceptibly, with older structures and ideas remaining intact. The metaphors of geological layers pressing into each other, or of subcurrents gradually becoming mainstream without older ideas disappearing overnight, are more appropriate ones than the images of 'birth' or 'flowering' that so often adorn textbooks discussing the eleventh and twelfth centuries. The older historiography about the monastery of Cluny, founded in 910 by Duke William of Aquitaine, is a case in point. William put Cluny under papal protection, guaranteeing the full dominion of its first abbot over its monks and property, as well as the free election of future abbots. From the mid-eleventh century onwards, Cluny was to play a key role in a new reform movement closely associated with the papacy, but as decades of scholarly work have shown, this did not mean the monastery was unique, exceptional, and influential right from the beginning. In many ways, Cluny was typical of a lively tenth-century monastic world heavily indebted to Carolingian monastic reform, and to a long tradition of immunities of various kinds defining sacred space. Perhaps Cluny was special in that its foundation charter and subsequent privileges made the most of this rich heritage, combining different elements that existed separately before. In Germany the emperors still took centre stage in monastic reform, as their Carolingian predecessors had done; when Otto I visited St Gallen in 972, he dropped his sceptre with a clattering noise among the monks who sang the *laudes* to welcome their monarch, to check whether anyone would be distracted. Nobody batted an eyelid; the emperor was satisfied.[17] This anecdote was recounted enthusiastically around 1050, by a monastic historian who deeply disapproved of the 'schismatics from

[17] Ekkehard, *Casus Sancti Galli*, c. 146, ed. H. F. Haefele, *Ekkehard IV. St. Galler Klostergeschichten* (Darmstadt, 1980), pp. 282–3.

Gaul'—that is, the radical reformers wishing to oust secular rulers from their sacred domains. In tenth-century France and Lotharingia the traditionally royal role of protecting and safeguarding the cloister was increasingly assumed by dukes, counts, and other noblemen now in charge of public power; to found or to reform a monastery had been an integral part of the trappings of true royal authority, which devolved upon the leaders of strong principalities. Monastic reform flourished, not only in Cluny, but also in Gorze, St Bavo in Ghent, and Fleury. The latter two monasteries were a crucial source of inspiration for a monastic movement in England building upon Carolingian models. The great English reformers of the tenth century—Æthelwold, Dunstan, and Oswald—cooperated closely with the king; it was King Edgar of Wessex who in c.970 promulgated the *Regularis Concordia*, turning the Rule of Benedict into the binding norm for monastic life in his kingdom. Likewise, Duke Alberic II of Spoleto invited Abbot Odo of Cluny (927–942) to reform the monasteries in and around Rome along Benedictine lines.

The tenth-century west was a lively religious landscape, featuring dramatic conversions of the powerful who put their armour upon the altar and renounced the world. In the far north, this was what Count Ansfrid did, before this formidable warrior, the scourge of robbers, became bishop of Utrecht in 995. But when he lost his eyesight, Ansfrid became a monk who followed Benedict's Rule. He had a hilltop cleared, six miles from Utrecht, and established himself there in a cell in order to escape the noise of the world. 'Once other cells had been built and thus a monastery had grown, he gathered a number of monks and put them under the guidance of an abbot.'[18] The religious fervour of Ansfrid and others converting from secular life was channelled along traditional lines, and incorporated in traditional structures: they moved away from the noise of the *saeculum*, and into the sacred and secluded space of the *claustrum*. Both domains, the secular world and the cloister, were equally hierarchical, and, moreover, intricately connected. Between these interconnected corridors of power—the palace and the monastery—secular rulers and bishops moved freely, heavily dependent upon the resources of the sacred and eager to extend its dominance. This pattern emerged

[18] Alpertus of Metz, *De diversitate temporum* I, c. 14, ed. H. van Rij (Hilversum, 1980), p. 30.

in late antiquity, it was established in the early medieval kingdoms in the west, and it came under attack in the century after Ansfrid established himself upon a modest hilltop near Utrecht. The intricacies of this long-term transformation await further investigation.

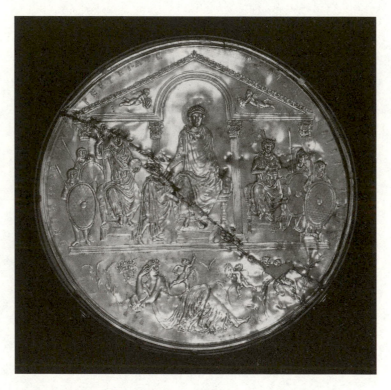

Figure 9 *Missorium* of the Emperor Theodosius I (379–395)

5

Culture

Ian Wood

The culture of western Europe and the Mediterranean in the year 400 was, at least for the elite, Roman and Imperial. It can be illustrated by an object of a decade earlier: the *missorium* of the Emperor Theodosius I (379–395), a silver-gilt dish bearing a picture of the seated emperor surrounded by his sons and guards. (Fig. 9). It was doubtless presented to some high-ranking member of the empire. For a rather smaller proportion of the population in the year 1000 culture was equally Roman and Imperial. One might take as a corresponding image the portrait from the Gospels of the Saxon Emperor Otto III (983–1002), where the young emperor sits in majesty, approached by personifications of Roma, Gallia, Germania, and Sclavinia (Fig. 11 and front cover). The iconography is in many respects classical and was intended to mark a Roman *Renovatio*. Yet its meaning is far removed from its prototypes—not least because it is contained within a Gospel Book.

The cultural history of the years between the production of these two objects is complex, but may reasonably be divided into five chronological sections: the closing years of the west Roman empire, which provided the basis for much of what was to follow; the period of the successor states; the cultural separation of Spain, marked by the Islamic takeover of much of the peninsula; the Carolingian Renaissance of the late eighth and ninth centuries, and finally the Ottonian *Renovatio* of the tenth century. Continuities across time are, of course, too easily ignored when the material is divided chronologically. On the other hand, the changes within the culture of western Europe between 400 and 1000 are such that it is important to give at least as much weight to the different periods within the early middle ages as to the continuities across those periods.

The last century of the western Roman empire

Despite the dramatic political changes which surrounded the arrival of the Visigoths and Vandals in the late fourth and early fifth centuries, the prevailing cultural image was one of stability—which is not to say that no writer noticed the disasters, for a number of historians and moralists—particularly in Gaul and Spain—recorded them in some detail, but others carefully avoided presenting an impression of catastrophe.

Nevertheless, imperial culture was not unchanging. There were novelties at the imperial court. The *magister militum* Stilicho, himself of barbarian extraction, is represented on an ivory diptych, wearing trousers—a style of clothing which was forbidden in Rome in 397 and 399! (Fig. 2). More significant, a new capital was created when Honorius moved from Milan to Ravenna, to profit from the security offered by the marshes of the river Po. As was appropriate for a capital, Ravenna gained new imperial buildings, if not under Honorius (395–423), at least under the influence of his sister Galla Placidia (d. 450). In 425 she built a palace chapel dedicated to St John, San Giovanni Evangelista, to commemorate the miraculous escape of herself and her infant son, Valentinian III (425–455) from a storm, as they returned from Constantinople to claim his throne. The decor of San Giovanni included a series of portraits of Christian emperors, and, in the apse, a depiction of the storm from which John the Evangelist had delivered the young emperor and his mother. She also founded a church dedicated to the Holy Cross, which had an adjacent chapel of St Lawrence, now wrongly known as the Mausoleum of Galla Placidia.

The Ravenna Annals, an apparently official record of events, which survive only in a later copy, but one whose marginal illustrations seem to be an accurate rendering of what was in the original, are illustrated with symbolic depictions of earthquakes and with the heads of executed traitors. The barbarians were ignored. The court art of Ravenna, which was essentially a *nouveau riche* city, much as Constantinople had been a century before, presented itself as a legitimate centre of power, triumphing over would-be usurpers, and untroubled by any external threats. Ravenna was the new imperial capital in the west. As such it would attract numerous later rulers, among them Charlemagne (768–814) and Otto III.

Imperial art in general was calculated to give an impression of stability, perhaps even of rigidity. Quite apart from buildings, there were statues and, rather more often, imperial portraits—displayed in public places much as photographs of presidential figures are still displayed in many countries. Imperial authority was also manifest in numerous occasions of gift-giving, New Year celebrations, inaugurations of consulships, birthdays, and anniversaries, when the emperor distributed gifts of silver, such as the *missorium* of Theodosius. Each object was of a value appropriate for its recipient. For high-ranking officials there would be brooches (*fibulae*), again of appropriate value. Similar objects could be sent to clients outside the Roman empire.

This court culture is as apparent in the written word as it is in objects. It is reflected in the preambles of laws, including those issued by Valentinian III and his successors, and it is also reflected in the court literature of the panegyric: prose or verse speeches delivered in praise of the emperor or a new consul, by orators like Symmachus (d. 402) or the poet Claudian (d. *c*.404). Such speeches provided the opportunity for the justification of a policy, even at times delicate criticism, but clothed in the imagery of Roman myth.

The culture of the court may seem rarefied but it was shared by the *literati* of the empire. Education for the elite was first and foremost an education in grammar and rhetoric. Rhetoric trained a man both for high office, where the art of persuasion was ever a necessity, and also for the leisure, *otium*, which was the ideal for any wealthy man. Business activity, *negotium*, was the negative of the leisured ideal, but it was generally reckoned that an aristocrat ought occasionally to deny himself the pleasures of *otium* to serve the state. A cultured senator was inevitably well-read, and he had the opportunity to show his literary skills not just in government or the law courts, or in the rows of books in his library, but also in his letter writing, since it was through such communication that he maintained the bonds of friendship, which lay at the heart of late Roman aristocratic society.

This literary culture was a long-standing one, which stretched back at least to the late Republic. It had been remarkably undisturbed by the Christianization of the Roman empire, even though the Bible, central as it was to the new religion, was anything other than a literary masterpiece by classical standards. Indeed literate Christians were more likely to improve the Bible by such tricks as versifying it, as they were to abandon their love of literature. Jerome (d. 419/420), the finest translator of the Bible, was a Latin stylist through and through—and he was aware of the potential conflict between literary studies and the Christian life, having a nightmare about being too much a follower of Cicero. Augustine of Hippo (d. 430), perhaps the greatest of all theologians, was a trained rhetor who had served his time at the imperial court. Rhetorical skills as well as Neoplatonic philosophy underpin his theology. Jerome and Augustine, like Ambrose of Milan (d. 397) and Basil of Caesarea (d. 379), were at the forefront of the fourth- and fifth-century patristic writers, Latin and Greek. Their works, especially biblical commentaries, provided a foundation for much early medieval scholarship. Like Jerome, Augustine was also a great writer of letters, as was Paulinus of Nola (d. 431), who did perhaps more than any other writer to transform the epistolary tradition into a vehicle for the expression of Christian love, by substituting the notion of *caritas* (misleadingly translated as 'charity' in the Authorized Version of the Bible) for *amicitia* (the traditional virtue of friendship).

The court and the aristocracy of the empire were bound together in a single, if multifaceted, literary culture. They present an image of the later Roman empire, which can blind us to the underlying importance of military power. Such power surfaces most clearly at moments of civil war and when the barbarian threat had run completely out of control. There was, however, always a military underside to Roman culture. It can be seen in the soldiers surrounding Theodosius on his *missorium,* and in the shield and spear held by Stilicho, the sword at his side and the great military *fibula* on his shoulder, all portrayed in detail on his diptych. It can be seen equally in the architecture of the frontier provinces, notably the Porta Nigra at Trier, and in the walls of the two capital cities, Rome and Constantinople, built in times of military crisis. It is also apparent in the numerous military buckles which are found in late Roman cemeteries of the frontier regions: buckles which in turn influenced the style of barbarian war-gear. By relieving most of its population of the duty of military service, and by keeping the majority of its forces near the frontiers, the empire had gone a long way towards splitting civilian and military culture, but it was a division which would be undermined in the fifth century.

Nor was the army the only focus for a culture other than the literate culture of the court and the senatorial aristocracy. Although the empire acknowledged two major literary languages, Latin and Greek, there were other languages in the provinces. To a large extent these had been pushed into obscurity, but such languages as Coptic and Syriac can already be found in the later empire. They appear as often as not in religious contexts and associated with marginal Christian groups, whether ascetics or heretics. They are a mark of the extent to which even Christianity was made up of numerous regional cultures, divided by language, doctrine, and the cults of local saints: microchristendoms as they have been called.[1] In the west, written evidence for this linguistic regionalism appears perhaps around 600, a little later than it does in the east. This chronological distinction may reflect the poorer survival of documents in the west, but it is more likely that, unlike the peoples of the Middle East, the Celts had previously had no significant tradition of writing. Nevertheless, in parts of Britain and in Ireland, Celtic cultures—literary and artistic— soon came into their own once the high culture of the imperial court and the senators had faded.

The successor states and the imperial tradition

The majority of the states which were established in what had been the western Roman empire tried in one way or another to continue imperial tradition or to ape it. The Ostrogoths, who established themselves in Italy in the 490s, took over the imperial capital of Ravenna, and their first king in Italy, Theodoric (493–526), in certain respects continued the work of Galla Placidia. Since the majority of the Ostrogoths, including the king, were Arian Christians—who saw the Three Persons of the Holy Trinity, Father, Son and Holy Spirit, as a hierarchy—they could not use the city's Catholic churches. A new Arian cathedral and baptistery were built, as was a new court chapel, dedicated to the Saviour, and decorated, like Galla Placidia's San

---

[1] P. Brown, *The Rise of Western Christendom* (Oxford, 1996).

Giovanni Evangelista, with sumptuous mosaics. Although some of the mosaics were replaced after the capture of the city for the Byzantine Emperor Justinian I (527–565), it seems that they originally included portraits of Theodoric and members of his court, set against representations of the palace of Ravenna and the city's port of Classe. This was something that Justinian's supporters would outdo, both by removing the Ostrogothic figures from the walls of Theodoric's chapel, and also by placing two of the most memorable images of an emperor, his empress, and their courts in the sanctuary of the newly completed church of San Vitale. This church seems particularly to have impressed Charlemagne and the architects of the palace chapel at Aachen at the end of the eighth century.

Nor was it only in terms of architecture that the Ostrogothic leadership aped the Roman past. Theodoric took over the institutions of government, and one of his administrators, the Roman senator Cassiodorus (d. 580), fortunately set down his official letters as models for future generations in a collection known as the *Variae*, which is as informative about late Roman government as it is about that of the Ostrogoths. The literary traditions of the senatorial aristocracy had also survived intact. Indeed, Boethius (d. 524) was one of the few great Latin philosophers of late antiquity. Quite apart from his *magnum opus*, the *Consolation of Philosophy*, written while awaiting execution, there were translations of Aristotle, and a number of short tractates on music, arithmetic and Christian theology.

Other barbarian kingdoms did not start with the advantage of taking over the capital city. In fostering governmental continuity, which they did, the kings of the Visigoths, Franks, and Burgundians were necessarily continuing the practices of regional rather than central government. Bishop Remigius of Rheims congratulated the Frankish king Clovis (481–511) on taking over the government of the old Roman province of *Belgica Secunda*.

Some kings of the new successor states of the west openly admitted their subordination to the emperor in Byzantium in their official correspondence, but that did not stop them emulating imperial style. Clovis's grandson, Theudebert I (533–548), usurped a little of the emperor's authority by issuing gold coins at one stage in his reign. Another grandson of Clovis, Chilperic I (561–584), imitated imperial *missoria*, having dishes made with inscriptions to the glory of the Franks.

The Merovingian kings were not boorish illiterates, but were able to read and write. One collection of letters, the *Epistulae Austrasiacae*, by various writers, survives from the east Frankish court. There is, in fact, an unbroken tradition of aristocratic letter-writing in Visigothic, Burgundian, and Frankish Gaul, stretching from Sidonius Apollinaris (d. *c.*480), through the works of his relatives Ruricius of Limoges (d. *c.*507) and Avitus of Vienne (d. 518), to the seventh-century bishop of Cahors, Desiderius (630–655). A collection of verse panegyrics and occasional poems for the Merovingian kings and their courtiers also survives from the pen of the late sixth-century Italian poet Venantius Fortunatus (d. *c.*600).

The late sixth century saw the resurgence of a royal court in Visigothic Spain. The Visigoths had openly aped the imperial court when King Athaulf married Galla Placidia in 411, a marriage celebrated by an official *epithalamium* (marriage-poem) delivered by a senator. The crises and civil wars of the early sixth century, however, undermined what court culture there was. A sense of imperial style was reasserted by Leovigild (569–586), who developed a royal regalia, and who also founded a city, Reccopolis, which he named after his son, Reccared. Reccopolis is reminiscent of Constantine's foundation of Constantinople. A later Visigothic king, Recceswinth (649–672), built a chapel which still survives, albeit somewhat altered, at San Juan de Baños, while a votive crown that he commissioned, probably for one of the great churches of Toledo, is one of the few examples of a type of object which is well attested in written sources from the days of Constantine onwards. By comparison with the Merovingians, the ideology of the Visigothic court in the late sixth and seventh centuries is rarely to be found in letters and poems: it is most apparent in the utterances of the Councils of Toledo, and in the *History of the Goths, Vandals and Sueves* of Isidore of Seville (d. 636) and the works of Julian of Toledo (d. 690), notably his *History of King Wamba*.

The Lombards were latecomers into the Roman world, but they too took over something of the imperial style—most notably in the representation of Agilulf (591–616/17) on the visor of a helmet, at present preserved in the Bargello Museum in Florence. Their palaces at Milan, Pavia, and Monza are unfortunately only known from written accounts, above all by the eighth-century writer Paul the Deacon (d. *c.*799).

Much weaker were the echoes of imperial culture in Anglo-Saxon

England. This is not surprising, since Britannia had been far less Romanized than provinces nearer the Mediterranean heart of the empire, and the takeover by the Anglo-Saxons was a much longer and more disruptive affair than was the case elsewhere. Nevertheless there are hints of imperial imagery in Bede's description of the Northumbrian King Edwin (c.616–633).

The courts of the barbarian kings of the successor states thus contained echoes, sometimes faint, but sometimes clear, of the imperial court. Yet louder were the echoes to be found in the culture of papal Rome. Although Ravenna had become the court capital for Honorius and his successors, Rome continued to be the imperial city, and, in the absence of the emperor, the papacy made more and more of the city's glorious past.

For the papacy Rome was, of course, the city of the apostles Peter and Paul. Constantine erected a great shrine for St Peter on the Vatican, and Pope Damasus (366–384) did the same for St Paul in the church of San Paolo fuori le Mura. Other popes were to add to the list of churches at the tombs of the martyrs. Their work was painstakingly recorded in the *Liber Pontificalis*, a collection of papal biographies, begun in the sixth century, and continued until the end of the ninth. Pelagius II (579–590) built the church of St Lawrence, and Honorius I (625–638) that of St Agnes, both of them extramural churches set over catacombs, with an eye to the needs of pilgrims. Gregory the Great (590–604) built little, but he did redesign the crypt of St Peter's. His cultural importance was to lie elsewhere, in his biblical commentaries, which continued the traditions of Augustine and Ambrose, in his administration of the papal estates and his defence of Rome—both of which are most apparent in the *Register* of his letters—and in his sending a mission to Christianize Anglo-Saxon Kent.

The popes had their eyes on the imperial as well as the Christian past. Pope Felix IV (526–530) transformed what had probably been the audience hall of the City Prefect into the church of SS Cosmas and Damian, which is dominated by a great mosaic of Christ at the Second Coming. At some point in the sixth century a ceremonial hall at the foot of the Palatine Hill was dedicated to the Virgin, to be known as Sta Maria Antiqua, whose sequence of frescoes provides a key to the history of painting from the sixth to the ninth centuries. Honorius I even turned the old senate house into the church of

S. Adriano. Shortly before that, Boniface IV (608–615) was the first pope to dedicate a major temple in the city to the Christian cult, with the consecration of the Pantheon to the Virgin, thus creating the church of Sta Maria Rotunda. In such ways the papacy not only Christianized the city, they also annexed its imperial past.

Kings and popes drew heavily on the Roman past, and the sub-Roman aristocrats who surrounded them were happy to cultivate the long-established traditions of a literary culture. Yet behind this façade of continuity much had changed. In the course of the fifth century most of the great urban schools of grammar and rhetoric seem to have failed: Gaul had boasted a great rhetorical tradition, which the fourth-century poet Ausonius (d. 393) had praised. By 500 the schools of Autun and Bordeaux had vanished from sight. Elsewhere in Gaul no more than an occasional orator is recorded. In so far as oratory survived, it did so in the homilies of clerics, although, responding to the standards of the time, Bishop Caesarius of Arles (502–542) deliberately cultivated a simple literary style in his sermons.

In Italy traditional education seemed less under threat around 500. Ennodius of Pavia (d. 521) praised both Rome and Milan as educational centres. A high level of schooling must also have been available in Ostrogothic Ravenna, for Theodoric's daughter Amalasuintha (d. 535) was regarded as being well educated. But if literary traditions continued in Italy into the sixth century, they were not to last through the long wars between the Byzantines and Ostrogoths, still less the subsequent arrival of the Lombards. Yet war was not the only cause of change. It may well be that the cities no longer had the resources to support a roster of teachers of grammar and rhetoric. Certainly the institutions that employed trained orators were themselves failing. With the decline and collapse of the imperial court, and with the break-up of the empire, there was a corresponding collapse of governmental jobs. Such offices had required oratorical ability. As a result, there was no longer the same incentive to master the rules of Latin rhetoric. Although education still continued in some households, it was increasingly associated with the church. Reading was taught at a parish level, and the Bible, especially the Book of Psalms, was used as a major text for teaching. More advanced learning could be found in the households of bishops, and, increasingly, in monasteries.

Even before the Ostrogothic wars, Cassiodorus considered the notion of creating a Christian school, by which he meant a centre of higher education, in Rome with the help of Pope Agapitus (535–536). In the event that was too optimistic a plan, and he retreated instead to the monastery he founded in 554 on his south Italian estate of *Vivarium* (Squillace), where he wrote a number of works, including a commentary on the Book of Psalms. He also commissioned the *Historia Tripartita*, which was compiled from the Greek histories of Socrates, Sozomen, and Theodoret. Cassiodorus's last work, the *Institutes*, provided his monks with what is effectively an annotated bibliography. It was to be a basic handbook during the early middle ages. Other writers also recognized the need to provide access to the learning of previous generations. Writing in Spain in the early seventh century Isidore of Seville, in his *Etymologies*, provided what was essentially a potted encyclopedia of classical knowledge for future generations. It was Isidore's most influential work, although he wrote much else besides, including works of theology and history. Just as encyclopedias were useful, so too were *florilegia*. Already in the early sixth century Eugippius (d. post 533) at the *Lucullanum*, outside Naples, put together a volume of quotations from Augustine's works. Around 700 Defensor, a monk from Ligugé, compiled his *Liber Scintillarum*, a book of extracts from the Church Fathers.

Cassiodorus' shift to church-based education was a sign of the times. So too was his decision to found a monastery. The origins of monasticism lay in fourth-century Egypt. Tales of the monastic life in Egypt, but also in Syria and Cappadocia, were brought back to the west, where Martin (d. 397) founded monasteries at Ligugé near Poitiers and subsequently in Tours. Further impetus was given to the western monastic tradition when a group of aristocrats led by Hono-ratus (d. c.430) set themselves up on the island of Lérins in the first decade of the fifth century. This Provençal movement received a further fillip when an easterner, John Cassian (d. c.435), who had lived in Egypt, moved to Marseilles. Cassian's two great spiritual works, the *Institutes* and the *Conferences*, were to be staples for the ascetic life. The monastic movement was, therefore, well established before Benedict wrote his *Rule* in the middle of the sixth century. The *Regula Benedicti* was one rule among many, and it was to take cen-turies before it eclipsed the alternatives. Monasticism in the fifth, sixth, and seventh centuries was not a motor for cultural uniformity, to compensate for the failure of the international court culture of the late Roman empire. Rather, its variety, which depended on the preferences and contacts of individuals, echoed the regional flavour of culture in the post-Roman period.

This cultural regionalism had its own compensations. It has been noted that the first surviving historical work of any length to come from Britain is the *De Excidio Britanniae* of the deacon Gildas, written at some point in the early sixth century, or just possibly a few years earlier. It may, of course, be an accident of survival that we have nothing comparable from earlier centuries. In the fourth century, however, Britain had produced the theological writer Pelagius (d. post 418), while two fifth-century letters have survived from the missionary Patrick. Pelagius is a good illustration of what could happen in imperial times: as a talented provincial he was sucked into the cosmopolitan life of Italy, and made his major impact while in Rome. Such opportunities were not open to later generations. Gildas' Latin suggests that he was well educated. His Latin is at least as good as that of his continental contemporaries, and he has much in common with a group of moralists writing in Gaul in previous generations. Nevertheless, he remained in Britain, perhaps moving later to Brittany, to write about the sins of his own people, and the resulting punishments inflicted on them.

Although not, strictly speaking, a historian, Gildas is one of the earliest of a group of western writers to set down a regional view of history. He was preceded by a handful of annalists, notably Hydatius in Galicia, and followed, among others, by Gregory of Tours (d. 594) and Fredegar (*c.*660) in Francia, Isidore in Spain, Bede (d. 735) in Northumbria, and Paul the Deacon in Italy. Closest in time to Gildas was Jordanes, who, in the middle of the sixth century, wrote a *Gothic History*, supposedly influenced by a now lost *History of the Goths* by Cassiodorus, but written from the vantage point of Constantinople. We have been told, quite rightly, to see each of these historians as embarking on an individual task, and not to see them as writers of a genre of national history.[2] At the same time we should not ignore the fact that they all limited their subject matter to particular regions or peoples, however much some of them (notably Gregory and Bede) were intent on charting the history of divine providence. Gregory did so by narrowing his focus from the history of the creation to that of

---

[2] W. Goffart, *The Narrators of Barbarian History (A.D. 550–800)* (Princeton, 1988).

Gaul, and ultimately of Merovingian Francia, while Bede concentrated on the Christianization of the Anglo-Saxons and the subsequent development of the Anglo-Saxon church. The fact of writing from within one of the successor states had an effect on their horizons: in Byzantium, however, Procopius (d. 562), and Agathias (d. c.580) after him, could still write imperial history.

Regionalism is also a factor in the ever-expanding world of hagiography, although it is an open question quite how much hagiography was written in this period. Visigothic Spain boasts few saints' Lives, as does post-Roman Italy: indeed Gregory the Great's *Dialogues* were written precisely because of a dearth of records about contemporary holy men. Francia seems at first sight to be very different because a good proportion of the hagiography dealing with the Merovingian period has been published in convenient editions. It is not clear, however, how much of this material was written before 750. For the sixth century there is the huge hagiographical output of Gregory of Tours and of Venantius Fortunatus. In Gregory's eyes, at least, Francia was filled with the shrines of holy men, giving access to numinous power, most of them supported by local cults, which ought ideally to be controlled by the clergy: each in its own way was a microchristendom. Gregory's interpretation of the world around him may have been less widely shared—and more deliberately constructed to enhance ecclesiastical power—than has been thought. There were certainly those who were sceptical about the power of the saints. Yet there can be no doubt that Gregory opens up a world even more local than Pausanias had observed in classical Greece. Seventh-century hagiography has other concerns, notably, in the *Passiones* of Bishops Praeiectus of Clermont (d. 676) and Leodegar of Autun (d. c.677), with politics.

Most of the changes described so far are developments within the existing culture of the empire. Even the histories of Germanic peoples and Germanic kingdoms were written from a largely Roman viewpoint, and in the Latin language. On the other hand, the Germanic incomers also brought with them non-Roman traditions, as well as Roman traditions which they had already transformed. All of these added yet more diversity. There are, however, problems in identifying, with the exception of certain archaeological artefacts, just what is and what is not Germanic. Although the barbarians were for the most part only converted to Christianity after their entry into the Roman empire, there is very little evidence to show what was the nature of their previous pagan religion. Old interpretations used to combine the first-century evidence of Tacitus with the thirteenth-century evidence of Snorri Sturlasson, and end up with an all-embracing Germanic paganism. What little evidence there is, however, suggests that it is wrong to amalgamate all the evidence, and that there was considerable variety. An equivalent problem attaches to the evidence for Germanic epic literature. The greatest of the early Germanic epics, the Old English *Beowulf*, only survives in one manuscript of *c*.1000, and although the poem, or a version of it, may well have been composed centuries earlier, it is impossible to deduce when the story originated, and whether its references to the migration period have any basis in fact. Some scenes from Germanic legend, however, are identifiable on metalwork, stone, and on the eighth-century Anglo-Saxon whale-bone box known as the Franks Casket, now in the British Museum, which has a clear depiction of the story of Weland the Smith. He is, however, depicted alongside the Virgin and Child, while other scenes on the Casket show Romulus and Remus and the Sack of Jerusalem by the Roman general, and later Emperor, Titus (Fig. 7).

However much one may question what is and what is not Germanic, two points are clear enough. The first is that the Germanic settlers had a linguistic impact on the regions in which they settled. The extent of the impact varied. It was most considerable in what was to become England, particularly eastern England, and in the territory adjacent to the Rhine. It was weaker the further one moved from the old frontiers of the empire towards the Mediterranean. One might note that the Germanic peoples had a comparable impact on the artistic language of decoration. Second, and of equal importance, because the barbarian incomers belonged to warrior societies, and because, in invading the empire, they caused the Romans themselves to mobilize, they effectively broke down the imperial division between civilian and military.

In some regions this seems to have prompted what was effectively a return to pre-Roman traditions amongst the indigenous populations of what had been the Roman empire. The native population of the highland zone of *Britannia*, for instance, revived a tradition of building hill-forts, although the new forts were rather smaller in scale than those of the pre-Roman Iron Age, and suggest a rather different social structure. The military ethos of the post-Roman world is captured in the epic poem called *The Gododdin*, which seems to have had its origins in the sixth century.

The Germanic incomers were not the only outsiders to have an impact on the culture of the post-Roman world. The Irish had never been conquered by Rome, which, ironically, exerted its greatest influence on them at precisely the moment that the western empire was in its final decline, through the Christianizing work of missionaries. The result was a Celtic tradition of Christianity, which was distinctive, even if it was not as different from other traditions as was once thought. Similarities between the legal books of the Old Testament and Irish law have led to Ireland being interpreted as a society not unlike that of the ancient Israelites. That it was archaic is clear enough from the great Irish saga, the *Táin Bó Cuailnge*, the *Cattle Raid of Cooley*, but it is now recognized that the similarities between Irish and Old Testament law may partly reflect borrowings from the Book of Leviticus.

Irish Christianity, as it developed in the sixth century, was strongly ascetic. In this it was drawing on patterns of desert asceticism, probably filtered through Gaul. Irish churchmen also championed a practice of penance which involved the use of tariffs set out in books of Penitentials. This practice seems to have been borrowed from the British church. What made these traditions important within a wider cultural world was a further Irish practice, the *peregrinatio pro Christo*, or pilgrimage for the sake of Christ, by which individuals seeking salvation followed the Gospel injunction to leave home, abandoning father and mother.

In around 590 this is exactly what the Leinsterman Columbanus (d. 615) did, settling first in the Frankish kingdom, founding the great monastery of Luxeuil, later moving to Italy, where he founded the monastery of Bobbio. In the generations after Columbanus Luxeuil and the related north Frankish monastery of Corbie were to play a major role in late Merovingian culture, not least because of their importance in manuscript production and, in Corbie's case, in the development of letter-forms which contributed directly to the evolution of Carolingian script.

Columbanus himself is sometimes regarded as a missionary figure, and certainly his monasteries contributed to an in-depth Christianization of the countryside. He was, however, primarily a holy man, who acted as a catalyst, invigorating the monastic traditions of Gaul and Italy. He was not the only such Irishman to have an impact on the ascetic standards of monasteries, or on the morals of kings. On the whole mission was not the *raison d'être* of these *peregrini,* although there were notable exceptions, above all Aidan, who worked in Northumbria in the reign of King Oswald (634–642), and, in the mid-eighth century, Virgil of Salzburg (d. 784), who played a significant role in organizing mission in eastern Bavaria and Carinthia.

The Irish were less significant for the developing notion of mission than were the people they inspired. The Anglo-Saxons, Christianized from Rome, Francia, and Ireland, thought they had a duty to evangelize their continental cousins without realizing quite how much Christianization had already taken place. It was a notion which Bede saw fit to include in his *Ecclesiastical History,* which, as it happens, was also the first extended account of the evangelization of a whole people.

Bede provides an interesting, if exceptional, illustration of the state of early medieval culture at the start of the eighth century. The monastery to which he belonged, the combined house of Wearmouth–Jarrow, had been founded by Benedict Biscop (d. *c.*690), with very considerable support from King Ecgfrith (670–685), who was to die fighting the Picts. It was subject to a monastic Rule which was influenced by that of St Benedict, but it was not Benedictine. It boasted a library of considerable riches, which had been built up of books recently collected on the Continent, and which allowed Bede himself to write works of biblical commentaries of such quality that he was regarded as the last of the Fathers of the Church. Bede's own scientific genius led him to gather information from a wide range of insular contacts, enabling him to be the first to write an account of the nature of the tides in his *On the Reckoning of Time.*

Among Bede's contacts were the monks of Lindisfarne, for whom he wrote a *Life of St Cuthbert.* Also created in honour of the saint was a manuscript which, rather more clearly than Bede, shows the complexity of early medieval culture. The scribe of the Lindisfarne Gospels certainly had access to one manuscript at Wearmouth–Jarrow, for the portrait of St Matthew in the former is thought to be derived from the depiction of Ezra in an Italian Bible of the sixth century, once owned by Cassiodorus and acquired by Benedict Biscop. The Lindisfarne Gospels also boast a profusion of ornament in the decoration of so-called carpet pages and of the opening phrases of each gospel. This ornament is derived from Germanic and Celtic tradition, not least from metalwork. Here, as in the other great insular gospel books, one gets a sense of the range of influences which underpinned the culture of the successor states. Despite the existence of a common elite culture which looked back to traditions of the fourth century and beyond, it is variety which is the dominant image of the cultural world of the post-Roman period.

Of course the range of influences differed from one part of the early medieval west to another. In the Frankish monastery of Echternach, founded for Willibrord (d. 739), an Anglo-Saxon who had spent years in Ireland, insular manuscript traditions combined with continental ones, most notably in the Trier Gospels, where a peculiarly Frankish style of initial, made up of animal-, notably fish-, forms, are to be found alongside the insular repertoire. It was a style which produced its own masterpieces in Frankish liturgical books of the eighth century (Fig. 8). A similar eclecticism can be seen in the surviving stone sculpture, in England and in the semi-subterranean Hypogée des Dunes, at Poitiers, whose decor boasts figure sculpture depicting the crucifixion, angels, and the Byzantine stylite saint, Simeon, as well as what appear to be apotropaic representations of intertwined fish, and a lengthy inscribed curse. Such eclecticism is a mark of the liveliness of culture in the British Isles and the northern half of Francia. In the southern half of Europe culture had remained more exclusively Roman. This is not to say that it was a cultural desert: rather it was a repository of tradition that was constantly drawn on in terms of books and in terms of the iconography of its monuments.

Spain after 711

The cultural developments of the successor states in the seventh century were little affected by the disaster which struck Byzantium: the rise of Islam. With the defeat of the Visigoths at the hands of an army of Berbers and Arabs in 711, however, the Muslim world impinged directly on the west. Islam carried with it its own religious traditions, notably an interest in the *Qu'ran*, in the Prophet, and in Islamic law. None of these traditions was monolithic, not least because of the politics of the Muslim world. In 750 the Umayyad caliphate in

Damascus was overthrown by the Abbasids. Six years later, however, a surviving Umayyad, Abd al-Rahman I (756–789), seized control of Muslim Spain. The rule of the Umayyads meant that Spain would be anything but a backwater in the Muslim world, but it also ensured that in certain respects it would adopt traditions different from those championed by the usurping Abbasids, now established in Baghdad. Thus, for instance, Muslim law in Spain followed the school established by Malik ibn Anas in Medina, and not the Hanafi school adopted by the Abbasids. In other areas of learning, however, the scholarship of Umayyad Spain derived from the east, where most Andalusi scholars spent some time. This is particularly true of astronomy, which was perhaps first adapted for conditions in al-Andalus by al-Maslama of Madrid (d. 1009). Some astronomical information found its way into the Calendar of Córdoba, which may have been based on one written for al-Hakam II (961–976), and which survives in Latin and Arabic versions.

The Umayyads long hankered after their lost caliphate. They tried to create in Córdoba a capital reminiscent of Damascus. To this end emir after emir expanded and embellished the great mosque. The glories of Córdoba itself were extolled, making it sound an infinitely greater city than archaeology reveals it to have been. Nevertheless, the ruins of the palace of Madinat al-Zahra, founded by Abd al-Rahman III (912–961), who reclaimed the title of caliph for the Umayyads, are an indication of the splendours and scale of Umayyad building in the neighbourhood of the city.

Abd al-Rahman III lamented the fact that the legitimacy of the Umayyads had been called into question by two centuries of silence. That is not to say that there had been no historical writing in the period since the conquest of Spain, but little survives. Much of the information that we do have is contained in later biographical dictionaries. Abd al-Rahman's son, al-Hakam II (961–976), determined to rectify the situation and encouraged the study of history and genealogy. In so doing he probably led to the championing of bogus Egyptian traditions relating to the conquest of Spain, which had been introduced into the peninsula a century earlier by Ibn Habib (d. 853). Al-Hakam also founded a great library, which was unfortunately purged by the puritanical vizier al-Mansur before 1002.

Our evidence for Umayyad Spain centres on Córdoba: we know little about other cities of al-Andalus. This is as true for the history of

the Christians as for the Muslims. Our knowledge of Christian culture under the Umayyad caliphate is dominated by a group of texts
associated with a martyr movement which erupted in the capital in
the 850s. These texts, written by Eulogius (d. 859) and his friend Paul
Alvar, give a superficial impression of considerable hostility between
Christians and Muslims, but the impression is only superficial: it is
clear that the martyr movement was frowned on by many Christians.
The church, in Umayyad Spain, indeed, had survived the Muslim
invasion remarkably well. Councils could still be held. Eulogius' own
writings reveal monasteries in the surroundings of Córdoba itself. A
recognition that Eulogius and Paul Alvar are not representative of
Christian culture calls into question the extent to which the Christianity in Umayyad Spain was under threat, and leaves wide open the
problem of the speed with which conversion to Islam took place. It
has also opened up the question of the date of a number of churches,
most notably of Santa María de Melque, outside Toledo, which used
to be assigned to the Visigothic period on no better grounds than that
it was assumed that they could not have been built under a Muslim
regime.

A rather less tolerant attitude, however, was to emerge on the
Christian side, in the north-eastern kingdom of the Asturias. This
was territory which, like other parts of the north and centre of the
peninsula, had remained outside Islamic control, albeit under threat
of Muslim raids. In the Visigothic period, Galicia seems to have been
a backwater: it was the Muslim conquest of the south which made it
the centre of a flourishing culture.

Although Asturian culture was to focus on the court at Oviedo, its
first product was to be a commentary on the Apocalypse written in
the late eighth century by Beatus, a monk of Liébana, on the edge of
the mountainous Picos d'Europa (Fig. 5). The monastic library there
afforded Beatus the opportunity to compile a sizeable work, drawing
on a considerable range of patristic authors. Whether Beatus thought
that the Muslims had brought the Apocalypse a stage closer is an open
question, for he nowhere mentions Islam. He did, however, mention
the evangelization of Spain by St James, who as the 'Moorslayer'
would become the presiding saint of the Christian reconquest.
Equally, one illustrator of Beatus—and the tradition of truly spectacular illustrations for his work may have begun in the Asturian
kingdom—did apparently link Muslims with the Apocalypse. A more

obvious sense of anti-Muslim feeling, however, is to be found in a group of texts associated with the court of Alphonso III (866–910), in particular the so-called Prophetic Chronicle, which indicated that the Muslims would be driven out of Spain in 883.

Asturian culture, however, is more marked by its building programmes than by its surviving literature. Although there is some debate over the precise chronology of Asturian churches, it is clear that the establishment of a capital in Oviedo by Alphonso II (788–842) at the end of the eighth century was the trigger for a succession of church buildings, most notably the church of San Julián de los Prados, which still survives, boasting a faint, but perfectly visible, set of frescoes depicting arcades with vistas opening onto images of churches. This *trompe l'œuil* style is derived ultimately from late antique decoration exemplified in both the orthodox baptistry in Ravenna and St George, Thessaloniki. The scheme centres on an image of a jewelled cross, reminiscent of a magnificent bejewelled cross, the so-called Cross of the Angels, commissioned by Alphonso in 808. The importance of this cross to Asturian ideology is marked by the fact that Alphonso III commissioned another, the Cross of Victories, exactly a century later.

The Asturian kingdom had its capital city in Oviedo, but one of its kings, Ramiro I (842–850) was responsible for building another cluster of royal buildings across the valley on Monte Naranco (Fig. 6). There is a mismatch between the documentary evidence for what Ramiro built and the surviving structures, making precise identifications difficult. What is certain is that the sculptors who worked on them had access to late Roman ivories and Sasanian metalwork, which provided the inspiration for their decorative schemes. Like the art of the successor states, that of the Asturian kingdom under Ramiro was remarkably eclectic.

The Carolingian Renaissance

While the Umayyads were establishing themselves in Spain, the Carolingians were doing the same in the Frankish kingdom, subsequently extending their authority into Italy as well as Saxony. Alongside these developments went the re-establishment of a dominant court culture, which in many respects meant a reinterpretation of the culture of the later, that is Christian, Roman empire.

Aspects of what we regard as the Carolingian Renaissance had their origins in the monastic culture of late seventh-century Francia. One of the most distinctive features of Carolingian learning was its production of books in an elegant script known as Caroline minuscule, which drew on Roman uncial, half uncial, and cursive letter forms, developed out of late Merovingian scripts (Fig. 10). So too, the reformed monasticism of the Carolingian period had its roots in the enthusiasm of certain Anglo-Saxons, most notably St Boniface (d. 754) for the *Rule* of St Benedict. Equally Alcuin (d. 804), who was summoned to Charlemagne's court to act as tutor to the then king and his daughters, was very much a product of the school of York, where he had been deeply influenced by the writings of Bede. The Carolingian Renaissance was not created *ex nihilo*. On the other hand, it was certainly fostered by Charlemagne himself, without whom it would scarcely have happened.

Despite the influence of Boniface, and despite the rather closer connections between Bishop Chrodegang of Metz and Pippin III (751–768), the first clear indication of the cultural revival that was to embrace the whole Frankish world came in 789 with Charlemagne's *Admonitio Generalis*. This lengthy capitulary, addressed to all the religious and secular officials of the kingdom, drew first on the canons of the late Roman church, setting out basic rules for the clergy and laity. It then turned to the Bible to produce a blueprint for Christian behaviour. The whole was prefaced with a statement in which the biblical king Josiah, in his visitations, admonition, and correction, is set out as the model for kingship.

Charlemagne was not the first to look to the Bible for his models. Late Roman emperors and the rulers of the successor states had been compared with such figures as Moses and particularly Melchisedek, the ideal priest king. The Carolingians, however, were to make much more of the image presented by the kings of the Old Testament, and not just of Josiah. David became a point of comparison for Charlemagne, and for his grandson Charles the Bald (840–877).

Much of the *Admonitio Generalis* is a restatement of canonical and biblical injunctions, but there are pieces of directly pragmatic guidance. In particular there are precise directives on teaching: schools were to teach the psalms, *notas* (writing or musical notation), *computus*

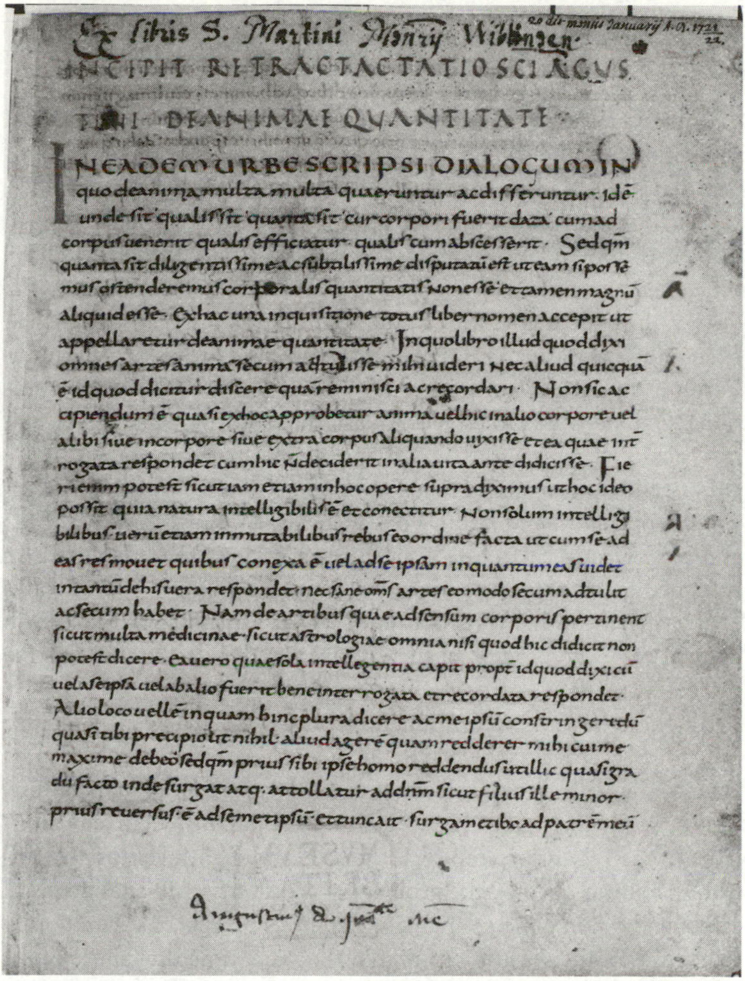

Figure 10 Caroline minuscule script. The main part of the text is written in Caroline minuscule. The 2-line heading beginning 'Incipit' is written in Rustic capitals, and the first line of the text, beginning 'In eadem urbe' is written in uncial script. Rustic capitals and uncial script are both scripts within the Roman system of scripts retained by the Frankish scribes of the Carolingian period and used in many of their books

(vital for calculation of the ecclesiastical year), and grammar. Books, particularly Gospels, Psalters, and Missals, were to be copied out with care. About ten years later Charlemagne returned to the association of good grammar and a proper understanding of scripture in another capitulary, 'on cultivating letters', *De litteris colendis.*

In many respects the programme, and specifically the educational injunctions, of the *Admonitio Generalis* are at the heart of Carolingian culture. Good grammar, good Latin, and good texts of books, especially Bibles and liturgical books, are recurrent elements. An immense amount of labour was put into creating a good text of the Bible at many centres in the Carolingian world. With regard to the liturgy, the issue was somewhat more complicated, because there had been no standardized liturgy in western Europe in the pre-Carolingian period, and different dioceses followed different traditions. One need was to establish a standard liturgy. This was not, in fact, achieved, but a start was made when Charlemagne secured a copy of the Roman Mass Book, known as the *Sacramentarium Gregorianum* or *Hadrianum*, from Pope Hadrian I (772–795) between 784 and 791. A concern to establish uniform ecclesiastical practice also stretched to an attempt to impose a single monastic rule, the *Rule of St Benedict*, or rather a version of it, which was made at the reform council of Aachen in 816, in the early years of the reign of Louis the Pious (814–840).

All these reforms were thought necessary to make the Frankish kingdom acceptable to God. Right religion, correctly, and to some extent uniformly, expressed, was at the centre of Carolingian culture. The need for this was made all the more apparent by current problems in the Byzantine empire. Since the early eighth century Byzantium had been riven by the problem of the status of images. Icons of saints had become increasingly important as objects of veneration in the course of the seventh century. At the same time the failure of the Byzantine armies in the face of the Muslims had led some to conclude that one cause of the empire's crisis was the veneration of images, which could be interpreted as idolatry. In the course of the eighth century Byzantium moved through phases both opposed to icons (iconoclasm) and in favour of them (iconodulism). In the last years of the eighth century an iconodule party was in power, and the ruler was a woman, the Empress Irene (796–802), who had achieved her position by having her son, the Emperor Constantine VI (780–797), blinded. The Carolingian court responded to affairs in the east in a work of theology entitled the *Libri Carolini*, written largely by Theodulf of Orléans (d. 821), which provides a remarkable critique of Byzantine ideology, as well as a theory of images. The Carolingian position was also set out at the Council of Frankfurt (794), which condemned both iconodulism and iconoclasm—allowing that images could be useful educational devices, but denying that they were worthy of veneration.

Rulers in the west had not entirely ignored Byzantium in the seventh century. Carolingian intervention in Italy, from the time of the conquest of the Lombard kingdom in 774, however, had meant that the Byzantine empire could not be ignored. Byzantine territory, of course, included substantial parts of southern Italy as well, theoretically, as Rome, though the city was largely left to the care of the popes. Carolingian support for the papacy, and involvement in its affairs, was necessarily a challenge to the Byzantines, not least when it led to Charlemagne being crowned emperor by Pope Leo III on Christmas Day 800. Intervention in Italy, and the concurrent development of an imperial ideal, also had direct repercussions on Carolingian culture.

Alongside the Bible, the Roman past was one of the foundations of Carolingian culture. While Rome, like the Bible, had been a recurrent influence for the successor states, its cultural legacy was the subject of renewed and intensified attention under Charlemagne. In certain respects the renaissance of things Roman went hand in hand with the reassertion of Christian education. A concern for Latin grammar and language was essential: the late Roman grammarians Donatus and Priscian were central to linguistic instruction. Just as Carolingian monasteries played a vital role in the creation of good biblical texts, and also in the transcription of the works of the Church Fathers, so too those same monasteries were responsible for the preservation of works of classical Latin literature. By the end of the ninth century most of what has survived to the present of classical Latin learning, works of some seventy authors, had been copied in Carolingian monasteries, and some Greek works were translated into Latin. There was also a revival of literary forms that had been central elements of late Roman culture. The court became a focus for poetry, sometimes on an epic scale, and of letter-writing, which is as distinctive a feature of the late eighth and early ninth centuries as it had been of the fourth to sixth. Alcuin and Lupus of Ferrières (d. *c.*862) were among the most notable writers. The social structures which sustained the new epistolary tradition were of course different from those of the later empire, but both societies depended on the regular exercise of communication.

The revival of Roman culture, however, was not just confined to literature. Roman architectural and artistic forms were seen as being appropriate to the new, increasingly imperial, culture of the north. This was expressed in small ways as well as large. Einhard (d. 840), for instance, who turned to Suetonius for inspiration when it came to writing his *Life of Charlemagne*, used the image of a Roman triumphal arch as a model for a small reliquary. The same architectural form was used at the abbey of Lorsch in constructing its gatehouse. Later on in the ninth century the main floor of the great western tower of the monastic church of Corvey, whose lowest storey was intended as an echo of the Holy Sepulchre in Jerusalem, was frescoed with scenes from classical legend. Not surprisingly it was royal buildings which most obviously drew on Roman antecedents. Charlemagne plundered Ravenna for marble and for columns, and he even used the church of San Vitale as a model for the new palatine chapel at Aachen. So strong was the notion of Rome that the epithet 'New Rome' was given to more than one place—Paderborn, for instance, as well as Aachen—adorned with Carolingian buildings.

Rome and the Bible underpinned the Carolingian Renaissance, but Rome meant more than one thing. It stood for classical culture. But it also stood for power, particularly imperial power, and as such could be exemplified by Ravenna as much as by the Eternal City itself. In addition it carried with it the notion of Christian, papal, power, with Rome being understood as the city of the apostles Peter and Paul. When the Abbot of Fulda, Ratgar (d. 835), decided to exploit a Roman model, he thought of the basilica of St Peter and sought to imitate it, to create a church to commemorate the Apostle of the Germans, St Boniface.

Neither Rome nor the Bible was monolithic. This is even apparent in the production of biblical manuscripts. In the middle decades of the ninth century scribes under successive abbots of Tours produced large-format, one-volume, Bibles, known as pandects, in a distinctive and elegant version of the standard Caroline minuscule, among them gospels for the Emperor Lothar I and a Bible for Charles the Bald. The text was for the most part Jerome's Vulgate Latin version, with spelling corrected and many organizing elements, such as headings, added. Although other centres such as Lorsch, Micy, and Metz also produced single-volume pandects, it was more usual for individual books or groups of books of the Bible to be copied. Gospels could receive particularly lavish treatment, and individual centres developed their own style of illumination. The Gospels of the so-called court school, the Ada and Coronation Gospels groups, are often distinguished by the splendour of their colour, while the latter group either had access to antique models or was subject to Byzantine influence. These Gospels had their echoes in manuscripts produced at other centres with court connections, notably the great monastery of Lorsch. During the reign of Louis the Pious, Archbishop Ebbo of Rheims (816–835, 840–841: Bishop of Hildesheim 845–851) presided over an atelier at the monastery of Hautvilliers, whose manuscripts were notable for the almost nervous quality of the figural drawing. A fine example is the Utrecht Psalter, which, when it reached Canterbury in the tenth century, exerted a profound influence on the Anglo-Saxon artists who saw it.

Book production was at the heart of the Carolingian Renaissance, and the most beautiful books were almost all Gospel books, although there were exceptions, not least the remarkable manuscripts of Hraban Maur's poetic contemplation of the Holy Cross, the *Liber sanctae crucis* (Fig. 12). As abbot of the monastery of Fulda, Hraban (d. 856) headed one of the great centres of Carolingian culture, as did the poet and theologian Walafrid Strabo (d. 849) at the Reichenau. They, and their contemporaries in other centres, produced an astonishing range of theological works, biblical commentaries, encyclopaedias, saints' lives, poetry, didactic and moral treatises, and school books. One intellectual who was trained at both Fulda and Reichenau was the monk Gottschalk (d. *c.*870), whose views on predestination caused a genuine theological debate, not least with the Irishman John Scottus Eriugena. The debate was concluded, however, as much by the ecclesiastical authority of Archbishop Hincmar of Rheims (845–882), the leading ideologue of the reign of Charles the Bald (840–877), as by intellectual consensus.

Historical writing had also been a matter of importance for the Carolingians from the middle of the eighth century, when members of the family were responsible for the continuations to the Chronicle of Fredegar. History was overtly used as Carolingian propaganda at the turn of the century, in the *Annales Mettenses Priores*. Thereafter a number of major sets of annals were kept up, not least those known as the Annals of St Bertin, which for a while were written by Hincmar himself. Annals, however, were not the only form of history writing cultivated during the ninth century. Einhard's *Life of Charlemagne* was followed at the end of the century by that of Notker of St Gallen (d. 912). In between, two authors, Thegan (d. *c.*850) and the so-called Astronomer, wrote biographies of Louis the Pious. Full-scale historical narrative was attempted in the reign of Charles the Bald by Nithard (d. 845).

The culture of the Carolingian empire was not confined to the court or the monasteries of Francia. Papal Rome, of course, had traditions of its own, particularly in the building of churches, which were decorated with mosaics harking back to the sixth century. The apse mosaics of Sta Prassede and Sta Cecilia, built by Pope Paschal I (817–824), copy those set up in SS. Cosmas and Damian by Pope Felix. Pope Gregory IV (827–844) used the same iconography in his foundation of San Marco, but adopted the colour scheme of Pope Honorius' seventh-century church of Sta Agnese.

Outside Rome, Italy boasted other traditions. By the late eighth century there was much to be said for the cultural achievements of the Lombards. Paul the Deacon, who wrote the history of his people, was one of the many leading scholars drawn into the world of Charlemagne's court. Lombard architecture is well illustrated by the fine monastic church of San Salvatore in Brescia, built by Duke Desiderius in *c.*753–756, with its elegant stucco work. Stucco, which was unquestionably of importance throughout the Carolingian world, as archaeology increasingly shows, is one of the glories of the Tempietto, probably to be dated to the early Carolingian period, at Cividale (Fig. 1), where there is also a fine collection of sculpture associated with King Ratchis (744–749, 756–757). In addition there would seem to have been a major tradition of fresco painting in Italy. The church of S. Maria foris portas at Castelseprio, however, would seem to be Carolingian, as, certainly, is the monumental fresco cycle at Müstair in the Upper Adige. Just down the valley, at Malles, is another church with two particularly impressive portraits, one military and the other religious. Nearby, the church at Naturns also boasts a cycle of paintings, albeit in a style that comes close to caricature.

Just as there was variety in art, so there was in language. Latin, like all languages, was in a constant state of evolution. The Latin of the seventh century was scarcely classical in its orthography or in its grammar. It was also becoming increasingly regional. In some places, because of the Germanic settlements of the fifth and sixth centuries, it had ceased to be spoken altogether. This was the case in England. Latin was, however, the language of the church, and when the Anglo-Saxons were Christianized, it became necessary to teach it from scratch. As a result the Anglo-Saxons, like other peoples who were taught Latin as a foreign language, learnt it from grammar books, and thus learnt a language which was out of kilter with the spoken Latin of native speakers. When good grammar was taken up by the Carolingians as part of the educational reforms of the period, this reinforced the divide between the two levels of the language; every day Latin speech became increasingly distinct from the Latin of the educated, developing increasingly into the Romance languages, that is early forms of Spanish, French, and Italian.

The beginnings of the Romance vernaculars were not the only linguistic spin-off from the Carolingian Renaissance. Concerns to spread Christianity among the non-Latin, Germanic speakers of the empire, led increasingly to the development of written forms of German. In England laws had been written in Old English as early as the seventh century, and Bede had embarked on translating parts of the Bible in the eighth. In Francia legal manuscripts acquired Germanic glosses, but no full-scale translation. In the course of the ninth century, however, ecclesiastics east of the Rhine, who had already begun to use the vernacular in such matters as baptismal catechism, began to write substantial Christian texts in Germanic dialects, such as Rhine Frankish and Old Saxon. Most important are the mid-ninth-century Old Saxon versifications of Genesis and of the Gospel story, which was retold in a poem called the *Heliand*, together with an Old High German version of the Gospels, the *Evangelienbuch* of Otfrid of Weißenburg. Secular poetry was also written down in the same period. Einhard tells us that Charlemagne himself commanded that ancient Germanic songs should be preserved. None of these survives, although there are fragments of a ninth-century epic, the *Hildebrandslied*, revolving around events of the fifth century. From perhaps the last decades of the century there is the first surviving Germanic poem on a contemporary subject, the *Ludwigslied*, which takes as its theme a battle against the Vikings.

The impact of Carolingian culture thus spread beyond the Latin and biblical renaissance of the court. Nor was it confined to the Frankish empire. It may be that the court culture of Alphonso II and Ramiro I in the Asturias was inspired to some extent by connections with the Carolingian world, though as we have seen there were more local influences. In the British Isles there are indications of Carolingian influence. This is not surprising, given the close political contacts between Offa of Mercia (757–796) and Charlemagne. Among the leading figures of the Legatine Synod of 786, sent by Pope Hadrian I to investigate the state of the English church, were a number of Frankish ecclesiastics, and there are close parallels between the canons of the synod and those of the *Admonitio Generalis* issued by Charlemagne three years later. The Book of Kells, the greatest insular manuscript of the years on either side of 800, and probably the product of the monastery of Iona, belongs firmly to the insular tradition. Other English manuscripts, such as the Royal Bible however, show Carolingian influence. Similarly, metalwork was inspired by the new continental classicism. In other media, chronological problems have prevented a clear understanding of the relation between the culture of the Carolingian world and that of the Anglo-Saxons. The Viking raids, which began in the 790s, but which did not become full-scale onslaughts until the 830s, used to be regarded as a reason for dating as little sculpture and architecture to the ninth century as possible. Although the assumption has been undermined in recent years, the extent to which the Carolingian Renaissance was echoed in England still remains to be established.

The tenth century

Although the Vikings did burn monasteries, the Scandinavian cultural impact of the ninth century was less than that of the Germanic settlements of the fifth and sixth. Certainly the Vikings set up new kingdoms in England and Ireland, and those kingdoms had their own cultures. The Anglo-Saxon sculpture of the north of England is easily divided into Anglian (i.e. pre-Viking) and Viking phases, with each having a very different repertoire of form and ornament. Classicizing vinescroll and interlace, for instance, is replaced by a rather debased

animal ornament. While the tradition of erecting stone crosses survives, furthermore, the iconography comes to include figures from
Scandinavian mythology and images of warriors. New types of funer-
ary monument, so-called hogbacks, also make their appearance. Of
the culture of the new courts ruled over by Viking kings we know a
little from later saga material. This sometimes includes fragments of
ninth- or tenth-century skaldic verse, some of it spoken in praise of
the new rulers. At the same time the Viking raids led to Anglo-Saxon
and Carolingian material being taken back to Scandinavia. Attempts
at Christianizing the Danes, moreover, as well as political contacts
with Germany, ensured that the culture of the royal centre at Jelling
came under increasing influence from the Frankish world.

In England, although the kingdoms of Northumbria, Mercia, and
East Anglia were dismembered, Wessex survived. Central to this survival was a renaissance. King Alfred (871–899), like the Carolingians,
to whom his own family was connected by marriage, thought that
God's favour, which included protection against the Vikings, was
dependent on proper religious observance. This in turn required
learning, and constant oversight by the clergy. Cultural reforms,
which included the translation into Old English of books which the
king thought all men should know (including Gregory the Great's
Pastoral Care, the Histories of both Orosius and Bede, and Boethius'
Consolation of Philosophy), as well as a concern for the poor knowledge of Latin, were at the heart of Alfred's reign. His reforms provided a base for the development of Old English literature, which
reached a peak in the homilies of Ælfric of Eynsham (d. 1025).

Alfred was the architect of West Saxon survival against the Vikings,
but it was left to his successors, notably Athelstan (924–939), to create
a united England—something which required more than simple war.
A central aspect of the unification was the translation from the north
to the south of the relics of saints, who both represented the Christian
past, as recorded in Bede's *Ecclesiastical History*, and also were the
focus of regional identities. Where the local power of the saint was
too great for a translation of relics to be achieved, as in the case of St
Cuthbert at Chester-le-Street, Athelstan instead showed his reverence
with endowments of precious manuscripts.

The tenth-century monastic reform which developed from such
centres as Cluny, Gorze, and Fleury, came to play a particular role in
English culture. One of the leaders of the movement in England,

Æthelwold (963–984), was bishop of the court city of Winchester, whose leading monastery was to become a major centre for the production of extremely costly Bibles and liturgical books of considerable beauty. Liturgy, architecture, especially that of the Old Minster, with its massive western tower looking back to a Carolingian tradition, and manuscripts, were to make Winchester under King Edgar (959–975) an appropriate capital for the newly united Kingdom of England.

West Francia and Lotharingia were at the heart of the monastic reform movement, and not surprisingly their monasteries boasted a number of major scholars, not least the hagiographer and abbot, Abbo of Fleury (d. 1004). Yet the episcopal schools, which had their origins in the ninth century, were equally important, especially that of Rheims in the time of Archbishop Gerbert of Aurillac (991–996), who later, as Pope Silvester II (999–1003), was to be one of the dominant figures of the Roman *Renovatio* of Otto III.

The Ottonians were a Saxon family, from what had been the eastern fringes of the Carolingian empire. One of the distinctive features of Ottonian culture was geographical. New cities, notably Magdeburg, were founded in the east, and with them new churches and monasteries, the most notable surviving monument being the great abbey church of Gernrode on the edge of the Harz mountains. But the Ottonians also had their eyes firmly on the old centres of Carolingian power. Otto I (936–973) was careful to appoint his brother Bruno archbishop of Cologne, where Theophano, widow of Otto II (973–983), founded the great church of St Pantaleon. More important still for the Ottonians was Charlemagne's old capital of Aachen. Otto III had a particular respect for Charlemagne, and even opened his tomb in the year 1000, exhumed the body and had it laid on Byzantine silks.

Like the Carolingians, the Ottonians also became involved in Italy and, inevitably, Rome. Once again northern intervention in the south caused a revival of the imperial title: Otto I was crowned emperor in 962. The imperial style of the Ottonians was further influenced by the fact that Theophano was the niece of the Byzantine Emperor John Tzimisces. Byzantium itself, however, received a scathing notice in the pages of the historian Liudprand of Cremona (d. *c.*970). Theophano's son, Otto III, embarked on a new Roman *Renovatio*, which was to lead to personal disaster in 1002, when he died of malaria having been driven ignominiously out of Rome. In the previous decade, however, Otto had been closely involved in an Italian ascetic movement, dominated by Romuald of Benevento (d. 1027), and he had been at the centre of a renaissance, which would continue under his cousin, the Emperor Henry II (1002–1024). At the heart of this renaissance was the production of incredibly lavish manuscripts, adorned with equally costly book covers, of Bibles, Gospels, and liturgical books. In many respects, but especially in their ruler portraits, they look back to Carolingian books, both to those produced in the court school of Charlemagne and such centres as Tours. Those which had been produced in the east Frankish kingdom, for instance in Regensburg, in the mid-ninth century, were also an inspiration. Stylistically, however, Ottonian illustrated books differ radically from what had gone before, not least in their use of gold, and in their increasing provision of considerable narrative cycles to illustrate the Gospel story.

The Ottonians paid particular attention to the narrative of Christ's Passion, and objects associated with it. The Holy Lance, supposedly that which had pierced Christ's side, became part of the imperial regalia, and was even carried into battle. Even more striking, when Otto III's body reached Cologne in Holy Week in 1002, it was, as we are told by the historian Thietmar of Merseburg (d. 1018), effectively treated as if it were Christ in the ceremonies which enacted the last week of His earthly life. This was a logical extension of a culture which emphasized the kingship and the suffering of Christ. It is an emphasis and a faith apparent in the manuscript illumination and the great crucifixes of the Ottonian period and expressed in the liturgy of the church. The texts and rituals of the liturgy itself were greatly enriched in the tenth century, building on the extraordinarily creative work of the Franks in the eighth and ninth centuries. The most dramatic developments, however, were in the music. In the late Merovingian and Carolingian periods a hybrid 'Roman' or 'Gregorian' chant repertory had been created by mixing older material, whose Roman-ness is disputed, with Frankish chant, and many additions were made. New syntheses of melody and prose known as sequences and tropes were added, particularly at such centres as Reichenau, Liège, St Gallen, and Winchester. Musical notation, which first appears in the ninth century, proliferated in many regional variants in the tenth. There were also major developments in music theory, a wider use of musical instruments, not least the organ, and the first records of liturgical drama to complement solemn ceremonies such as the Holy Week observances in Cologne in 1002.

Members of the Ottonian family, men and women, were considerable patrons in their own right. As a result they were the dedicatees of a number of major literary works, including the *Chronicle* of Widukind of Corvey (d. *c.*973). Yet there was no court school, and no officially-sponsored programme for the revival of learning. Instead the Ottonians relied solely on a limited number of monasteries for the production of their great manuscripts, notably on Reichenau, Corvey, and Fulda, all of them monasteries with strong imperial connections, and, in the case of the Reichenau, also involved in the Gorze reform movement. In this respect the Ottonian renaissance lacked the depth of its Carolingian counterpart. Nevertheless both the Carolingians and the Ottonians embarked on a *Renovatio*, which in each case involved the recreation of an imagined Christian imperial past. Through the overarching monastic reforms and intellectual developments, not least the music and the educational curriculum, moreover, connecting strands were spun across Latin Europe. The Carolingians and Ottonians created the impression of a dominant culture, determined by Rome and by the Bible, and thus provided moments of coherence in a world of extraordinary cultural variety.

Figure 11 Otto III, king (983–996), emperor (996–1002), enthroned

6

Europe and the wider world

Jonathan Shepard

The rulers of imperial Rome prided themselves on their organization of space, and their road systems and border controls substantiated their pretensions. In the fifth century the world could still be conceived of as revolving around two cities, Rome and Constantinople, although the empire's centre of gravity lay in its eastern provinces, while the north-western parts were left to fend for themselves. The eastern empire underwent drastic changes in the seventh century and became culturally 'isolationist'. Lines of communication with the west remained open, but close encounters tended to show up how the different parts of Christendom were diverging. Charlemagne's feats evoked ancient Rome and Byzantium, but his power-base, culture, and vision were distinctive. The term *Europa* defined the Christian west better than did the vocabulary of 'empire', being applicable to peoples beyond the rule of ancient Rome. Many of their notables were taken with the idea of 'membership' and, unlike the barbarians fended off by Rome, were not kept out of the 'club'. Attempts at participation could take the form of spectacular raids, but the trading and religious contacts between western centres and Scandinavians and Slavs proved resilient, and even the Byzantines responded to 'barbarian' approaches with missions and trade agreements. If the Mediterranean was still in the later tenth century virtually a Muslim lake, *Europa* encompassed power- and population-clusters reaching to Iceland and the Middle Dnieper. For all the ebbs and flows, this was ultimately a period of expansion.

Empire without end?

Europa was one of three continents known to classical geographers. Neither Europe nor the other two, Asia and Africa, was regarded as falling wholesale beneath the sway of the Roman emperor. But it was widely assumed that the whole inhabited world was his for the taking. Appian wrote: 'Possessing the best part of the earth and sea [emperors] . . . have, on the whole, aimed to preserve their empire through exercising prudence, rather than to extend their sway indefinitely over poverty-stricken and profitless tribes of barbarians.'[1] Writers highlighted the contrast between full 'subjects' and the inhabitants of the *barbaricum*. The concept of zones rippling out from a centre-point was enshrined in the political culture of the city of Rome: its inner boundary, the *pomerium*, screened off the military zone with a ring of markers. The *pomerium* was ritually redrawn in new imperial foundations, the civilian nucleus being marked out by a plough drawn by a bull and a cow. Through sacred rites and layouts, the towns gained the character of symbolic miniatures of Rome, particularly the Capitoline Hill.

The empire's outer boundaries were not marked out so ceremonially, but the outlying regions bristled with fortified towns and other military installations. In part they served a practical purpose, regulating cross-border trade and deterring aggression. But the towns, fortifications, and bridges also had symbolic significance, staking the emperor's claim to regions, for example the walls from coast to coast in Britain. They served notice that no one lay wholly beyond the emperor's remit. Virgil's vision of the empire as 'without end' in space and time[2] was refracted in the ritual of the fifth-century Christian empire. The reliefs at the base of Arcadius' Column in Constantinople show three different imperial encounters: with the senators of the key imperial cities, Rome and Constantinople; with subjects of the provinces; and with conquered foes. Such was the perspective of the imperial 'establishment'. Flaunting the rulers' hegemony over the

---

[1] Appian, *Roman History*, Preface 7, trans. H. White, I (London and New York, 1912), pp. 10–11. Appian was writing in the second century AD.

[2] Virgil, *Aeneid*, 1. 279 ff.

wider world was a key means of cementing together the disparate inhabitants of the rural northern provinces and the teeming urban centres of the eastern Mediterranean. Rome and Constantinople, personified as enthroned women on coins and consular diptychs, offered a focus for all these subjects' loyalties, being consubstantial with the empire and the emperors, centres of wealth, wisdom, and God-given authority.

Their aura of world dominion continued to matter to emperors in the sixth century, although the western provinces were now fragmenting into a patchwork of regimes of varying provenance. The cult of victory was reinforced with the symbolism of Christianity to which imperial regimes were committed. The Barberini diptych shows a mounted emperor with Christ above him and, below, a barbarian in Iranian dress raising his hand towards the emperor. The peak of triumphalism was reached by Justinian. Outside his church of St Sophia an equestrian statue showed Justinian in military costume, pointing his hand eastwards. This orientation eastwards was significant, albeit not just for the reasons intended by the emperor. Court rhetoric might extol the 'new Rome' as the centre of all things and the Barberini diptych might display Indians and Persians as subjects making offerings to the emperor, but the reality was less flattering. To the east, the Roman empire had to reckon with Sasanian Persia, a superpower capable of devastating incursions into its eastern provinces. Justinian's most solid and sumptuous fortifications were built in areas at risk from the Persians, notably along the Euphrates valley. More generally, the sizeable populations and—in Iraq—extensive urban centres under the Shah's sway made up a wealthy trading zone, with which the Roman cities of the Middle East were linked commercially. Many of the merchants of 'the two eyes' of the world[3] could deal with one another through common languages—Syriac, spoken across the Fertile Crescent from Ctesiphon to Antioch, or Greek, the language of urban elites throughout the area.

Competition was keen between the east Roman and Persian businessmen and also between their rulers. Justinian tried hard to gain access to Oriental silk via routes bypassing Persian dominions and procured silk worms' eggs from central Asia, India, or still further

---

[3] Theophylact Simocatta, *Historiae*, 4. 11, ed. C. de Boor and P. Wirth (Stuttgart, 1972), p. 169; trans. M. Whitby and M. Whitby (Oxford, 1986), p. 117.

east. His successors exchanged several embassies with Turk leaders in central Asia. On a more mundane level, merchants from the Roman world vied with Persian counterparts for a share of the luxury trade across the Indian Ocean. The Persians' intervention there prompted Procopius' complaint that 'the Persian merchants always locate themselves at the very harbours where the Indian ships first put in . . . [and] are accustomed to buy the whole cargoes'.[4] The vitality of commerce in the Indian Ocean rim is emerging from excavations at ports on the Egyptian coast of the Red Sea and the eastern shore of the Persian Gulf. Merchantmen converged on Sri Lanka. According to Cosmas Indicopleustes, 'the island, being in a central position, receives many ships from the whole of India, Persia and Ethiopia, and equally sends ships out, too', between the two halves of the Indian Ocean.[5] Its 'great emporium', seemingly housing Persian Christians, is probably identifiable as Mantai, which looks onto the reefs separating Sri Lanka from the mainland. Substantial amounts of Sasanian ceramics have been found there as well as Roman pottery, and traders from Egyptian cities made their way east. Cosmas, himself from Alexandria, while telling of the commodities and creatures to be found around the ocean, assumed that the region would not be wholly unfamiliar to his readers. For all their rivalries, the Sasanian and Roman worlds shared aesthetic and cultural values as well as overlapping economic interests. Sasanian and imperial Roman silks have very similar designs, and a shared taste for luxury furs from the far north probably accounts for the finds of Persian and Byzantine silver vessels and coins in the regions of Perm and the Kama basin.

There was, in other words, a multiplicity of contacts between east Mediterranean urban centres and the advanced cultures still further east in the fifth, sixth, and early seventh centuries. In fact Byzantine and Sasanian rulers were hard-put to regulate exchanges between the local populations of their borderlands in the Fertile Crescent. The treaty between Justinian and Chosroes I of 562 indicates a common interest in confining trade to a few points where tolls could be levied and also in containing the religious enthusiasm of communities

---

[4] Procopius, *History of the Wars*, 1. 20. 12, ed. and trans. H. B. Dewing, I (London and New York, 1914), pp. 192–3.
[5] Cosmas Indicopleustes, *Topographia Christiana*, 11. 15, ed. W. Wolska-Conus, III (Paris, 1973), pp. 344–5.

straddling the borderlands. The treaty allowed Christians in Persia to 'worship freely' provided that they did not try to make further converts. Most of them were 'heretics', subscribing to doctrines at variance with those of the 'orthodox' hierarchy. The network of the predominant Christian community in Persia, the Nestorians, stretched along the 'Silk Road' via Samarkand as far as China. Attempts by emperors like Justinian to devise a broadly acceptable formulation about Christ's nature met with obstruction from communities in cities such as Alexandria, while the patriarch of Constantinople itself could, on occasion, swing its citizens against the imperial doctrinal line. Yet the waywardness of these urban populations of the Roman east was a mark of vigour and their external affiliations generated what seems to have been mounting prosperity in the sixth century. They yielded taxes which helped emperors fund wide-ranging diplomatic and religious missions and formidable armies, despite the toll inflicted by bubonic plague that spread from the Indian Ocean via the Red Sea from 542 onwards. Attracting numerous barbarian auxiliaries through generous payments, Justinian managed to reconquer much of Italy and the coastal strip of southern Spain, bolstering his claim to be reviving the empire's glory. From his vantage point on the Bosphorus, Justinian could view western warlords' regimes as merely provisional. Their leaders were, when circumstances allowed, ritually disrobed as interlopers. Such was the fate of the Vandal king, Gelimir, paraded through Constantinople in 534 in a procession evoking the triumphs of ancient Rome.

The days of an inter-continental empire encompassing the world's choicest regions and projecting the emperor's presence through roads and military installations were, however, numbered. The conflict between Sasanian Persia and Byzantium which broke out in 603 became a fight to the death and brought massive disruption to the cities and trading nexuses of the Byzantine east, the empire's richest provinces. Emperor Heraclius eventually brought about the overthrow and death of the Shah in 628, events celebrated in biblical terms in his victory bulletins. But Byzantine tactics and military organization proved unequal to the challenge that arose immediately afterwards from desert-based Arab raiders, lightly-equipped but highly mobile and showing unprecedented purposefulness thanks to their new common creed, Islam. Nowhere within striking distance of the desert was secure from their demands for tribute and submission to the Will of God. By 650 they had put paid both to the Sasanian empire and to Byzantine dominion over the Middle East. Arab raiders were edging across the Western Desert towards Carthage while other war-bands probed into Armenia, another former conduit of commerce between Byzantium and Persia.

The business confidence of the sixth century was now lacking in the urban centres of Egypt and Syria and their contacts with the Indian Ocean rim abated. Some trade may have persisted with territories remaining under the authority of the emperor. But this did not compare in value or variety with what had gone on before, especially once the constant warfare with the Arabs brought a change over patterns of settlement and wealth distribution in the Byzantine lands. Towns shrank in size and in Asia Minor many were transferred to hilltops that were less accessible to Arab raiders but also to potential shippers of goods for the market and to ideas or information about the world beyond. The 'Roman' provinces—most of Asia Minor, Thrace, and a pattern of islands and enclaves along the Balkan and Italian coastlines (including Sicily)—were by 700 organized on a flexible, cost-effective basis against Arabs to the east, Slavs and Bulgars to the west. But the empire had receded visibly. Already in the 640s a character in a fictional dialogue between a converted Jew and his former co-religionists observed: 'Until today the territory of the Romans stretched from the Ocean, that is Scotia, Britannia, Spain, Francia, Italy, Greece and Thrace . . . as far as Antioch, Syria, Persia and all the East, . . . Egypt, Africa and Inner Africa, . . . and one sees there still the statues of their emperors in bronze and marble. For all the nations were subjected to the Romans by God's command. Now, however, we see Romania humbled'.[6] Later in the century the Syriac *Apocalypse* of Pseudo-Methodios of Patara prophesied that the man-eating peoples of the north would burst forth from the gates behind which Alexander the Great had penned them, 'and the earth will shake before their presence.'[7] The thought-world of frontiers and imperially guaranteed tranquillity was on the ebb.

The author of the fictional dialogue, *The Doctrine of Jacob the*

---

[6] *The Doctrine of Jacob the Newly Baptised*, 3. 10, ed. G. Dagron and V. Déroche, 'Juifs et Chrétiens dans l'Orient du VII siècle', *Travaux et Mémoires*, 11 (1991), p. 168.

[7] *Die Apokalypse des Ps.-Methodios*, ed. A. Lolos, Beiträge zur Klassischen Philologie 83 (Meisenheim am Glan, 1976), pp. 128, 130.

Newly Baptised, was overstating the early seventh-century empire's possessions, but not the scale on which client-potentates, customers, and ever adaptable traders still operated in rumbustious synergy. In part, the demand for eastern goods among the prominent and well-to-do in the empire's wake sprang from their intrinsic aesthetic qualities, appetizing tastes, or rarity value. But it also fed on their associations with a *régime* still not irredeemably *ancien,* and with its authority symbols. Gelimir had, while king of the Vandals, dined as a Roman judging by Procopius,[8] and what seem to have been Roman-style dinner services have been found at Martynovka and Malaia Pereshchepina in Ukraine as well as Sutton Hoo.[9] Scandinavian aspirants to status from the fourth century onwards had imitations of imperial medallions—gold 'bracteates'—made for themselves, and the fashion became most pronounced around the mid-sixth century, when the influx of Byzantine coins into Scandinavia peaked. Some appropriated 'imperial' qualities for the commissioner of the medallion, depicting him in the pose of the emperor, but wearing finger-rings or other ornaments of distinctively local type. These attempts to take imperial symbols as a template of lordship were made in regions which not even the flightiest rhetorician had claimed for Rome. The regimes occupying former imperial territory were not, of course, necessarily more inclined either to adapt imperial symbols to their own requirements or to concede any formal obligations to the emperor. In fact the Visigoths in Spain were quick to exploit the empire's humiliation at the hands of the Persians and in 624 they ousted the emperor's men from Cartagena. But the flurry of embassies bearing subsidies in gold and of exiles toing and froing between Constantinople and Merovingian courts in the sixth and early seventh centuries attests the emperor's continuing capacity for intervention in Frankish affairs. Against this background, and while merchants from the eastern Mediterranean still frequented Marseilles, few aspirants to stable kingship could afford to ignore the *basileus.* In the late sixth century, King Childebert II of the Franks still found it politic to call him 'our most pious father, the

---

[8] Procopius, *History of the Wars,* 3. 21. 1–7, ed. and trans. H. B. Dewing, II (London and New York, 1916), pp. 176–9.

[9] M. Mango, 'Silver plate among the Romans and among the barbarians', in F. Vallet and M. Kazanski (eds.), *La noblesse romaine et les chefs barbares du IIIe au VIIe siècle* (Paris, 1995), p. 81.

emperor'[10] and in 668 the mayor of the palace, Ebroin, detained Hadrian, a churchman of North African origin bound for England, upon suspicion of going 'on some mission for the emperor to the kings of Britain, to the detriment of his [own] realm.'[11] Ebroin soon released Hadrian but his apprehensions sprang from experience. It cannot be proved that the 'nest of silver bowls' manufactured in the Byzantine lands c.600 and deposited within a generation or so in a mound at Sutton Hoo were themselves some form of imperial gift or subsidy. And neither they nor the various other eastern Mediterranean or Oriental products—cowrie shells, amethysts, bronze and copper vessels—arriving in south-east England around this time need to have come directly from the Levant. But the evidence of contacts between the Byzantine lands and Celtic south-west Britain, notably finds of Aegean and eastern Mediterranean amphorae and fine red-slipped tableware, raises at least the possibility of occasional contacts with Anglo-Saxon ports and courts further east.

It is, however, probably vain to try to determine which objects arrived by way of traders from Egyptian and Levantine centres, which by way of imperial gift-givers and which via intermediaries in Francia and elsewhere. What is significant is the multiplicity of ways by which goods, persons, and ideas could reach north-western elites from eastern Mediterranean centres as late as the mid-seventh century. There is no neat name to denote this powerhouse, but it generated a kind of gravitational field. One further item which both points to its functioning and perhaps thereby gains explication is the helmet of the notable excavated at Sutton Hoo. Its overall design is ultimately Sasanian and even the garments worn by the 'dancing warriors' shown on the helmet's decorative plates are identifiable as the uniforms of Sasanian warriors.[12] The modalities of the appearance of these designs at Sutton Hoo are lost somewhere in the dynamics of emulation and exchanges between the two superpowers of the

---

[10] Childebert II, Letter to Patriarch John of Constantinople, ed. W. Gundlach, *MGH, Epistolae* III (Berlin, 1892), p. 151.

[11] Bede, *Historia ecclesiastica gentis anglorum*, 4. 1, ed. and trans. B. Colgrave and R. A. B. Mynors, *Bede's Ecclesiastical History of the English People* (Oxford, 1969), pp. 332–3.

[12] J. Campbell, 'The impact of the Sutton Hoo discovery on the study of Anglo-Saxon history', in C. B. Kendall and P. S. Wells (eds.), *Voyage to the Other World: The Legacy of Sutton Hoo*, Medieval Studies at Minnesota 5 (Minneapolis, 1992), p. 92 and p. 100, n. 97.

Middle East. But it is these exchanges and the essentially open nature of the Roman empire's eastern approaches which made a commonality of elite culture feasible, and the Sasanian–Byzantine helmet an object of respect among the East Angles. So long as they lasted, the claims made for the empire in *The Doctrine of Jacob the Newly Baptised* made sense: for some while it seemed possible that the 'humiliation' inflicted first by the Persians, then the Arabs, might be redressed and that the statues would, as it were, come alive. After Carthage fell to the Arabs in 698 and the entire North African coast became enemy territory, Sicily still gave the emperor a base from which to monitor affairs in the west. And, in the seventh and eighth centuries, the church and people of Rome still prayed for the emperor's dominion to return, 'more complete'.[13]

The Mediterranean as a barrier to east–west travel

Nonetheless, the emperor was diminished once he lost purchase on the three eastern patriarchates beside Constantinople itself which had until the mid-seventh century functioned beneath his aegis: Alexandria, Jerusalem, and Antioch. The lands and small towns now beneath his sway no longer amounted to a 'generator', putting out waves of sometimes mutually incompatible cultural, religious, and 'political' initiatives. Those routes which remained viable for officials, diplomats, and churchmen towards the end of the seventh century were more circuitous and hazardous than had ever been the case in antiquity. The Egnatian Way and other Roman-built highways were no longer maintained and the proximity of Slavs, Avars, and other incomers made the land routes unappealing if not hazardous for the next century and a half. From the seventh century Slavs' picking off boats in the Gulf of Corinth and marauding the outskirts even of important towns such as Patras and Corinth induced travellers between east and west to take the slower, stormier route round the southern capes of the Peloponnese. They could

---

[13] *Liber diurnus Romanorum pontificum*, ed. H. Foerster (Bern, 1958), p. 117, lines 15–17.

expect sporadic havens along this route but the hinterland of the Peloponnese appeared alien to the English-born pilgrim, Willibald, around 723: his *Vita* mentions only the stronghold of Monemvasia as a landfall between Syracuse and the Aegean, and regards it as lying 'in the land of *Slawinia*', without inklings of imperial rule there.[14]

The assaults of unbelievers from every direction and mass-displacements of Christian people may well have fostered a greater sense of community among those afflicted. Sicily and many districts as far north as central Italy harboured individuals and sometimes whole communities of Greek-speakers. During the seventh and early eighth centuries, the number of Greek monasteries founded at Rome rose from nil to eight and until the end of the tenth century, churches and monastic houses filled or frequented by eastern Christians continued to be prominent, if not particularly numerous, in and around Rome. Several persons of eastern origin or Greek background were installed on the pontifical throne and some were able and active in sponsoring the copying of manuscripts and spreading the Word. Thus, Pope Zacharias (741–752) translated into Greek the *Dialogues* of Gregory the Great, and these straightforward stories about saints' lives, wonders, and personal salvation struck a chord. Pope Gregory, who was apparently revered in the east within a generation of his death, became known to Greek-speakers as 'the Dialogue'. Nonetheless, the easterners, esteemed as they were for book learning and asceticism, were ultimately only guests, whose manners might be admirable but must not flout basic house rules. One migrant from the upheavals of the mid-seventh-century eastern Mediterranean, Theodore of Tarsus, was ordained archbishop of Canterbury as being well-instructed in Greek, Latin, and both secular and sacred writings. Yet he had to give up his existing tonsure, shaven 'after the manner of the easterners' and one of the tasks enjoined by the pope on his guide, Hadrian, in 668 was that Theodore 'should not introduce any Greek customs contrary to the true faith'.[15] These two Greek-speakers proceeded to expound the Scriptures and the Greek Fathers to the

---

[14] Huneburc of Heidenheim, *Hodoeporicon (Vita Willibaldi)*, ed. G. H. Pertz, *MGH, SS*, XV.1 (Hanover, 1887), pp. 93–4; trans. C. H. Talbot, *The Anglo-Saxon Missionaries in Germany* (London, 1954), p. 160.

[15] Bede, *Historia ecclesiastica*, 4. 1, ed. Colgrave and Mynors, *Bede*, pp. 330–1.

Anglo-Saxons in a distinctively eastern mode, giving pride of place to rhetoric.

In the seventh and subsequent centuries, the notion that earthly suffering of communities and the debacles of imperial regimes were God's punishment for sins and might actually offer the means to correction and redemption gained the prominence in the east which it enjoyed in Latin-speaking regions. It is expressed in the writings of Anastasius of Sinai and also in the *Apocalypse* of Pseudo-Methodius, a work probably written in Arab-dominated Mesopotamia towards the end of the seventh century. However, for all the points at which the *Apocalypse* 'spoke' to contemporary Christians elsewhere— tellingly enough for it to be translated into Latin in the eighth century—this work contained distinctive eastern features: the Christian empire would eventually prevail despite the triumphs of other powers, the 'Roman' victor emerging from across the eastern, 'Ethiopian', sea; and the empire's indestructibility would be due to its faith in Christ. The belief remained entrenched in the east, notably among the ruling elite (including most senior churchmen), that the emperor had a primary role in guiding men's souls towards salvation. This was not an assumption shared by many religious thinkers living in Rome or further west. Moreover, the very preoccupation of communities with staving off God's wrath and propitiating the saints heightened their concern with the modalities of worship. At a time when communications were difficult and earthly relief forces uncertain, this opened the door to local idiosyncrasies and downright deviation from the practices of metropolitan churches. Anxiety about deviant forms of worship led Emperor Leo III to heed those churchmen who, in the 720s, maintained that images of Christ and the saints were idols—and not extensions of the divine to help repulse Saracen invaders (see Chapters 4 and 5). The Iconoclast Controversy did not, in itself, draw an insurmountable dividing line between the papacy and the empire, but it illustrates the divergent ways in which ecclesiastical centres were moving. Under pressure of events, each looked to its own means of salvation, both material and spiritual. At a practical level, Leo III sought to secure Sicily and Calabria for correct worship by transferring them, together with Illyricum, away from papal authority to the Constantinopolitan patriarch's jurisdiction. This was tacit recognition that most of Italy and the west lay beyond Leo's effective remit.

Out-of-body experiences in east and west

Another form of self-help—presenting ordinary folk with an immediate sense of the next world—underlay an initiative taken by Gregory the Great. Visions of heaven and hell circulated among eastern Christian communities in the first centuries after Christ, elaborating upon Paul's vision of Paradise.[16] Living on the alert for the world's end, Gregory turned stories of journeys to the other side and back into a popular genre. His *Dialogues*' fourth book relates out-of-body experiences of individuals whose souls had returned with reports of flowery meadows and fires crackling with real flames. Soon, further travelogues of souls on the verge of death were composed in the west. Thus, demons clawed back the winged soul of Barontus which Archangel Raphael was guiding up to heaven, but flight over a monastery during vespers gave it a decisive upwards boost. And at the end of the seventh century a Northumbrian layman, Drythelm, was led through a vale of suffering to 'a very great wall . . . whose length and height in every direction seemed altogether boundless'; beyond lay the joyful mansions of the good but not wholly perfect, and further on still an extraordinarily beautiful light could be discerned.[17] According to Bede, Drythelm returned to this world with his experiences of the next.

Travel reports such as this filled in the landscape which theology left vague. They offered information essential for any mortal and many more were composed in the Carolingian west, advising how to avoid the tortures of the damned. Visions of rulers in the next world became a feature of ninth-century political discourse. A more fundamental theme was the value of masses for the dead, held to be especially potent in relieving the agonies of those in the vale, and this enhanced the mediating role of the clergy and, above all, monks as intercessors with this unseen world. So realistic were the reports that sporadic attempts were made to locate the entrance to the region of suffering: the twelfth-century *Purgatory of St. Patrick* made it out to be in Ireland. More generally venerated as a contact point with the

---

[16] St Paul's Letter: 2 Cor. 12: 2–4.
[17] Bede, *Historia ecclesiastica*, 5. 12, ed. Colgrave and Mynors, *Bede*, pp. 492–3.

next world was the Holy Land, and fascination with 'the Land of Promise' spanned western Christendom. The holy places contained physical traces of scriptural events and the monuments in this sacred space offered allegorical hints as to Revealed Truth, intimations of the ultimate reality. Travellers' descriptions of biblical landmarks were avidly collated with what the Scriptures related, partly for guidance in the re-creation of sacred space, church buildings and especially altars being charged with symbolism. Some were fired to retrace events of sacred time for themselves. The early ninth-century scholar Dicuil recorded a journey of pilgrims whose piety led them beyond Jerusalem to the Nile and the pyramids, or rather 'the seven barns built by holy Joseph, according to the number of the years of abundance, four in one place and three in another'.[18] However, for the vast majority of ordinary persons—peasants—in the west, communication with the divine through the offices of the priesthood was the norm, as Gregory the Great had intended.

Gregory's attempts to dramatize, even sensationalize, the Christian faith's message and bring the reality of the next world home to his flock sprang from pastoral concerns in an insecure, fragmented society where a readily intelligible moral lead seemed wanting. His stories were in no way aimed against the idea of empire and in fact proved popular in the east, while from the eighth century onwards a Latin version of the eastern *Vision of Paul* circulated widely. Yet this sort of approach to the other side set western piety on a different track from that of Christians in the east. There, the belief that heaven could be found on earth and that Constantinople was a kind of New Jerusalem was no mere conceit of imperial propaganda, but engrained in the political culture. Visions and reports of trips to heaven tended to portray it as a well-walled city, housing a yet more splendid version of the palace in Constantinople, replete with eunuchs and reception halls. Archangels were customarily portrayed in the garb of the emperor's officials. In other words, God's authority was immanent in the imperial order. So entrenched was the state's management of earthly affairs that the journey of the soul upon leaving the body was envisaged as a series of halts at 'customs posts'; demons examined it with the aid of ledgers of past sins, counterparts of the bureaucracy of

---

[18] Dicuil, *Liber de mensura orbis terrae*, 6. 12, ed. and trans. J. J. Tierney and L. Bieler, Scriptores Latini Hiberniae 6 (Dublin, 1967), pp. 62–3.

angels. The Byzantines' conviction that their forms of worship and hierarchy reflected the heavenly scheme of things rubbed off on some outsiders. Rus emissaries sent by Prince Vladimir of Kiev in the 980s to investigate Byzantine Christianity reported on the service they attended in Constantinople, 'We knew not whether we were in heaven or on earth. . . . We only know that God dwells there among men.'[19]

The eastern empire's survival tack

The standing alert of the Byzantine rulers in the face of threats from the east and the influx of Slavs and other 'barbarians' into the Balkans made them keenly interested in these peoples from a military perspective. The *Strategikon* apparently commissioned by Emperor Maurice at the end of the sixth century differs from earlier tactical treatises in devoting a chapter to 'the tactics and characteristics of each people'. Maurice shows awareness of the different forms of culture among 'the nations', treating the Persians as virtually on a par with the Romans, in contrast with loosely organized Slavs. He stresses the need to adapt, particularly to Slav guerrilla tactics, and he is explicit about weaponry and techniques borrowed from barbarians, for example, the short, composite bow and the round 'Avar-style tents which are both stately and useful'.[20] Iron stirrups, too, were adopted from the Avars who had, only two or three generations before Maurice's time, been sparring with the armies of China. The empire's soldiery could no longer count on well-maintained highways to speed them to troublespots, but they could make the most of their situation and practise fighting in loose formation with the utmost tactical flexibility. The value of intelligence about enemy intentions is highlighted by Maurice and this extended to monitoring goings-on at foreign courts. Constantine V maintained 'secret friends' among the Bulgars to keep abreast of the leaders' plans and was swift to react to new links forged between Pippin and the papacy,

[19] *Povest' Vremennykh Let*, ed. V. P. Adrianove-Peretts and D. S. Likhachev (St Petersburg, 1996), p. 49.

[20] Maurice, *Strategikon*, 1.2, ed. G. T. Dennis; German trans. E. Gammillscheg (Vienna, 1981), p. 82.

sending an organ—a kingly symbol—and a proposal of marriage between the emperor's son and Gisela, daughter of Pippin. A function of the emperor's stand-in during his absences from the capital was 'to guard against sudden attacks by the enemy . . ., and in this connection . . . constantly to write to and receive reports from the border themes, and to keep an eye on neighbouring hostile peoples'.[21] The ruses which a mid-tenth-century treatise, *Skirmishing*, recommends to regional commanders presuppose that they will often be facing numerically superior Muslim raiders. Against this background of insecurity and involuntary contacts, it is understandable that the 'image' which the imperial court sought to convey through ceremonies and other propaganda was one of order. Equally, as a corollary to the relics and hymns which became so prominent in public life from the early seventh century onwards, strict observance of religious ritual and doctrine was a tool of survival. Through avoidance of deviationism the Christians would retain God's support.

Those who showed too free-ranging a familiarity with the literature of the pre-Christian past or some affinity for 'barbarian' peoples were apt to incur suspicion, ridicule, or worse from the politico-ecclesiastical elite prevailing in Constantinople. Patriarch Photius was castigated for setting his heart on 'an unsound and sandy foundation, profane learning'.[22] The members of that elite were not above making major *de facto* concessions to 'barbarian' rulers, as the situation required. But for this very reason they were disinclined to write it up, or cause it to be recorded in court literature. Occasionally, disaffected sources draw attention to what were probably unexceptional modes of doing business with outsiders. Thus, the iconoclast emperor Leo V is berated by an icon-venerating chronicler for the way he ratified a peace treaty with invading Bulgars in 816: the ritual included oaths sworn over slaughtered dogs, Bulgar-style.[23] It is from a treaty incorporated in the Rus *Primary Chronicle* that we learn of the

---

[21] Constantine VII Porphyrogenitus, *Three Treatises on Imperial Military Expeditions*, ed. and trans. J. F. Haldon (Vienna, 1990), pp. 86–7.

[22] Nicetas David, *Vita Ignatii*; *PG* 105, col. 509.

[23] Theophanes Continuatus, 1. 20, ed. I. Bekker (Bonn, 1838), p. 31; D. Sinor, 'Taking an oath over a dog cut in two', *Altaic Religious Beliefs and Practices, Proceedings of the 33rd Meeting of the Permanent International Altaistic Conference, Budapest June 24–29, 1990*, ed. G. Bethlenfalvy et al. (Budapest, 1992), p. 302, repr. in Sinor's *Studies in Medieval Inner Asia* (Aldershot, 1997), no. 17.

proviso that a Rus who violates the terms, whether pagan or Christian, 'shall merit death by his own weapons and be accursed of God and of Perun'.[24] In fact, these tenth-century treaties are remarkable testimony not merely to Byzantine officialdom's acquaintance with foreigners' customs but also to their readiness to accommodate them. Disputes were to be resolved and amends made for crimes in accordance with norms prevailing in the world from which the Rus sprang. 'Romans' who fell out with the Rus were subject to their alien legal procedures. For example, there was to be a search through their houses if stolen goods allegedly lay inside and the proprietor refused to open up, and thieves could be dealt with more summarily than overt robbers. This accommodation of northerners' ways reflects Byzantine anxiety to accustom the Viking Rus to trading as an expedient road to riches. But it also helps explain why the public image more commonly projected was of the emperor receiving tribute from foreigners, or parading prisoners-of-war in triumphs redolent of ancient Rome.

The literary convention was to designate foreign peoples by classical names—partly to keep one's Greek in high-style 'Attic' but also from reluctance to ascribe to these often amorphous groupings intrinsic worth or to detach oneself from the cultural landscape which the classics still provided and which did have things of relevance to teach. Moreover, carrying on with the classical literary order was a means of mitigating the downturn in Roman affairs since the days of the ancients. Writers such as Constantine VII were well aware that their empire had once stretched to the Tigris and the furthest west and maintained that 'the emperor of Constantinople rules the sea as far as the Pillars of Hercules'.[25] The Saracens could still be deemed intruders to whom 'the war of the Romans with the Persians gave . . . the opportunity to seize the land', in the words of Constantine's father.[26]

---

[24] *Povest' Vremennykh Let*, ed. Adrianova-Peretts and Likhachev, p. 26.

[25] Constantine VII, *De thematibus*, 10, ed. A. Pertusi, Studi e Testi 160 (Rome, 1952), p. 94.

[26] Leo VI, *Tactica*, XVIII. 110; *PG* 107, col. 972.

Byzantine reports on 'barbarians': the focus narrows

The Byzantine elite, conscious of their empire's lost territories and glories, were not inclined to dignify 'barbaric' peoples with a description in high-style Greek—even though many of those carrying out diplomatic missions despatched by the emperor possessed literary talents. The dearth of such reports after the sixth century is worth a little further discussion; for it marks the transfiguration of eastern Christian cultural perspectives after the age of Justinian. It was in part a question of one's approach to the seen world. Careful descriptions and empirical analysis of human events and natural phenomena as a means to explaining the way of the world had been the essence of ancient science and historical writing, and they were already under attack from Cosmas Indicopleustes in the sixth century. Cosmas denounced the prevailing opinion that the earth was a sphere as being of pagan origin and contrary to plain good sense. Instead, he maintained, the sky is draped like a tent over the flat, stationary earth and above it is another, heavenly, tabernacle inhabited by God and the angels. Cosmas' anti-empirical outlook is an early instance of what became the prevailing orthodoxy in eastern cosmography. It compounded the disinclination of the Byzantine elite to describe in detail the differing manners and *mores* of those living beyond their own circle. The official line was that 'barbarian' regimes were essentially illegitimate, liable to go the way of Gelimir's. But the reticence also sprang from a certain lack of assurance as to how to discuss barbarians' ways, both among individual members of the elite, fearful of being denounced for deviation or treachery, and engrained in the political culture as a whole.

Thus, scholars sent on embassies to Baghdad sometimes engaged in discussions with Muslim sages ranging beyond their brief of demonstrating imperial wisdom and know-how and presenting the case for Orthodox doctrine against Muslim errors. There is evidence suggesting that John the Grammarian could have obtained astronomical data while on a mission to Damascus, perhaps readings from the

Caliph's own observatory.[27] Such scholarly collaboration would not have looked good in literary accounts of embassies. Polemics against Islam were their principal 'published' product. Nor were disquisitions composed of the sort that Priscus of Panium or Menander the Guardsman had written in, respectively, the later fifth and the later sixth centuries. Priscus spiced his historical work with an account of his sojourn at Attila's camp in 449. Interweaving ethnographical observations and moral themes in the manner of Herodotus—whose remarks about the nomad way of life he draws upon—Priscus recounts conversations with individuals, including an expatriate merchant and a Hunnish chieftain. The expatriate voices his preference for the 'better life' that he now enjoys as against conditions among the Romans, where justice is for the rich, taxes are oppressive and 'since . . . not all men carry weapons, they place their hope of safety in others and are thus easily destroyed in war'.[28] Priscus represents the chieftain, Onegesius, as rebuffing an invitation to defect: 'do the Romans think that . . . I shall betray my master, turn my back upon my upbringing among the Scyths, my wives and children and think that slavery to Attila is not preferable to wealth among the Romans?'[29] Portraying 'barbarians' as noble savages was a means of indirectly criticizing or at least putting into a new perspective the *mores* of the 'civilized' world, and it had precursors reaching back to Herodotus. More than a century later, Menander the Guardsman presented the barbarians' point of view, drawing on diplomats' accounts of negotiations. The Turkish khagan reportedly put his fingers in his mouth and told an envoy: 'As now there are ten fingers in my mouth, so you Romans have used many tongues. Sometimes you deceive me, sometimes my slaves. . . . To lie is foreign and alien to a Turk.'[30]

Barbarian 'arrogance' could be depicted in this way so long as the

---

[27] P. Magdalino, 'The road to Baghdad in the thought-world of ninth-century Byzantium', in L. Brubaker (ed.), *Byzantium in the Ninth Century: Dead or Alive?* (Aldershot, 1998), pp. 198, 208–10.

[28] Priscus, in *The Fragmentary Classicising Historians of the Later Roman Empire*, ed. and trans. R. C. Blockley, II (Liverpool, 1983), pp. 268–9; M. Maas, 'Fugitives and ethnography in Priscus of Panium', *Byzantine and Modern Greek Studies*, 19 (1995), pp. 146–60.

[29] Priscus, in *Classicising Historians*, ed. and trans. Blockley, II, pp. 274–5.

[30] Menander the Guardsman, *History*, ed. and trans. R. C. Blockley (Liverpool, 1985), fragment 19. 1, pp. 174–5.

world still lay at the Romans' feet. An oration of Agathias maintained in the 560s that the 'Ausonian' traveller could traverse the earth without fear, drinking from a tributary of the Indus or visiting the Pillars of Hercules: 'nowhere will you find a region which is foreign . . . but everywhere you go you will be in the possessions of the wise emperor, who encompasses the world with his dominion. The Tanais (river Don) forms a frontier for the continent in vain.'[31] A couple of generations later such bravado would be hard to sustain. Constructing histories of the emperors' feats ceased to carry much conviction and literary representations of diplomatic encounters with barbarians also went out of fashion: not because they were rare, but because the improvisation and manoeuvring involved was no longer performed from a position of strength.

Reports about the borderlands and beyond streamed into the imperial palace in the tenth century, but focused quite narrowly on matters of military intelligence and were for the emperor's eyes only. It was axiomatic to the emperor's hegemony that he was better informed than his subjects about the movements of foreigners in general. It is no accident that the surviving attempts at panoramas of foreign peoples emanate from emperors or their research assistants. The emperor and his staff could pick and choose between incoming despatches and earlier, 'canonical' descriptions of peoples, including those of Priscus and Menander. But the task of integrating the truths of the ancients with ephemeral reports was formidable, as witness the treatise which Constantine VII compiled for his son and heir, Romanus. The preface sets out his objective—to consider 'in which way each nation is able to benefit the Romans, and in which to harm', their customs, 'and the position and climate of the land they inhabit'.[32] Even allowing for Constantine's deficiencies as a collator, the gap between design and execution is glaring. No post-sixth-century overview seems to have been available to supply a framework and the emperor and his assistants relied on bare narratives of chronicles for their coverage of such momentous events as the Arabs' subjugation of the Near East and Spain.

Constantine VII's *De administrando* nonetheless reveals how an

---

[31] Agathias, *Anthologia Graeca*, 4. 3(b), ed. and German trans. H. Beckby, I (Munich, 1965), pp. 248, 250.

[32] Constantine VII, *De administrando imperio*, prooemium, ed. and trans. G. Moravcsik and R. J. H. Jenkins (Washington, DC, 1967), pp. 44–7.

assiduous emperor viewed the world around him. Balkan Slav groupings liable to come under Bulgarian hegemony receive detailed coverage. So do northern peoples who have molested Byzantine possessions recently, the Hungarians, Khazars, and Rus. Special attention is paid to the Rus, who can be prevented from sailing against 'this imperial city of the Romans' if the emperor courts the Pechenegs.[33] The Rus mattered because they could terrorize the capital: peoples who only harassed outlying possessions were, ultimately, of lesser consequence. Constantine takes in the length and breadth of the Mediterranean basin. Little is said about contemporary powers north of the Alps, and the overall scene is kaleidoscopic. Beyond the 'imperial city' and 'Romania' swirl motley groupings of marauders. From a few fixed points their movements are watched and forestalled, for example, Cherson on the Crimea and strongholds in Armenia. This defensive stance could involve contacts with faraway peoples, such as the Alans—potential adversaries of the Khazars—who lived north of the Caucasus. Extensive mission work had been carried out among them by Byzantine churchmen earlier in the tenth century. And Constantine himself oversaw the baptism in his palace of Hungarian chieftains and the Rus princess Olga. But developments such as these could not be smoothly integrated into Constantine's ideal of Solomonic kingship and 'Roman' dominion, any more than could the concessions that had, in practice, to be made to outsiders. Constantine's treatise makes no mention of the treaties with the Rus or the missionary enterprises which he sponsored.

Christians across the sea: Bishop Liudprand's viewpoint

Constantine VII does have positive things to say about one foreign 'nation': 'the Franks' may at times be brutish or disorderly but imperial marriages with them were permissible, 'because of the longstanding fame and nobility of those lands and peoples'.[34] A

---

[33] Constantine VII, *De administrando imperio*, 2, ed. Moravcsik and Jenkins, pp. 50–1.
[34] Constantine VII, *De administrando imperio*, 13, ed. Moravcsik and Jenkins, pp. 72–3.

comparable sense of affinity was expressed a few years later by a churchman hailing from Italy. Liudprand of Cremona's *Antapodosis* puts forward a vision of cooperation between the Christian powers of the Mediterranean world, among whom the emperor to the east is a distant yet potent figure, sending ships equipped with Greek Fire to attack one of Liudprand's *bêtes noires*, the Saracens at Fraxinetum. Liudprand's work ends with his own visit to the palace 'surpassing not only in beauty but also in strength all the strongholds I have ever seen',[35] and his vignettes of recent imperial history highlight the piety of the Greeks. Moreover, the compass of his work is not so very different from Constantine's *De administrando*, namely, the Christian potentates and population centres of the Mediterranean, and the Saracens and others who harassed them. Nonetheless, to Liudprand the Greeks are strangers as well as brothers and the details which he offers serve partly as a kind of background briefing for the Spanish bishop to whom the *Antapodosis* is dedicated and for members of the German elite among whom he is writing. Otto I and his fellow-Saxons were virtual novices to the power play in the Mediterranean world, but even magnates further south were probably worse informed about Byzantium than their Carolingian predecessors had been.

The closure of most land routes to the east by the Hungarians from the end of the ninth century had compounded the hazards which travellers anyway faced at sea. The seizure of Byzantine Crete by Muslim adventurers in 824–827 and the Muslims' gradual reduction of Byzantine Sicily and seizure of enclaves along the Calabrian and Campanian coasts made the Mediterranean more of a Muslim lake than ever before. The Byzantine reconquest of other portions of southern Italy from the mid-870s onwards did not really make up for the higher risks and costs that now beset the traveller. It was from the later ninth century on that 'the sons of Ishmael ruled the waves and preyed on all the gulfs, beaches and promontories'.[36] For this epoch evidence of sea journeys between the Latin west and the Byzantine lands is sparsest. Thus, Liudprand was writing after the obstacles to direct east–west contacts had proliferated. Not all the manifold

[35] Liudprand of Cremona, *Antapodosis*, V. 21, in *Opera Omnia*, ed. P. Chiesa, Corpus Christianorum, Continuatio mediaevalis 156 (Turnhout, 1998), p. 135; trans. F. A. Wright, *The Works of Liudprand of Cremona* (London, 1930), p. 190.

[36] *Osios Loukas: O bios tou osiou Louka tou Steiriote (Life of St Luke the Steiriote)*, 3, ed. D. S. Sophianos (Athens, 1989), p. 160.

strands linking the central Mediterranean with Byzantium were cut. Senior officials, soldiers, and churchmen made the journey to and from administrative bases and ecclesiastical centres in southern Italy in sizeable numbers and the Italian-born Patriarch Nicholas Mysticus kept up links with friends and relations as far north as Rome. More-over, the very challenge of the Muslim predators fostered a certain sense of commonality between eastern and western Christian poten-tates. Emperor Theophilus was invoking this in 841 after the Saracens began to seize Sicily, in an attempt to bestir Emperor Lothar to combined operations against them.

To some extent, then, Liudprand belonged to a series of writers and statesmen whose sense of the common beliefs of the Christians in east and west—of 'Christendom'—was sharpened by the obtrusive Muslim presence in the central Mediterranean region. But the sequence is fitful and on those occasions when joint operations came close to implementation, mishaps were liable to open up broader issues of relative status and degrees of *romanitas*. Thus, Emperor Louis II and Basil I traded insults concerning a recent debacle at Bari even while plans were being laid for further liaison against the Sara-cens. Carolingian accounts of visits to Constantinople such as Ama-larius of Trier's are cursory about the place itself, although eloquent about the sea voyage's hazards.[37] In contrast, Liudprand's *Antapodosis* treats goings-on in the *basileus'* court with mawkish fascination, almost as if he had alighted on a 'lost world', half-familiar from history books. Liudprand and his presumed audience were eager to update their acquaintance with the Greeks and *arrivistes* such as his lord, Otto I, were impatient to exchange respects and formalize rela-tions. But eagerness and unfamiliarity with the Greeks' ways could themselves lead to misunderstandings and reactions such as those vented by Liudprand after his bid to gain a *porphyrogenita* for Otto I's son was rebuffed in 968. Now the different—'effeminate'—clothing, manners, and lifestyles of the eastern elite became objects of re-proach, the inverse of the plain-living, soldierly ways of Liudprand's Saxon masters.[38]

---

[37] Amalarius of Trier, *Versus maritimi*, MGH, *Poetae latini aevi carolini* I (Berlin, 1881), pp. 426–8.

[38] Liudprand of Cremona, *Relatio de Legatione Constantinopolitana*, 12, 37, in *Opera Omnia*, ed. Chiesa, pp. 192–3, 203; trans. Wright, *The Works of Liudprand of Cremona*, pp. 225, 256–7.

Views from the fringes: Orosius, Isidore, Bede

Liudprand's accounts of Byzantium and the Mediterranean world were written from the point of view of a royal employee. If Liudprand was answerable to Otto I, many of the western Christian recorders of contacts with 'others', narrators of travels or expounders of the 'nature of things' were neither writing directly in the entourage of a king nor much taken with the vagaries of the seen world. There is diversity and fluctuation in the places where they wrote, a 'polycentrism' which ceased to characterize the eastern empire. This does not, of course, amount to 'multiculturalism' or moral relativism; the outlook even of those few writers about 'outsiders' who were not themselves monks or churchmen was unimpeachably Christian. But the fact remains that there was no lasting western equivalent of the near-monopoly on 'higher' literary activity and political power over which the *basileus* presided in Constantinople. In the archipelago of power clusters and writing- and copying-points which stretched across the west, there was a multiplicity of shifting affinities, many of them unarticulated and local or familial, others still casting an eye back at the overarching framework provided by the emperor's rule at Constantinople. As late as the mid-eighth century, popes were dating their letters by the eastern empire's regnal years, yet by that time the papacy itself was regarded in many of the more influential quarters of the west as the repository of collections of canon law and arbiter of good religious teaching. Individual attempts were made to make sense of current events and to reconcile them with the received wisdom of privileged texts, the Scriptures and other 'sacred' writings, on the one hand, and what could be culled from the mass of information and exegesis left by pre-Christian writers, on the other. Considering the lack of hierarchical supervision and diversity of milieux in which these attempts were made, the disagreements and rivalries are less noteworthy than the coherence attained. The Christian consensus was largely self-imposed, bolstered by respect for written 'authority'.

This respect is apparent in the first major exegesis of events since the Creation to be made from a Christian point of view. Orosius, writing his *Histories against the Pagans* in the early fifth century, sought to show God's hand at work in current events. In response to the allegation of pagans—'strangers from the City of God'—that the Christian religion had brought on 'the disasters of the present day', he sought to demonstrate that 'men's misery started with original sin'.[39] Yet he accepts the organization of space made by 'the pagan ancients' and offers their (not wholly consistent) versions of the world divided into three parts. The Mediterranean is at the heart of matters, its towns, islands, and adjoining provinces being described in some detail; beyond live 'the nations' (*gentes*), fifty-four of them in Europe which stretches from the Don in the east to the northern part of the ocean and thus includes a sizeable portion of the *barbaricum*.[40] Orosius' outline was not original, save in the way it consistently viewed the world from east to west, recognizing perhaps the Christian significance of this orientation. But this made his exhaustive historical account more accessible to readers lacking direct experience of the Mediterranean world, and before long it was being copied and circulated north of the Alps. Northern readers would find little about their own lands in Orosius' pages, but the careful sets of directions were of value for communities and scholars still trying to find themselves and creating their own 'micro-Christianities'.

A further reason for Orosius' resonance lay in his ambivalence. He was writing only just after serious fissures had appeared in the imperial order, and his *Histories* were intended to prove that Christianity brought greater benefits to emperors than paganism had done. But at the same time, following St Augustine to whom he dedicated his work, he declared prime allegiance to the City of God, and could interpret all earthly disasters as corrective measures necessary for bringing men closer to salvation. The very omissions of Orosius made his scheme of things more malleable to those seeking to bolster their own regimes and to Christian apologetics: his survey does not even mention Constantinople as an imperial city and he does not treat the empire as key to salvation.

---

[39] Orosius, *Historiarum adversum paganos libri vii*, Prologue 9, 13; 1. 4, ed. and French trans. M.-P. Arnaud-Lindet, I (Paris, 1990), pp. 8, 9, 10; English trans. I. Raymond, *The Seven Books of History against the Pagans: The Apology of Paulus Orosius* (New York, 1936), pp. 30, 32.

[40] Orosius, *Historiarum libri vii*, 1. 52–4, ed. Arnaud-Lindet, I, pp. 24–5; trans. Raymond, *Seven Books of History*, pp. 34–5.

Some of the other most effective theorizers as to the meaning of earthly things and their place in time and space wrote, like Orosius, on or beyond the fringes of effective imperial dominion, and did not place much weight on the empire or its bouts of Reconquista. Isidore of Seville was, like Orosius, combative and his numerous written works, among them the *De natura rerum* and the uncompleted *Etymologiae*, were just one facet of his strivings as bishop of Seville and counsellor to Visigothic kings in the early seventh century. Drawing on numerous classical as well as Christian works, he put a Christian gloss on all objects, observations, and calculations known to man, supplying diagrams of, for example, the elements, the terrestrial world (made up, as for Orosius, of Asia, Europe, and Africa) and the five zones of heaven: 'let us imagine . . . [the zones] as our right hand in such a way that the thumb is the arctic circle . . .; the little finger the antarctic circle'.[41] Isidore offered a kind of 'rule-of-thumb' guide to the divine unity behind the apparent confusion of things for persons enjoying little access to stocks of books or conversation about abstractions. Knowledge is not upheld for its own sake, any more than is open-ended speculation and not all the data is accurate. But Isidore allows for inquisitiveness and his assemblage of classical and biblical concepts and lore intermingled with disquisitions on everyday things was voluminous enough to function like a kind of 'floating observatory' in space. It is, so to speak, programmed not only to answer queries, iron out errors, and set the course but also to supply checklists against which new and alien-seeming phenomena can be evaluated and categorized in terms of Christian allegory. The 'observatory' is not tied to a single fixed geographical centre—although it places the earthly Paradise in Asia—and the intended universality of its application made it transferable to a variety of milieux, from king's courts to bookman's cells. For all his vaunted intimacy with the workings of everything and glorification of Spain as 'queen of all provinces',[42] Isidore was himself something of a migrant, trying to provide for the unpredictable. To far-flung scholars and wielders of

---

[41] Isidore, *De natura rerum*, 10. 1, ed. and French trans. J. Fontaine, *Isidore de Seville: Traité de la nature*, Bibliothèque de l'École des Hautes Études Hispaniques 28 (Bordeaux, 1960), p. 209.

[42] Isidore, *Historia Gothorum, Wandalorum Sueborum, MGH, Auctores Antiquissimi* XI (Berlin, 1894), p. 267; trans. K. B. Wolf, *Conquerors and Chroniclers of Early Medieval Spain* (Liverpool, 1990), p. 81.

earthly power, Isidore offered a kind of 'hitch-hiker's guide' to the cosmos.

One such reader and, in part, copier of Isidore's works lived on the outermost fringes of the western lands. The Venerable Bede spent nearly all his life in Wearmouth-Jarrow, at work on Bible commentaries, the computation of sacred time, and the *Ecclesiastical History of the English People*. This is basically a story of how 'outsiders' became 'insiders': Anglo-Saxon leaders, descendants of Germanic invaders, were one by one converted to Christianity, whether by missionaries or fellow-kings, and led their people into membership of the 'universal Church' under the headship of 'the Apostolic See' (see Chapter 4). It was not inevitable that the various Anglo-Saxon warrior-elites would alike accept the form of Christian belief and observance on offer from so far away, as against the looser-knit ways embodied by Celtic holy men such as Aidan. Moreover, the seventh century was precisely the time when the Byzantine–Sasanian symbiosis collapsed and the eastern Mediterranean lost much of its 'locomotive' power, in political, cultural, and economic terms. There is little doubt that this had a dulling effect on commerce between the Mediterranean and lands north of the Alps. Now, centres of political gravity and trading zones were forming around the North Sea instead, and although the Christian cult soon gained high-placed adherents after the arrival of Augustine's mission in England in 597, this might have served to aggravate rivalries and consolidate divisions between the miscellaneous kings and aspirant kings. Bede was, in effect, celebrating the fact that this did *not* happen and that the 'universal' way prevailed. One of his *History*'s most dramatic scenes is set at Whitby, the debate between advocates of the Celtic and Roman positions over 'the observance of Easter and the rules of ecclesiastical life'. The speech put into Wilfrid's mouth invokes the Easter observance maintained in various far-away places, besides Rome itself, and witnessed by Wilfrid with his own eyes.[43] His arguments are represented as carrying the day, and it was Bede's own *De ratione temporum* that would put a scholarly full stop to the controversy.

---

[43] Bede, *Historia ecclesiastica*, 3. 25, ed. Colgrave and Mynors, *Bede*, pp. 300–7.

Travelling and converting

Travel or communications feature in about a quarter of the chapters of Bede's *History*. Many of the contacts which he records with approval are to do with the Christian Mediterranean world. But he also proclaims the moral worth of 'preaching to the Gentiles', mission work among the Germanic peoples on the Continent, 'from whom the Angles and Saxons . . . are known to derive their origin'.[44] Representing one's subject matter as a kind of chosen 'people' whose origins lay far away was a commonplace among the historians of emerging polities in the early middle ages.[45] Bede takes the theme further and devotes several chapters to Anglo-Saxon priests' 'apostolic work' among the inhabitants of Frisia and further inland. Two of them, both named Hewald, who were put to death are treated as martyrs by Bede, and their miracles are recorded.

The dynamic for travel could be directed 'inwards' or 'outwards' more or less interchangeably, the journey itself and the attendant perils and detachment from earthly commitments being at least as important as the arrival. Thus, the priest Egbert is depicted as resolving to sail to the German peoples to see 'whether he could deliver any of them from Satan' or, 'if this could not be done, to go to Rome and . . . worship at the shrines of the holy apostles and martyrs of Christ'.[46] The notion of venerating faraway relics and undergoing trials if not 'martyrdom' for their sake was closely allied to that of conversion work. Such an outlook was not unique to the north-western islands. It features in the *Life* of Amandus, who *c*.630 crossed to the Slavs on the far side of the Danube 'greatly hoping that he might win the palm of martyrdom'.[47] He travelled round 'freely preaching the Gospel' in a language which his hagiographer does not specify. But the sense that a life of constant wandering and deprivation was a higher form of devotion pervaded Celtic Christianity with peculiar intensity. St Patrick expressed it thus: 'I am a slave in

---

[44] Bede, *Historia ecclesiastica*, 5. 9, ed. Colgrave and Mynors, *Bede*, pp. 476–7.
[45] See Introduction, pp. 7–8.
[46] Bede, *Historia ecclesiastica*, 5. 9, ed. Colgrave and Mynors, *Bede*, pp. 476–7.
[47] *Vita S. Amandi*, 16, ed. B. Krusch, *MGH, Scriptores rerum merovingicarum* V (Hanover, 1910), p. 440.

Christ to a foreign people for the ineffable glory of the everlasting life which is in Christ.'[48]

Such sentiments found wide resonance and help explain a paradoxical feature of the north-western approaches of the former Roman empire. Communications grew more arduous as the north's commercial ties with the Mediterranean world frayed and travellers across the Frankish lands faced hefty tolls from royal officials and poorly maintained roads and bridges. These obstacles and endemic risks of violence seem actually to have stimulated a significant number of individuals, many of them monks, to make a virtue of travelling as being a form of suffering for Christ. The English-born monk Boniface's self-identification with the early Christian martyrs was finally vindicated when he and his companions were put to death by pagan Frisians in 754. But combining enthusiasm for saving heathens' souls with a vision of an enlightened order anchored in the Mediterranean world was not the prerogative of activists of Boniface's stamp alone. It informs a letter written to him in the early years of his evangelizing by Bishop Daniel of Winchester (see Chapter 4).[49] Daniel writes as a member of this 'Christian world', although his own see lies far from lands yielding olives or, even, vines in abundance. Such zest for the wider community overrode the geo-political obstacles and allowed for the inclusion of others, not merely the Saxons of whom Boniface remarked that 'we are of one blood and one bone',[50] but also the Slavs and Avars. In this way, enthusiasm for ancient, authoritative centres of piety and learning together with the spiritual interpretation placed upon travel could fuse, and impel individuals and small groups of monks outwards. The tendency for the 'inwards'—or 'backwards'—looking aspirations of the northerners to spawn contacts, not always intended, with other peoples, living north of the vine line and beyond the old Roman borders, is a defining characteristic of Latin Christendom in the early middle ages.

The papacy was pre-eminent as a kind of 'exemplary centre', exerting allure upon those whose Christianity was relatively new-found

[48] *Letter*, 10, in *St. Patrick: His Writings and Muirchu's Life*, ed. and trans. A. B. E. Hood (London, 1978), pp. 36, 57. See also Chapter 4, pp. 145–6.
[49] Boniface, *Epistolae*, no. 23, ed. M. Tangl, *Die Briefe des heiligen Bonifatius und Lullus, MGH, Epistolae Selectae* 1 (Berlin, 1916), p. 40; trans. E. Emerton, *The Letters of Saint Boniface*, 2nd edn. (New York, 2000), p. 28.
[50] Boniface, *Epistolae*, no. 46, ed. Tangl, pp. 74–5; trans. Emerton, p. 53.

and who were conscious of the amorphousness of their local church structures. Popes were ready enough to remind potentates of St Peter's standing as 'prince of the apostles' and of other churches' debt to his successors. Leo II informed the Visigothic king Erwig that 'from this holy apostolic Church . . . all lands, including your lord-ship's, have arrived at knowledge of the Truth and the way of Life'.[51] Individual popes showed a feel for the local customs and preoccupa-tions of converts. Thus, Nicholas I dealt patiently with Khan Boris of Bulgaria's anxieties as to whether the Bulgars' garments were in keeping with Christian worship and how to reconcile the new religion with his conduct of war.[52] Nicholas and his successors showed interest in the Byzantine brothers, Constantine-Cyril and Methodius, who had translated passages of the Scriptures and litur-gical texts into Slavonic during their mission to Moravia during the mid-860s: they were invited to Rome in 867. Methodius was later made archbishop of 'the Pannonians'. But while these and other gestures of interest in evangelization carried weight, they were made largely in response to the initiatives of local rulers such as Boris, or in competition with the Byzantines, whose claims to Illyricum rankled. The papacy laid claim to an 'apostolic' role in relation to the Slavs as to other peoples, but there is no evidence of systematic training of preachers in Rome or a 'missionary strategy'. On the whole, popes' perspectives were still orientated along the traditional axes of the Mediterranean world. When papal apologists sought to formulate a position in the later eighth century, they concocted it in the form of an imperial decree. The places allegedly handed over to Pope Syl-vester by Constantine the Great comprise his palace, the city of Rome, and 'all the provinces, districts and towns of Italy and the western regions'.[53] There is no mention of the north, although the document was drafted while relations between popes and Frankish rulers were intensifying.

---

[51] *Leoni Papae Epistulae*, no. 7; *PL* 96, col. 418.

[52] Nicholas I, *Responsa*, MGH, *Epistolae* VI (Berlin, 1925), pp. 579–82, 585, 587–8, 590–1, 593.

[53] *Constitutum Constantini*, 17, ed. H. Fuhrmann, *MGH Fontes iuris Germanici antiqui in usum schol.* 10 (Hanover, 1968), p. 93.

Charlemagne's ambit

Rome and Constantinople held a place in the thought-world of the mightiest of Frankish rulers, Charlemagne. His biographer records that he almost doubled the extent of the realm he had inherited while a later eulogist observed that peoples 'whose names the Romans had not known' came under his sway.[54] At war for much of his reign, Charlemagne displayed overlordship by sending spoils to offshore rulers and subsidies to the patriarch and other Christians living in Jerusalem. The Irish kings who received his 'gifts' 'called themselves his slaves and subjects'.[55] Charlemagne's building projects sometimes evoked eastern or ancient imperial monuments. His church of the Virgin at Aachen had an eastern-style plan while his bridge across the Rhine at Mainz mirrored Roman emperors' responsibility for communications. Charlemagne's testament bespeaks fascination with two cities. On one of the silver tables mentioned therein was engraved a map of Constantinople, while another showed the city of Rome. A third depicting the cosmos was perhaps the subject of Theodulf of Orleans' verses on a 'picture, in which the image of the earth was rendered in the form of a circle'.[56] Charlemagne and his contemporaries supposed a connection between these cities and the universe: the cities brought focus to God's creation, even while gaining significance from it. Not surprisingly, Charlemagne's own court was sometimes labelled a 'new Rome'.

Such belief in the court's God-given centrality was not absurd and Charlemagne's Aachen palace complex remained pivotal through the reign of his son, Louis the Pious. Their respective sons and other agents had to forward envoys 'from outside peoples' to them, without

---

[54] Einhard, *Vita Karoli Magni*, 15, ed. G. Waitz, *MGH, Scriptores rerum germanicarum* (Hanover-Leipzig, 1911), p. 17; trans. P. E. Dutton, *Charlemagne's Courtier* (Peterborough, Ontario, 1998), p. 25; Poeta Saxo, *Annalium de gestis Caroli Magni Imperatoris libri quinque, MGH, Poetae latini aevi carolini* IV.1 (Berlin, 1899), p. 70.

[55] Einhard, *Vita Karoli Magni*, 16, ed. Waitz, p. 19; trans. Dutton, *Charlemagne's Courtier*, pp. 25–6.

[56] Theodulf of Orleans, *Carmina, MGH, Poetae latini aevi carolini* I (Berlin, 1881), p. 547.

attempting diplomacy for themselves.[57] Southern borders in Italy were demarcated grandly with boundary markers. Religious missions were sent out, such as Anskar's to Sweden, while much was made of Louis' role as converter. The Danish king Harald's ceremonial baptism looms large in Ermoldus Nigellus' portrayal of Louis' court: 'Realms of their own accord now seek you, which neither powerful Rome nor Frankish laws could subjugate. You keep them all in the name of Christ, father.'[58] Charlemagne had nursed a vision of general 'peace', enforced by himself alone in fulfilment of God's will. Charlemagne's notion of bringing this about through a single law code— reminiscent of ancient Rome or Byzantium—failed to take off. But a standard 'computus' was probably compiled soon after consultations at his court in 809 and it circulated widely. Drawing on Isidore, Pliny, and especially Bede, it gives instructions on how to calculate Easter, an account of the six ages of world history, the number of years since the Creation and Incarnation, and copious astronomical data.

Concerns with time and place were closely allied and several attempts at describing the world were made at Carolingian courts. Here, too, the aim was to provide definitive guidelines, creating a 'canonical geography' from the welter of information in earlier writings. Hraban Maur's *On the Nature of Things* offered an allegorical explanation for phenomena, placing Jerusalem at the centre of the earth and focusing on the reality behind the seen world, much as Cosmas Indicopleustes and eastern cosmographers did. Other writers were content to delineate the surface of the earth, reworking authorities such as 'the book of the blessed presbyter Orosius and the book of the lord bishop Isidore'.[59] One or two put old texts to new uses, notably the Irish-born Dicuil at Louis the Pious' court in his quest for precise measurements. His curiosity occasionally led him to cite eyewitness reports, not only about the 'barns' of Joseph (above, p. 213) but also the ends of the earth, Ultima Thule. Dicuil notes that around the summer solstice the setting sun 'hides itself as though behind a

[57] 'ab exteris nationibus', *Ordinatio imperii*, c. 8, ed. A. Boretius, *MGH, Capitularia regum Francorum* I (Hanover, 1883), no. 136, p. 272.

[58] Ermoldus Nigellus, *In honorem Hludovici*, ed. and French trans. E. Faral, *Ermold le Noir* (Paris, 1964), p. 190, lines 2517–19.

[59] *Situs orbis terrae vel regionum*, ed. P. Gautier Dalché, 'Situs orbis terre vel regionum: Un traité de géographie inédit du haut Moyen Âge (*Paris, B.N. latin 4841*)', *Revue d'Histoire des Textes*, 12–13 (1982–3), p. 162 (*praefatio*), repr. in his *Géographie et culture: La Représentation de l'espace du VIe au XII siècle* (Aldershot, 1998), no. 3.

232 | JONATHAN SHEPARD

small hill in such a way that there was no darkness . . . and a man could do whatever he wished as though the sun were there, even remove lice from his shirt'. Dicuil corrects earlier writers who maintained that the sea was permanently frozen around Thule (probably Iceland) from the autumnal to the spring equinoxes, although his clerical informants assured him that 'one day's sail north of that [island] they did find the sea frozen over'.[60] Dicuil was far from alone in his curiosity: he owed these observations to others. He thus lets slip how much was noted at Carolingian courts yet never placed on the written record.

Charlemagne's lead made curiosity about distant goings-on respectable, although the data was not codified for its own sake. Thus, in his *Commentary* on Matthew's Gospel, Christian of Stablo shows awareness of the respective conversions of the Bulgars and the Khazars to Christianity and Judaism in the 860s.[61] A generation later in Wessex some of the blanks in Orosius' description of the world were filled in with information brought to King Alfred's court by a Norwegian, Ohthere. At Alfred's behest, the Anglo-Saxon translator of Orosius recounted Ohthere's voyage round the North Cape 'to find out how far the land extended due north, or whether anyone lived to the north of the unpopulated area'.[62] Sailing directions and the peoples and creatures of the White Sea region were thought worth describing. Such interest was quite compatible with conventional piety and veneration of traditional shrines. Alfred, himself the translator of Boethius, journeyed to Rome—leaving his name in a commemorative book in Brescia[63]—and corresponded with Patriarch Elias of Jerusalem, seeking his advice about medicinal remedies.[64] But these diverse initiatives also suggest how the Christian west was developing in permutations unlike those of Byzantium or imperial Rome. Veneration for older seats of learning and sanctity fused with

---

[60] Dicuil, *Liber de mensura orbis*, 7. 11, 13, ed. and trans. Tierney and Bieler, pp. 74–5.

[61] Christian of Stablo, *Expositio in Matthaeum*; PL, 106, col. 1456; L. S. Chekin, 'Christian of Stavelot and the Conversion of Gog and Magog', *Russia Mediaevalis*, 9 (1997), pp. 13–34.

[62] Ohthere's Account in *Two Voyagers at the Court of King Alfred*, ed. and trans. N. Lund and C. E. Fell (York, 1984), p. 18.

[63] S. Keynes, 'Anglo-Saxon Entries in the "Liber Vitae" of Brescia', in J. Roberts, J. L. Nelson, and M. Godden (eds.), *Alfred the Wise: Studies in Honour of Janet Bately on her Sixty-Fifth Birthday* (Cambridge, 1997), pp. 107–16 .

[64] J. Harris, 'Wars and rumours of wars: England and the Byzantine world in the eighth and ninth centuries', *Mediterranean Historical Review*, 14 (1999), pp. 37–9.

explicit admiration for travel and with travellers' tales as sources of information. Such tendencies were fostered by the proliferation of courts and cultural centres in the west in the generations following Charlemagne. Itinerant kingship and the need for precisely calculated distances gave rulers different viewpoints from that of the emperor on the Bosphorus. In the meantime the 'trickledown' of literacy equipped relatively humble writers to commemorate local encounters with pagans and to record depredations of 'pirates' and other raiders against fellow-Christians further afield.

This commonality of faith and key texts was not coterminous with a particular regime or dependent on specific frontiers. Nor did it radiate exclusively from any one city or cultural centre. Nowhere could the survival of scholarship or learning be taken for granted: Alcuin could describe himself as 'battling daily against ignorance in Tours'.[65] Yet the very lack of territoriality of these shifting centres implied resilience and potential for expansion. Karl Leyser pointed out that in the later eighth century *Europa*, a classical term not much used previously, came to be applied to the dominions of Charlemagne.[66] Its vagueness and elasticity denoted Charlemagne's ambit more aptly than references to 'new Rome' or any other purportedly central point. Charlemagne himself allowed for diversity amongst his subjects even in his *Admonitio generalis*. While recommending certain canons from the *Dionysio-Hadriana*, he also suggested that bishops use 'whatever others you know to be necessary'.[67] Aiming for Christian hegemony, he acknowledged in practice the polycentric nature of his dominions and fostered a unique politico-cultural configuration.

If the liturgies sung in western churches remained strikingly varied towards the end of the ninth century, *Europa*'s approaches were no less conspicuously exposed to the hit-and-run raiding of Vikings and others. It was hard to maintain effective control points, not least near waterways where the Vikings were in their element. This was as true of peaceful contacts as of defence-works, and such capitularies as that

---

[65] Alcuin, *Epistolae*, no. 172, ed. E. Dümmler, *MGH, Epistolae* IV (Berlin, 1895), p. 285.

[66] K. Leyser. 'Concepts of Europe in the early and high middle ages', repr. in Leyser's *Communications and Power in Medieval Europe*, ed. T. Reuter (London, 1994), pp. 6–8.

[67] *Admonitio generalis*, ed. A. Boretius, *MGH, Capitularia regum Francorum* I (Hanover, 1883), no. 22, p. 54; R. McKitterick, 'Unity and diversity in the Carolingian church', *Studies in Church History*, 32 (1995), pp. 59–82, at p. 81. See also Chapter 5.

issued in Thionville in 805 ban the sale of 'arms and armour'[68] to the Slavs and others. It is likely that these regulations and the raids themselves are mere outcrops of diverse contacts towards which few participants were inclined to draw attention—exchanges of *Europa*'s manufactures and slaves for goods from far to the north and east. Tating-style pitchers are found in emporia ranging from England to Dorestad (where over fifty vessels are attested), Hedeby, Birka, and Staraia Ladoga. Produced in several kiln centres they represent fairly high-value exchanges.[69] Finds of what seem to be European-made glass-beads in Scandinavian emporia and east of the Baltic hint at wider nexuses of exchanges of beads for furs. That trade reached still further east is shown by finds of swords along such riverways as the Dnieper and Volga. Some have blades inscribed with western workshops' names, most commonly 'Ulfbehrt'. Ibn Khurradadhbih regarded swords as a principal commodity of the Rus while another ninth-century Baghdad-based writer, al-Kindi, described in detail 'Frankish' swords that seemingly reached the Muslim world via the Rus lands.[70]

That Carolingian *Europa* was far from 'leakproof' does not betoken overall 'weakness', any more than finds of Roman weaponry in Danish peat-bogs diminish imperial Rome. Rather this points to the repute of manufactures issuing from the Rhineland and the vitality of exchanges that brought Muslim silver to the Baltic and still further west in the ninth and tenth centuries. Since much of the carrying trade was left to Frisian-based vessels or Scandinavians on seaways remote from writing centres, few clerically minded writers had cause to describe it. They were more apt to chronicle—for moralizing purposes—the failures, when the authorities were worsted by Vikings, flagrant challengers to the Christian order of things. The effect is to obscure the substratum of regular exchanges and widely diffused wealth upon which these raiders preyed.

---

[68] *Capitulare missorum in Theodonis villa datum secundum, generale*, c. 7, ed. A. Boretius, *MGH, Capitularia regum Francorum* I, no. 44, p. 123.

[69] R. Hodges, *The Hamwih Pottery: The Local and Imported Wares from 30 Years' Excavations at Middle Saxon Southampton and their European Context* (Southampton, 1981), pp. 64–8.

[70] Ibn Khurradadhbih, *Kitab al-Masalik wa'l Mamalik [Book of Ways and Realms]*, ed. T. Lewicki, *Źródła arabskie do dziejów słowiańszczyzny* I (Wrocław–Cracow, 1956), pp. 76–7; A. N. Kirpichnikov, *Drevnerusskoe oruzhie*, I (Moscow–Leningrad, 1966), p. 46 and n. 199.

The keen interest which Scandinavian 'kings', war-bands, and bar-terers showed in *Europa* is ultimately a tribute to the magnetism which it exerted. Their ability to conduct surprise raids presupposed close familiarity with currents, beaches, and locations of population centres. This had probably more often been gained from prior trad-ing contacts than systematic spying. Youthful members of Scandina-vian elites sought loot, fame, and status from expeditions and the value of slaves as commodities gave an extra incentive for raiding. But these enterprises were variants of many less glamorous attempts by outsiders to partake of the Christian west's wealth and aura, through trading or placing their martial talents at the service of western employers. Louis the Pious' baptism of King Harald was only the most fêted of numerous receptions of Scandinavian 'royalty' at Carolingian courts: sometimes the newcomers were assigned coastal districts to defend.[71] There were probably many other commen-dations and deals at lowlier levels.

The missions to Scandinavia formally sponsored by Carolingian rulers had little immediate impact. More headway was made among the Slavs of central Europe, aided by the relative ease of access and the penumbra of Carolingian power. Their leaders sought spiritual as well as political confirmation from Frankish rulers as the groups of stone churches excavated in Moravian strongholds bear witness. But the leaders' miscellaneous connections with Frankish nobles and royal malcontents could subvert. Rastislav was placed in charge of the Moravians by Louis the German in 846, yet he proved wayward and fended off a punitive expedition of Louis in 855. By the early 860s he was requesting a bishop successively from the papacy and the Byzan-tine emperor, and the latter démarche elicited the mission headed by Constantine-Cyril and Methodius. Rastislav was looking for an alternative ecclesiastical structure to that provided by the east Frankish bishoprics. Other ecclesiastical centres were within his reach. The 'patriarchate' of Aquileia, for example, carried out mission work in Carinthia and the names of Moravian notables feature in the Cividale monastery's Gospel Book.[72] However, it was Bavarian

---

[71] S. Coupland, 'From poachers to gamekeepers: Scandinavian warlords and Carolingian kings', *Early Medieval Europe*, 7 (1998), pp. 85–114.

[72] O. Tůma, 'Great Moravia's trade contacts with the eastern Mediterranean and the mediating role of Venice', *Byzantinoslavica*, 46 (1985), pp. 75–6.

churchmen who took the most sustained interest in pacification of the Danubian basin's Slavs. The surviving ninth-century translations of prayers and texts for baptism and confession from Latin into Slavonic (using Latin characters) probably emanate from their milieu. It was the archbishop of Salzburg and his suffragan bishops who protested vigorously at the involvement of Cyril and Methodius and their pupils in the pastoral care of the Danubian Slavs. In their eyes, this amounted to intrusion into their sphere of jurisdiction, aggravated by the novelty of Slavonic used as a formal language of worship. Under Methodius' auspices, a *Life* of his brother was composed, offering a passionate justification of their preaching and translation work. Methodius seems, however, to have been outmanoeuvred by the Frankish-born bishop of Neutra, Wiching, and after his death in 885 his pupils and associates were dispersed, some of them finding employment with Boris of Bulgaria. The Frankish bishops' line on their past missionary achievements and present jurisdiction had been set out trenchantly after Methodius' imprisonment. The *Conversio Bagoariorum et Carantanorum* rested the case for the archbishopric of Salzburg's rights in Carinthia and Pannonia on copious details of the priests sent out to preach, the princelings converted, and the churches founded, reflecting the self-sufficiency and self-confidence of the borderland sees.[73] Interest in neighbouring peoples is also registered by the 'Bavarian Geographer''s list of numerous Slav 'towns' and groupings,[74] and by the reports of new waves of attacks by nomads from the east. Regino of Prüm shows awareness that 'the most ferocious people of the Hungarians' had occupied the Don steppes before migrating westwards under pressure from the Pechenegs and possible over-population.[75]

---

[73] *Conversio Bagoariorum et Carantanorum*, ed. H. Wolfram (Vienna, Cologne, and Graz, 1979), pp. 34–59 (text with German trans.).

[74] *Descriptio civitatum*, ed. in E. Herrmann, *Slawisch-Germanische Beziehungen im südostdeutschen Raum von der Spätantike bis zum Ungarnsturm*, Veröffentlichungen des Collegium Carolinum 17 (Munich, 1965), pp. 220–1.

[75] Regino of Prüm, *Chronicon*, ed. F. Kurze, *MGH, in usum schol.* (Hanover, 1890), p. 131.

Ends of empire and Otto III

The irruption of the Hungarians and their confederates into the Pannonian plain dammed the eastwards flow of Frankish Christianity. Numerous Slav groupings succumbed or came to terms with them. The differences between the responses of east and west are noteworthy. To Byzantine statesmen the Hungarians represented just one of various 'barbarian' threats and their diplomacy averted most of the raids and drew some chieftains into the emperor's orbit as religious converts and *patrikioi*. The looser-knit, poorer structures in the west bore the brunt of the pillaging and their leaders were mostly caught off-guard. An exception was Henry 'the Fowler', the Saxon duke elected king of the Germans in 919. He organized strongholds and well-maintained cavalry units which hindered the Hungarians' hit-and-run tactics, relaxed their hold over their Slav tributaries and diverted them into districts not yet enjoying his close supervision. During the reign of Henry's son, Otto, the raids grew fitful and Otto's victory over a Hungarian host at Lechfeld and subsequent worsting of the Abodrites and other Slavs at Recknitz broke the habit of raiding. Otto was, apparently, acclaimed as 'emperor' on the battlefield.[76]

For Otto, as for Charlemagne, it was essentially spectacular victory over rank outsiders that earned paramount status. But Otto and his father were 'borderers' in a sense that Charlemagne had not been. What Saxon-based rulers lacked in legitimacy and long-standing patronage could partly be made up for with a 'forward' policy towards neighbouring pagans. Soon after his accession Otto founded a monastery at Magdeburg and this became a forepost for mission work beyond the Elbe. Following his victory at Lechfeld, Otto sought papal approval for a new archbishopric based in Magdeburg. His bid was initially stymied by the archbishop of Mainz and other senior churchmen: only in 968 did Magdeburg become headquarters of an archbishopric. Such episodes suggest both the political 'clout' of the established German bishops and the revenues to be raised from the newly conquered peoples to the east.

---

[76] Widukind, *Rerum gestarum Saxonicarum libri tres*, 3. 49, ed. H.-E. Lohmann and P. Hirsch, *MGH, SS in usum schol.* (Hanover, 1935), p. 128.

Otto's martial prowess attracted the attention not only of the papacy but also of the Byzantine emperor and the Umayyad ruler of Spain. Exchanges of embassies and gifts were a useful way of showing off Otto's ascendancy to his fellow German magnates. He also measured himself against past masters and imperial landmarks, being crowned king at Aachen in 936 and making much of his possession of the Holy Lance, which had associations with Constantine the Great. In 961 he heeded John XII's call for help much as Charlemagne had responded to papal appeals against local enemies. Like Charlemagne, his reward was coronation as emperor by the pope in Rome. Numerous individuals sought to implicate him in 'the Old World'. Liudprand's *Antapodosis* was written partly for this purpose and by 967 Otto was seeking a Byzantine *porphyrogenita* as bride for his son and heir, Otto II. Saxon military involvement in Italy was welcome to many Byzantines and they fancied that 'the cub'—Otto—might join with 'the lion'—Nicephorus II—in exterminating the 'jack-ass', driving the Saracens from the central Mediterranean.[77] In the event Otto overestimated his ability to bludgeon the Byzantines into a marriage agreement on terms of his making and in 972 he had to settle for a niece of the current, non-porphyrogenitan, emperor, reportedly to the derision of Italian and Saxon magnates.[78] However, an ivory plaque of Christ blessing Otto II and Theophano shows how the match could dignify Saxon imperial pretensions. Otto, styled 'emperor of the Romans *augustus*' on the ivory and in charters from 982, regarded his rights as encompassing the entire peninsula and acted accordingly. He led an army into the Byzantine south in the name of extirpating Saracen marauders. Near the Messina Straits he was defeated by Muslims operating by land and sea, lost numerous commanders and himself only narrowly escaped. The Saxon 'cub', for all his audacity, lacked sea-power. Saracen raiders continued to wreak havoc on Calabria and within a few months rebellious Slavs had expelled the Germans from most of their strongholds east of the Elbe, even sacking Hamburg. The full extent of their eastern holdings was only regained in the twelfth century.

If expansion in the sense of Germanic emperors' conquests abated

[77] Liudprand, *Legatio*, 40, in *Opera Omnia*, ed. Chiesa, pp. 204–5; trans. Wright, *The Works of Liudprand of Cremona*, pp. 258–9.

[78] Thietmar of Merseberg, *Chronicon*, 2.15, ed. R. Holtzmann, *MGH, SS*, nov. series 9 (Berlin, 1935), p. 56.

in the late tenth century, the diffusion of Christian worship and organization gathered pace and the nexuses of Viking trade routes acquired a culturo-political overlay. It is not wholly accidental that several prominent potentates adopted Christianity in the generation following Lechfeld—and not earlier. Otto's victories over Hungarians and Slavs gave them reasons for taking the plunge. On the positive side, it was a matter of joining up with the religion of 'winners', those structures which had best withstood the outsiders' raids and made them unprofitable. Anglo-Saxon missionaries played an important part in evangelizing among the Norwegians. But apprehensiveness about the scale of Ottonian striking power was probably influential in turning potentates towards Christianity. Through gaining the favour of a God with a proven 'track record', a potentate could bind subjects and confederates more tightly to his cause. At the same time, his adoption of Christian rites and authority symbols made it harder for the Ottos to attack him outright. A mixture of motives is discernible with the Danish king, Harald Bluetooth. Around 965 he staged a trial of Christ's powers. After a priest carried red-hot iron in his bare hands unscathed, Harald ordered his subjects to give up their idols: 'from then on he gave due honour to the priests and servants of God'.[79] While claiming that he had 'won all Denmark for himself, and Norway'[80] Harald extended earlier earthworks raised against Frankish aggression, the Danevirke, and built several fortresses to a uniform design. Other potentates followed suit, notably Miezko, who imposed Christianity on the more important of his fellow Poles in the 960s and, in the earlier 970s, the Hungarian, Géza, who gave his infant son Waik the Christian name of Stephen. German churchmen were involved in these developments, but they seem to have been invited in by local leaders and were not acting upon the emperor's sole initiative.

Shortly after Lechfeld the Rus princess Olga sought from Otto a religious mission. Her démarche is a reflection of Otto's stature at that time. Nonetheless, he had trouble finding a suitable head for the mission. His eventual choice, Adalbert, lacked experience, was reluctant to set off, and soon returned, alleging trickery on the Rus'

[79] Widukind, *Rerum gestarum Saxonicarum libri tres*, 3. 65, ed. Lohmann and Hirsch, p. 141.

[80] Jelling Stone inscription, trans. in E. Roesdahl, *Viking Age Denmark* (London, 1982), p. 172.

part. The fiasco suggests a shortage of devoted missionaries, but the Rus could be regarded as a special case. Olga made her approach to Otto while leader of a political structure that had been consolidating along the Volkhov, Lovat, and Dnieper riverways since the early tenth century. The elite, now based on the Middle Dnieper, was directly involved in bartering primary produce and slaves for luxury goods from Byzantium and individual notables adopted eastern Christianity. Olga herself was baptized and became Constantine VII's goddaughter some time in the later 940s or 950s and probably only after being denied a full-blown Byzantine mission did she turn to Otto. However, some Rus questioned her policy and her own son, Sviatoslav, adopted the guise of a Eurasian nomad and attempted to relocate to the Danube delta. Nonetheless, Christians of diverse provenance continued to ply the eastern riverways and when Sviatoslav's son, Vladimir, tried to legitimize his regime by getting the inhabitants of Kiev to worship prescribed gods, he encountered resistance. Tury, a Scandinavian Christian who had lived in Byzantium, would not give up his son for sacrifice and both were slain.

Vladimir's bid for a compulsory cult suggests both cognizance of and reaction against Christianity's pulling-power. After examining monotheistic worship practised among the Germans as well as the Byzantines and Muslims, he eventually opted for a link with Byzantium. In return for sending military aid, he received a *porphyrogenita* to wed, and also a religious mission headed by a metropolitan. It was probably a particular convergence of interests between Vladimir and Emperor Basil II in the 980s that forged this liaison. But Vladimir would also have been aware of the baptism of Baltic potentates over recent decades. He may have aimed to outshine them all through a deal that brought not only churchmen but also masons, mosaicists, and strikers of coins.

With the Rus elite's adoption of Christianity c.988, other outsiders seeking high status had all the more incentive to profess the cult of 'winners'. Captains of large predatory war-bands in Scandinavia could regard propagation of Christianity as an attribute of rulership. Thus, Olaf Tryggvason, baptized after campaigning in England in the mid-990s, set about imposing the new religion together with his own authority upon fellow Norwegians. Against this fast-moving background was played out an attempt at ordered hierarchy. The phenomenon of Otto III can be seen as an intensification of the tendency already discernible in his father to make imperial rule more palpable in Italy; as the product of an able youth whose quest for salvation fused with the zeal for spiritual renewal and evangelization of holy men and scholars; and as a calculated recourse to mystique and spiritual ties after forcible territorial expansion ceased to be profitable. These facets of Otto are not mutually incompatible and one might anyway expect an adolescent ruler to have had intensive urges, themselves fast-shifting: Otto was dead at 21. He both drew on ancient hallmarks of imperial and sacred order *and* made allowances for the drive for self-improvement manifest among the elites forming to his east and north. He devoted time and attention both to established seats such as Rome and Aachen and to rising powers such as Venice and Poland. Within this skein of associations he could hope to wrap the German lands.

The city of Rome was not in itself of overriding importance to Otto when he paid his first visit in 996. His pressing concern was to secure the papacy for his cousin, Gregory V and thus be able to count on papal cooperation in resolving ecclesiastical problems, ranging from Rheims to Prague and the bishoprics east of the Elbe. However, to ensure such collaboration Otto had to involve himself more directly in Roman affairs. In 998 he deposed and mutilated an anti-pope and beheaded his chief backer, the 'prefect of the city', John Crescentius. By the late 990s Otto was trying to 'bond' with the city. Installing himself on the Palatine, where the Caesars' palaces had stood from the time of Augustus, and sponsoring flamboyantly 'imperial' ceremonial, Otto signalled his right to reside within the city walls, in defiance of the *Donation of Constantine*. The portentous dignities bestowed upon officials and sympathizers were partly for Roman consumption, setting Otto up as arbiter of status and palace-based master of the city. He promoted the Virgin as its protectress, commissioning a hymn in her honour, and incurred criticism from Bruno of Querfurt for 'favouring the Roman people above all others with money and honours'.[81] The pomp was also intended to project Otto's bid for hegemony beyond the ancient empire's confines. This is manifest in his journey to Poland to venerate the relics of his former confidant, Adalbert, bishop of Prague, slain by the Prussians in 997.

---

[81] Bruno of Querfurt, *Vita quinque fratrum*, 7, ed. J. Karwasińska, Monumenta Poloniae Historica, nov. ser. 4.3 (Warsaw, 1973), p. 43.

At Gniezno, Otto prayed before Adalbert's tomb, declared the church of Gniezno to be an archbishopric, and exchanged gifts with the Polish ruler, Boleslaw. In creating a separate archbishopric, Otto helped bring definition to Boleslaw's polity. In further ceremonial, Otto gave Boleslaw a copy of the Holy Lance and set his own crown on Boleslaw's head, as being 'brother and partner in the empire'.[82]

Regal status and a church hierarchy were the objectives of several dynasties emerging on the periphery. Otto could not halt the trends but he could cap them—literally, in the sense of conferring a crown together with other authority symbols. In 1000 he sent a crown and gilded lance to Waik-Stephen, ruler of his grandfather's foes, while also approving the creation of a separate archbishopric to encompass the Hungarians' land. Such measures were the more resonant thanks to the collaboration of his new pope, Gerbert, who had assumed the name of Sylvester. No pontiff had taken this name since Constantine the Great's time and the implication was that Otto was a new Constantine. Otto was styled 'most devoted and faithful propagator of the holy churches' in 1001, and other charters termed him 'servant of the apostles', alluding to his missionary activities.[83]

Otto's combination of mastery of Rome with 'hands-on' mission work was unprecedented. It struck a chord with potentates ambitious to partake of the political culture of the Christians while retaining—in fact consolidating—their own regimes. Boleslaw, 'friend and ally of the Roman people',[84] for example, accompanied Otto to Aachen and witnessed his opening of Charlemagne's tomb (see Chapter 5). Otto was harnessing such aspirations to a largely consensual structure, a 'virtual empire'. He was, at the same time, negotiating a marriage tie with Byzantium and early in 1002 a *porphyrogenita* arrived in Italy. Their wedding would have symbolized accord between the masters of Rome and Constantinople in flesh and blood and their offspring might have upheld this equilibrium. Otto died, however, before he met his bride to be. The prospect of eastern and western Christian emperors presiding in a kind of partnership over ancient seats of empire and numerous far-flung peoples faded with him.

---

[82] Gallus Anonymus, *Cronicae et gesta ducum sive principum Polonorum*, 7, ed. C. Maleczyński, Monumenta Poloniae Historica, nov. ser. 2 (Cracow, 1952), p. 20. See also below, p. 247.

[83] See G. Althoff, *Otto III.* (Darmstadt, 1996), p. 136, n. 36.

[84] Gallus Anonymus, *Cronicae et gesta*, 7, ed. Maleczyński, p. 20.

Figure 12 Hraban Maur, *Liber sanctae crucis,* with portrait of Louis the Pious, emperor of the Franks (814–840) as *miles Christi*

Conclusion: into the eleventh century

Rosamond McKitterick

The identification of the year 1000 as a major divide is primarily a modern one. For contemporaries, it was just another year. Thus, the *Anglo-Saxon Chronicle* recorded that 'The king went into Cumberland and ravaged very nearly all of it; and his ships went out round Chester and should have come to meet him, but they could not. Thus they ravaged the Isle of Man. And the enemy fleet had gone to Richard's kingdom that summer.' Ralph Glaber (980–1046), writing his *Libri historiarum* at Auxerre in the 1030s, on the other hand, offers his own conviction of the numerical importance of the year 1000 as a focus for his history. Around 1000, Ralph tells us

men, especially in Italy and Gaul, began to construct churches . . . it was as if the whole world were shaking itself free, shrugging off the burden of the past and cladding itself everywhere in a white mantle of churches . . . a multitude of people . . . began to travel to the sepulchre of the Saviour at Jerusalem. At the same time a great many eminent men of Italy and Gaul died, among them bishops, dukes and counts.

How approximate Ralph's dating is, and how much he exaggerates, can be gathered from extant evidence of church building in the early eleventh century and the actual death dates of three of those he mentions as dying 'at about this time', namely Pope Benedict VIII (d. 1024), Robert II, king of the Franks (d. 1031), and Fulbert of Chartres (d. 1028). All these—the churches, the pilgrimages, the deaths of great men—are, moreover, portents rather than the consequence of the year 1000 having been reached. Even so, Ralph regards the significance of 1033, the millennium of the Passion, as far greater. He acknowledges that after the year 1000 in Italy and Gaul, men of both orders (that is, lay and cleric) emerged whose lives and works provide an example worthy of imitation by posterity, just as his own history recounts events and achievements before the year 1000.

Nor was Ralph alone in his anchoring of the events of his own day in his immediate past. In the cultural sphere in the eleventh and twelfth centuries there was a lively sense of continuation, if not continuity. Many eleventh- and twelfth-century historians started their account of their own day with sections going back to the eighth or the fifth century or even beyond, though the use by them of their early medieval past has still not been fully explored. The eleventh and twelfth centuries, moreover, saw a notable resurgence of the copying of older histories, such as Einhard's *Life of Charlemagne* and Paul the Deacon's *History of the Lombards*, into new books and historical compilations. The scholars of the eleventh and twelfth century, however much they were developing new patterns of thought and new emphases in their theology and philosophy, felt a deep sense of indebtedness to the learned scholars of the early medieval and Carolingian period, and list them respectfully among their predecessors and mentors.

So too, the power and prowess of the rulers of the early middle ages, as well as the circumstances of their conversion to Christianity and promotion of the Christian religion, continued to inspire their later successors and emulators. Certainly Otto III had opened up the tomb of Charlemagne. But it was in 1165 that Frederick Barbarossa had the Frankish emperor Charlemagne canonized and a liturgical cult spread across Europe thereafter. After Otto I until 1531, moreover, no fewer than thirty German rulers were crowned at Aachen.

By contrast, many modern historians have evoked contradictory and far too generalized images of disorder, turmoil, and dramatic change at the beginning of the eleventh century, perhaps too much influenced by events in a small part of France. It is self-evident that a complex social, political, and religious system embedded in the accretion of legal rights requires a long slow process of adaptation and change. Even in the second half of the ninth century, the east and west Frankish kingdoms differed greatly in their style of government, with the former making far less use of capitularies or coinage than the latter. Royal leadership in the east Frankish kingdom moreover may have been enhanced as a consequence of the Magyar attacks, just as it was strengthened in England in the face of Viking armies, or so the *Anglo-Saxon Chronicle* would have us believe.

That there was change and discontinuity as well as continuity into the eleventh century, however, is clear, not least in the clearer definition of the boundaries of the aristocracy in terms of military activity, the consolidation of local power, and legal entities and the impact these had on the power of central government. As Chris Wickham remarks, local building blocks were the basis for new forms of centralizing government in the twelfth century. These were in the future but they signal difference. The year 1000, and the decades following, were the point at which this shift began to take place. Even in England and Germany, where Carolingian continuities were stronger, many of these developments took place as well, across the next century or so. So 1000 in terms of social and political developments is as good a point as any to stop, at least in these parts of western Europe; from here on, any lay political actor, and indeed any peasant or ecclesiastic, would of necessity take as a starting point the unchallenged hegemony of local aristocratic power.

The extended process of economic expansion on either side of the year 1000 is stressed by Jean-Pierre Devroey. As he remarks, it is essential to take a very long view in investigating medieval economic institutions, not least because of the very patchy nature of the source material. Further, Mayke de Jong has reminded us of the many tributaries from far distant sources that were fed into the river of the eleventh-century church reforms and how useless a landmark the year 1000 is when it comes to the transformation of religious belief and practice. Although the reformers of the eleventh century were quite convinced that they were putting what they regarded as the decadence of the previous centuries behind them, their rhetoric should be rejected. It was the very interconnectedness of the sacred and secular worlds in the early middle ages which provided such a strong base for the future when those boundaries began to be redrawn.

Otto III's reign, moreover, as Jonathan Shepard comments, for all the recognition of change in the political landscape, marked in many respects the end of an old order. *Europa* was putting out shoots in a multitude of directions and on diverse planes. Missionary work carried on in the east. In 1008 Bruno of Querfurt, who had disparaged Otto's penchant for Rome, attempted to convert the Pechenegs, 'cruellest of all pagans'. Bruno took it for granted that the land of the Rus, from whose 'limit' he set forth into the steppes, was Christian. The new polities on Europe's outer approaches provided a spring-board for propagating Christianity still further afield. Eastern churchmen were not yet seen as alien to the process. In the mid-eleventh century, Armenian bishops were active in Iceland and there were small churches on Greenland, albeit not in the Scandinavian outposts along the North American seaboard.

Around the time the earliest churches were being built on Green-land, in 996, 160 'Amalfitan' traders were reportedly massacred in Cairo. The figure may well be inflated, but the presence of Italian merchants having some sort of 'factory' well up the Nile suggests a quickening in exchanges between the central Mediterranean and the Levant. Amalfitans already had an establishment in Constantinople by 944. Another hint of activity comes from a Byzantine chrysobull of 992 granting privileges to Venetian merchantmen and the goods of other peoples carried in Venetian vessels. This suggests burgeoning demand for access to Constantinople's markets, as well as a high-lighting of the 'leverage' which Venetian vessels—potential troop transports—were beginning to exert. The scale of commerce was still modest and confined to intermediaries such as the Amalfitans and Venetians. But it would be small, often mutually competitive units of traders, freebooting adventurers, and penitential pilgrims who would make the running in the Mediterranean. Europe, though riven by numerous rival elites, was cross-woven by common cultural and religious aims, customs and values. By the tenth century's close, Europe was germinating forces which no imperial sleight of hand could have harnessed, and which would soon bear down on Muslim Sicily and Spain and the eastern empire itself.

This book has stressed the many separate and independent devel-opments in the transformation of the Roman world and emergence of early medieval Europe. There was a dynamic interaction between the ever-expanding horizons of Latin Christendom with its encircling realms and territories, and with the other world, throughout the six hundred years we have discussed in this volume. A world of great richness and diversity, its common elements notwithstanding, was created. A fuller historical understanding of this period and the following centuries can only come from a fully integrated study of political, social, economic, religious, and cultural matters and a recognition of the range as well as the limitations of our evidence. With all the continuities and discontinuities outlined in our separate chapters, this period was clearly fundamental for the subsequent development of Europe. Indeed, it was in the early middle ages that the Europe we have inherited was formed.

Further reading

General

Although the suggestions for further reading below are mostly of work in English, it is important to stress that modern work on the early middle ages, on which the content of the chapters in this volume draws, is produced in all the major languages of Europe. Detailed bibliographies which give some indication of the great wealth of this modern scholarship are to be found in the collaborative volumes of *The New Cambridge Medieval History*. The available volumes covering the period of this book are R. McKitterick (ed.), vol. II, *c.700–c.900* (Cambridge, 1995) and T. Reuter (ed.), vol. III, *c.900–c.1024* (Cambridge, 1999). Vol. I, *c.500–c.700*, ed. P. Fouracre, is in preparation. P. Garnsey (ed.), *The Cambridge Ancient History*, vol. XIII (Cambridge, 1998) covers the period 337–425. Reference works such as E. A. Livingstone (ed.), *The Oxford Dictionary of the Christian Church*, 3rd edn. (Oxford, 1997); A. P. Kazhdan (ed.), *The Oxford Dictionary of Byzantium* (1991); G. W. Bowersock, Peter Brown, and Oleg Grabar (eds.), *Late Antiquity: A Guide to the Postclassical World* (Cambridge, Mass., 1999); *Lexikon des Mittelalters*, 9 vols. (Stuttgart, 1999); and M. Lapidge (ed.), *The Blackwell Encyclopaedia of Anglo-Saxon England* (Oxford, 1999) have useful articles and bibliographies on topics, events, and individuals. For historical atlases that include the period, see A. Mackay (ed.), *Atlas of Medieval Europe* (London, 1997); M. Parisse (ed.), *Atlas de la France de l'an Mil* (Paris, 1994); *The Times Atlas of European History*, 2nd edn. (London, 1998); *The Times Atlas of World History*, 5th edn. (London, 1999); and J. Engel (ed.), *Grosser historischer Weltatlas II Mittelalter* (Munich, 1970). The periodical *Early Medieval Europe*, established in 1991, is devoted to the period *c.400–c.1100*. Political, economic, social, religious, or cultural issues are most commonly integrated in studies of this period. Many of the items listed for one chapter, therefore, are as helpful for another.

Sources

The New Cambridge Medieval History volumes listed above also include comprehensive sections on the source material. For the period before 800, some have been translated in the Liverpool Latin Texts for Historians. The Frankish *Annals of St Bertin* and *Annals of Fulda*, trans. J. L. Nelson and T. Reuter, respectively, appear in a series of texts in translation by Manchester University Press. Nevertheless, some of the principal texts available in English translation may be indicated here. The regional histories of the various barbarian kingdoms include Isidore of Seville, *History of the Goths, Sueves and*

Vandals, in Kenneth Wolf (trans.), *Conquerors and Chroniclers of Early-Medieval Spain* (Liverpool, 1991); Gregory of Tours, *History of the Franks*, trans. L. Thorpe (Harmondsworth, 1974); Jordanes, *History of the Goths*, trans. C. C. Mierow (Princeton, 1915); Bede, *Ecclesiastical History of the English People*, trans. B. Colgrave and R. A. B. Mynors (Oxford, 1969); Paul the Deacon, *History of the Lombards*, trans. W. D. Foulke (Philadelphia, 1907); B. Scholz (trans.), *Carolingian Chronicles* (Ann Arbor, 1970). The *Anglo-Saxon Chronicle* is available in many editions. One of the most useful, because accompanied by a host of other English sources (including the law codes) in translation, is D. Whitelock (ed.), *English Historical Documents, c.500–1042*, 2nd edn. (London, 1979). S. Keynes and M. Lapidge, *Alfred the Great: Asser's Life of King Alfred and Other Contemporary Sources* (Harmondsworth, 1983) is excellent with very full notes. Compilations of late-antique sources in translation include Michael Maas (ed.), *Readings in Late Antiquity: A Sourcebook* (London and New York, 2000). The best collections of Carolingian sources in translation are P. D. King, *Charlemagne: Translated Sources* (Kendal, 1986) and Paul E. Dutton, *Carolingian Civilization* (Peterborough, Ontario, 1993). Most of the early medieval law codes have been translated, including S. P. Scott, *The Visigothic Code* (Boston, 1910); K. Fischer Drew (trans.), *The Lombard Laws* (Philadelphia, 1973) and *The Laws of the Salian Franks* (Philadelphia, 1991). These can be compared with C. Pharr (trans.), *The Theodosian Code* (New York, 1969). Only a small proportion of the legislative, theological, philosophical, educational, literary, or scholarly texts from the period after Charlemagne's reign for anywhere in Europe have as yet been translated into modern languages, though most from continental Europe, with the notable exception of the charters of the Emperor Louis the Pious, are available in modern editions of the original Latin texts, largely in the series Monumenta Germaniae Historica, Fonti per la Storia d'Italia, Les Classiques de l'histoire de la France, Corpus Christianorum and Sources Chrétiennes. A taste of the literary works, letters, and philosophy can be gained from E. Emerton, *The Letters of Saint Boniface*, 2nd edn. (New York, 2000); Peter Godman (trans.), *Poetry of the Carolingian Renaissance* (London, 1983); S. Allott (trans.), *Alcuin of York* (a small selection of Alcuin's letters only) (York, 1974). G. W. Regenos (trans.), *The Letters of Lupus of Ferrières* (The Hague, 1970); H. P. Lattin (trans.), *Gerbert, Letters with his Papal Privileges as Sylvester II* (New York, 1961); E. G. Doyle (trans.), Sedulius Scotus, *On Christian Rulers* (Binghamton, NY, 1983); I. P. Sheldon Williams and E. Jeauneau (ed. and trans.), John Scotus Eriugena, *Periphyseon* (Dublin, 1968–); J. J. Tierney (ed. and trans.), Dicuil, *Liber de mensura orbis terrae* (Dublin, 1967). The selection of tenth-century documents made by Boyd Hill, *Medieval Monarchy in Action: The German Empire from Henry I to Henry IV* (London, 1972) has a representative sample. Many saints' lives, however, have been translated, and two useful collections are Thomas Head and T. F. X. Noble, *Soldiers of Christ* (Philadelphia, 1995) and Paul Fouracre and Richard Geberding, *Late Merovingian France: History and Hagiography 640–720* (Manchester, 1996). Key texts for Byzantium and its neighbours are Constantine VII Porphyrogenitus, *De administrando imperio*, ed. and trans. G. Moravcsik and R. J. H. Jenkins (Washington, DC, 1967); Liudprand of Cremona, *Antapodosis* and *Legatio*, in *Opera Omnia*, ed. P. Chiesa (Turnhout, 1998); trans. F. A. Wright (London, 1930); Maurice, *Strategikon*, ed. G. T. Dennis with German trans. by E. Gammilscheg (Vienna, 1981); English trans. G. T. Dennis (Philadelphia, 1984); Menander the Guardsman (Protector), *History*, ed. and trans. R. C. Blockley (Liverpool, 1985); *Povest' Vremennykh Let*, ed. V. P. Adrianove-Peretts and D. S. Likhachev (Moscow–Leningrad, 1996); trans. S. H. Cross and O. P. Sherbowitz-Wetzor, *The Russian Primary Chronicle* (Cambridge, Mass., 1953); *Skirmishing: Three Byzantine Military Treatises*, ed. and trans. G. T. Dennis (Washington, DC, 1985); Theophanes Confessor, *Chronographia*, ed. C. de Boor, I (Leipzig, 1883); trans. C. Mango and R. Scott (Oxford, 1997); Theophylact Simocatta, *Historiae*, ed. C. de Boor and P. Wirth (Stuttgart, 1972); trans. M. and M. Whitby (Oxford, 1986); N. Golb and O. Pritsak, *Khazarian Hebrew Documents of the Tenth Century* (Ithaca, NY, 1982).

Introduction

Leslie Webster (ed.), *The Transformation of the Roman World, AD 400–900* (London, 1997), an exhibition catalogue from the British Museum and British Library provides a clear illustrated introduction to many of the key issues of the period. On ethnogenesis, see Walter Pohl and Helmut Reimitz (eds.), *Strategies of Distinction* (Leiden, 1999). An indication of the wealth of new archaeological material is provided in Richard Hodges, *Light in the Dark Ages: The Rise and Fall of San Vincenzo al Volturno* (London, 1997) and K. Randsborg, *The First Millennium A.D. in Europe and the Mediterranean: An Archaeological Essay* (Cambridge, 1991). Rosamond McKitterick and Roland Quinault (eds.), *Edward Gibbon and Empire* (Cambridge, 1997); Donald R. Kelley, *Foundations of Modern Historical Scholarship* (New York, 1970); R. Howard Bloch, *God's Plagiarist: Being an Account of the Fabulous Industry and Irregular Commerce of the Abbé Migne* (Chicago, 1994); and Simon Keynes, 'The cult of King Alfred', *Anglo-Saxon England*, 28 (1999), pp. 225–356, provide various insights on older historical scholarship. Walter Goffart, *The Narrators of Barbarian History A.D. 500–800* (Princeton, 1982); Patrick J. Geary, *Phantoms of Remembrance: Memory and Oblivion at the End of the First Millennium* (Princeton, 1994); and Y. Hen and M. Innes (eds.), *The Uses of the Past in the Early Middle Ages* (Cambridge, 2000) address aspects of the construction of the past by early medieval writers. The contributors to R. McKitterick (ed.), *The Uses of Literacy in Early Mediaeval Europe*

(Cambridge, 1990) address a central issue in early medieval history, closely related to the themes of R. Wright (ed.), *Latin and the Romance Languages in the Early Middle Ages* (London and New York, 1991). Histories of early medieval Europe are generally tackled by region, of which the following comprise excellent studies: Edward James, *The Origins of France* (London, 1982) and *The Franks* (Oxford, 1988); I. N. Wood, *The Merovingian Kingdoms, 450–751* (London, 1994); R. McKitterick, *The Frankish Kingdoms under the Carolingians, 751–987* (London, 1983); Timothy Reuter, *Germany in the Early Middle Ages, c.800–1056* (London, 1991); Roger Collins, *Early Medieval Spain: Unity in Diversity, 400–1000*, 2nd edn. (London, 1995), *The Arab Conquest of Spain, 710–797* (Oxford, 1989), and *The Basques* (Oxford, 1986); Hugh Kennedy, *The Prophet and the Age of the Caliphates: The Islamic Near East from the Sixth to the Eleventh Century* (London, 1986) and *Muslim Spain and Portugal: A Political History of al-Andalus* (London, 1996); C. J. Wickham, *Early Medieval Italy: Central Power and Local Society 400–1000* (London, 1981); James Campbell (ed.), *The Anglo-Saxons* (London, 1982); Wendy Davies, *Wales in the Early Middle Ages* (Leicester, 1982); A. P. Smyth, *Warlords and Holy Men: Scotland AD 80–1000* (London, 1984); D. O Cróinín, *Early Medieval Ireland, 400–1200* (London, 1995); P. Sawyer (ed.), *The Oxford Illustrated History of the Vikings* (Oxford, 1998); Mark Whittow, *The Making of Orthodox Byzantium, 600–1025* (London, 1996); Simon Franklin and Jonathan Shepard, *The Emergence of Rus, 750–1200* (London, 1996).

Politics

In addition to the chapters in the *New Cambridge Medieval History*, vols. II and III, and the regional studies listed above, see John Matthews, *The Roman Empire of Ammianus* (London, 1989). Stimulating interpretations of government and politics in the tenth century are Karl Leyser, *Rule and Conflict in an Early Medieval Society* (London, 1979); *Communications and Power in Medieval Europe: The Carolingian and Ottonian Centuries*, ed. T. Reuter (London, 1994); and Jack Bernhardt, *Itinerant Kingship and Royal Monasteries in Early Medieval Germany, c.976–1075* (Cambridge, 1993). For the British Isles, Thomas Charles-Edwards, *Early Irish and Welsh Kingship* (Oxford, 1993); Wendy Davies, *Patterns of Power in Early Wales* (Oxford, 1990); James Campbell, *Essays in Anglo-Saxon History* (London, 1986). On the problems of identity and assimilation in the successor states, see e.g. Walter Pohl (ed.), *Kingdoms of the Empire: The Integration of Barbarians in Late Antiquity* (Leiden, 1997), and Patrick Amory, *People and Community in Ostrogothic Italy, 483–554* (Cambridge, 1997). Our understanding of the political behaviour and ideologies of the early middle ages, notably in the ninth century, has been greatly enhanced by the seminal work of Janet L. Nelson, now in three volumes of collected studies: *Politics and Ritual in Early Medieval*

Europe (London, 1986), *The Frankish World, 750–900* (London, 1996), and *Rulers and Ruling Families in Early Medieval Europe* (Aldershot, 1999), as well as her monograph on *Charles the Bald* (London, 1992). Many of the most useful contributions to the politics of this period are in the form of collaborative volumes, such as I. N. Wood and P. Sawyer, *Early Medieval Kingship* (Leeds, 1977); P. Wormald (ed.), *Ideal and Reality in Frankish and Anglo-Saxon Society* (Oxford, 1983); Hartmut Atsma (ed.), *La Neustrie: Les Pays au nord de la Loire de 650 à 850*, Beihefte der Francia 16 (Sigmaringen, 1989); P. Godman and R. Collins (eds.), *Charlemagne's Heir: New Perspectives on the Reign of Louis the Pious (814–840)* (Oxford, 1990); J. L. Nelson and M. T. Gibson, *Charles the Bald: Court and Kingdom*, 2nd edn. (Aldershot, 1990); Regine Le Jan (ed.), *La Royauté et les élites dans l'Europe carolingienne* (Lille, 1998). On law and charters, see I. N. Wood and Jill Harries (eds.), *The Theodosian Code* (London, 1993), Rosamond McKitterick, *The Carolingians and the Written Word* (Cambridge, 1989); Matthew Innes, *State and Society in the Early Middle Ages: The Middle Rhine Valley 400–1000.* (Cambridge, 2000). On politics from the ecclesiastical perspective and the involvement of the papacy, see T. F. X. Noble, *The Republic of St Peter: The Birth of the Papal State 680–825* (Philadelphia, 1984) and J. M. H. Smith (ed.), *Early Medieval Rome and the Christian West* (Leiden, 2000). On money, see P. Grierson and M. Blackburn, *Medieval European Coinage, Vol. I The Early Middle Ages, 5th–10th Centuries* (Cambridge, 1986).

Society

Averil Cameron, *The Mediterranean World in Late Antiquity, 395–600* (London, 1993); A. Dopsch, *The Economic and Social Foundations of European Civilisation* (London, 1937); and A. H. M. Jones, *The Later Roman Empire* (Oxford, 1964) provide stimulating general surveys. For the most part, an understanding of society in this period is gained from a wealth of specific regional and thematic studies. Among these can be mentioned: Herwig Wolfram, *History of the Goths* (Berkeley, 1988); R. van Dam, *Leadership and Community in Late Antique Gaul* (Berkeley, 1985); Ross Balzaretti, *The Lands of St Ambrose* (Turnhout, 2000); T. S. Brown, *Gentleman and Officers: Imperial Administration and Aristocratic Power in Byzantine Italy A.D. 554–800* (Rome, 1984); J. F. Haldon, *Byzantium in the Seventh Century*, 2nd edn. (Cambridge, 1997); R. M. Karras, *Slavery and Society in Medieval Scandinavia* (New Haven, 1988); Regine Le Jan, *Famille et pouvoir dans le monde franc (VIIe–Xe siècle)* (Paris, 1995); E. Manzano, *La frontera de al-Andalus en epoca de los Omeyas* (Madrid, 1991); P. Pastor, *Resistencias y luchas campesinas en la época del crecimiento y consolidación de la formación feudal: Castill y Léon, siglos X–XIII* (Madrid, 1980); G. Tabacco, *The Struggle for Power in Medieval Italy* (Cambridge, 1989); P. Cammarosano, *Nobili e re* (Bari, 1998). Further, the following range widely both geographically and over the period in discussions of key issues: Wendy Davies and Paul Fouracre (eds.), *The Settlement of Disputes in Early Medieval Europe* (Cambridge, 1986); Wendy Davies and Paul Fouracre (eds.), *Property and Power in the Early Middle Ages* (Cambridge, 1995); and M. Parisse (ed.), *Veuves et veuvage dans le haut moyen âge* (Paris, 1993). Note the extensive glossaries of technical terms contained in each of the Davies and Fouracre volumes. These are also pertinent for matters discussed in the chapter on the economy. On specific issues, see H. W. Goetz, ' "Nobilis" ', *Vierteljahrschrift für Sozial- und Wirtschaftsgeschichte*, 70 (1983), pp. 153–91; A. Ja. Gurevic, *Le origini des feudalismo* (Bari, 1982); W. I. Miller, *Bloodtaking and Peacemaking* (Chicago, 1990); T. Reuter (ed.), *The Medieval Nobility* (Amsterdam, 1979); Susan Reynolds, *Kingdoms and Communities in Western Europe 900–1300*, 2nd edn. (Oxford, 1997) and *Fiefs and Vassals* (Oxford, 1994); Chris Wickham, *Land and Power: Studies in Italian and European Social History, 400–1200* (London, 1994).

Economy

On the early medieval European economy, the best and most accurate general surveys are provided by the relevant chapters in the *New Cambridge Medieval History*, vols. II and III referred to above. Several volumes in the *Settimane di Studio del Centro Italiano di studi sull'alto medioevo* offer theoretical and regional contributions within the limits of Christian and Muslim Europe, such as the city: 6 (1958) and 21 (1973); money and exchange: 8 (1961); agriculture, the rural world, animals and vegetation: 13 (1965), 31 (1983), 37 (1989); crafts and technology: 18 (1970); markets and merchants: 40 (1992). For a conceptual approach, see C. J. Wickham, 'Problems of comparing rural societies in early medieval western Europe', *Transactions of the Royal Historical Society*, 6th series, 2 (1992), pp. 221–46. H. Pirenne, *Mahomet and Charlemagne* (New York, 1968; translated from the posthumously published French edition of 1937); M. Bloch, *Feudal Society* (Chicago, 1964; French original 1939); G. Duby, *The Early Growth of the European Economy: Warriors and Peasants from the Seventh to the Twelfth Century* (London, 1974; French original of 1973) and *Rural Economy and Country Life in the Medieval West* (London, 1968; French original of 1966) are still stimulating. For regional surveys, see, in addition to those mentioned in previous sections, R. Latouche, *The Birth of Western Economy* (London, 1981); E. Zanini, *Le Italie bizantine: Territorio, insediamenti ed economia nella provincia bizantina d'Italia VI–VIII secolo* (San Spirito, 1998); and M. Kaplan, *Les Hommes et la terre à Byzance du VIe au XI siècle* (Paris, 1992). On demography, the best survey is P. Toubert, 'The Carolingian momentum', in his *A History of the Family* (Cambridge, Mass., 1996; French original 1986). M. Montanari, *The Culture of Food* (Oxford, 1994; Italian original 1994) is a useful general account. An interesting perspective is provided by P. Squatriti, *Water and Society in Early Medieval Italy, AD 400–1000* (Cambridge, 1998). W. Rösener, *Peasants in the Middle Ages* (Urbana, Ill., 1992; German original 1992), offers a good general introduction on agriculture; see also *La Croissance agricole du haut moyen âge*, in *Flaran* 10 (Auch, 1990) and G. Astill and J. Langdon (eds.), *Medieval Farming and Technology: The Impact of Agricultural Change in Northwest Europe* (Leiden, 1997). On urban aspects, see A. Verhulst, *The Rise of Cities in Northwest Europe* (Cambridge, 1999); H. Clarke and B. Ambrosiani (eds.), *Towns in the Viking Age* (Leicester and London, 1991); and R. Hodges and R. Hobley (eds.) *The Rebirth of Towns in the West, AD 750–1050*, CBA Research Report (London, 1988).

Religion

Inspiring introductions are Robert A. Markus, *The End of Ancient Christianity* (Cambridge, 1990) and Peter Brown, *The Rise of Western Christendom: Triumph and Diversity, AD 200–1000* (Oxford, 1996). Judith Herrin, *The Formation of Christendom* (Oxford, 1987) is invaluable, not least for its full treatment of Byzantium. Michael Wallace-Hadrill, *The Frankish Church* (Oxford, 1983) is eminently readable, as is Richard Fletcher, *The Conversion of Europe: From Paganism to Christianity, 371–1386 AD* (London, 1997). On influential individuals see, e.g. Robert A. Markus, *Gregory the Great and his World* (Cambridge, 1997); D. N. Dumville (ed.), *Saint Patrick A.D. 493–1993* (Woodbridge, 1993); M. Lapidge (ed.), *Columbanus: Studies on the Latin Writings* (Woodbridge, 1997). A recent approach to Christian attitudes to Jews is Jeremy Cohen, *Living Letters of the Law: Ideas of the Jew in Medieval Christianity* (Berkeley and Los Angeles, 1999). On theology, an excellent case study is J. Cavadini, *The Last Christology of the West: Adoptionism in Spain and Gaul, 785–820* (Philadelphia, 1993). The history of sanctity has yielded a vast body of literature since the 1970s: see Peter Brown, *The Cult of the Saints* (London, 1982) and J. Howard-Johnston and P. A. Hayward (eds.), *The Cult of the Saints in Late Antiquity and the Early Middle Ages: Essays on the Contribution of Peter Brown* (Oxford, 1999). Spiritual parenthood has been investigated by Joseph H. Lynch, *Godparents and Kinship in Early Medieval Europe* (Princeton, 1986). On rituals of death, see F. S. Paxton, *Christianizing Death: The Creation of a Ritual Process in Early Medieval Europe* (Ithaca, NY, 1990). On celibacy, see M. Frassetto (ed.), *Medieval Purity and Piety: Essays on Medieval Clerical Celibacy and Religious Reform* (New York and London, 1998). Sacred space being claimed by royal power is explored by Barbara Rosenwein, *Negotiating Space: Power, Restraint and Privileges of Immunity in Early Medieval Europe* (Ithaca, NY, 1999) and M. de Jong, C. van Rhijn, and F. Theuws (eds.), *Topographies of Power in the Early Middle Ages* (Leiden, 2000). On pastoral care and councils, esp. in England, see John Blair and

Richard Sharpe (eds), *Pastoral Care before the Parish* (Leicester, London, and New York, 1995) and C. R. E. Cubitt, *Anglo-Saxon Church Councils, c.650–850* (London and New York, 1995). Recently, the impact of the Old Testament on early medieval religious practice, discussed by German historians such as Raymund Kottje and Arnold Angenendt, has been taken up elsewhere: see e.g. M. de Jong (ed.), *The Power of the Word: The Influence of the Bible on Early Medieval Politics*, in *Early Medieval Europe*, 3 (1998), pp. 261–357, and see also R. Gameson (ed.), *The Early Medieval Bible: Its Production, Decoration and Use* (Cambridge, 1994).

Culture

The collaborative volume R. McKitterick (ed.), *Carolingian Culture: Emulation and Innovation* (Cambridge, 1994) has essays on the Frankish reform, literature, grammar, philosophy and theology, art, music, book production, historical writing and political thought, all with bibliographies. Books with many colour reproductions of sculpture, buildings, artefacts, and painting from the period include: J. Hubert, J. Porcher, and W. Volbach, *Europe in the Dark Ages* (London, 1969) and *Carolingian Art* (London, 1970); L. Grodecki, F. Mütherich, J. Taralon, and F. Wormald, *Le Siècle de l'an Mil* (Paris, 1973). On buildings, see R. Krautheimer, *Early Christian and Byzantine Architecture*, 2nd edn. (Harmondsworth, 1975) and *Rome: Profile of a City, 312–1308*, 2nd edn. (Princeton, 2000). Interpretative studies primarily concerned with art are Henry Mayr-Harting, *Ottonian Book Illumination: An Historical Study* (London, 1991); H. Hoffmann, *Buchkunst und Königtum im ottonischen und frühsalsichen Reich*, Schriften des MGH 30 (Stuttgart, 1986); Lawrence Nees, *A Tainted Mantle: Hercules and the Classical Tradition at the Carolingian Court* (Philadelphia, 1991); and Mireille Mentre, *Illuminated Manuscripts of Medieval Spain* (London, 1996). On early medieval intellectual life, see P. Riché, *Education and Culture in the Barbarian West from the Sixth through the Eighth Century*, trans. J. J. Contreni (Columbia, SC, 1978); R. Crocker and D. Hiley (eds.), *The New Oxford History of Music*, Vol. II, *The Early Middle Ages to 1300*, 2nd edn. (Oxford, 1990); Donald Bullough, *Carolingian Renewal: Sources and Heritage* (Manchester, 1991); J. Marenbon, *From the Circle of Alcuin to the School of Auxerre: Logic, Theology and Philosophy in the Early Middle Ages* (Cambridge, 1981); J. J. Contreni, *Carolingian Learning, Masters and Manuscripts* (Aldershot, 1992). The master of the study of early medieval script and book production was Bernhard Bischoff. Some of his essays are trans. M. Gorman, *Carolingian Manuscripts in the Age of Charlemagne* (Cambridge, 1994). Many lavishly illlustrated recent exhibition catalogues offer interpretative essays and new research as well as useful syntheses, such as L. Webster and J. Backhouse (eds.), *The Making of England: Anglo-Saxon Art and Culture, AD 600–900* (London, 1991); C. Stiegemann and M. Wemhoff (eds.), *799:*

Kunst und Kultur der Karolingerzeit (Paderborn, 1999); A. von Euw and P. Schreiner (eds.), *Kaiserin Theophanu: Begegnung des Ostens und Westens um die Wende des ersten Jahrtausends* (Cologne, 1991); and K. van der Horst, William Noel, and W. C. M. Wüstefeld (eds.), *The Utrecht Psalter in Medieval Art* (Utrecht, 1996).

Europe and the Wider World

On visual perceptions of the world, see J. B. Harley and David Woodward (eds.), *The History of Cartography, Vol. I. Cartography in Prehistoric, Ancient and Medieval Europe and the Mediterranean* (Chicago, 1987) and P. G. Dalché, *Géographie et culture: La Représentation de l'espace du VIe au XIIe siècle* (Aldershot, 1997). A useful atlas in addition to those mentioned above is P. R. Magosci (ed.), *Historical Atlas of East Central Europe* (Toronto, 1995). On communications, see R. Chevalier, *Roman Roads*, rev. edn. (London, 1989); J. H. Pryor, *Geography, Technology and War: Studies in the Maritime History of the Mediterranean, 649–1571* (Cambridge, 1988); E. D. Hunt, *Holy Land Pilgrimage in the Later Roman Empire* (Oxford, 1982); Evangelos Chrysos and Ian Wood (eds.), *East and West: Modes of Communication* (Leiden, 1999); and (in terms of writing) M. Mostert (ed.), *New Approaches to Medieval Communications* (Turnhout, 1999). On science and time, D. Gutas, *Greek Thought, Arabic Culture* (London and New York, 1998); Faith Wallis, *Bede: The Reckoning of Time* (Liverpool, 1999) (an edition of Bede's text with extensive introduction and commentary); and P. Butzer and D. Lohrmann (eds.), *Science in Western and Eastern Civilization in Carolingian Times* (Basel, 1993), which includes Arno Borst on the Carolingian encyclopaedia of time of 809. On knowledge of Greek in the west, see Walter Berschin, *Greek Letters and the Latin Middle Ages*, trans. J. Frakes (Washington, DC, 1988). On Byzantium, see J. F. Haldon, *Byzantium in the Seventh Century: The Transformation of a Culture*, 2nd edn. (Cambridge, 1997); Robin Cormack, *Writing in Gold: Byzantine Society and its Icons* (London, 1985); and N. G. Wilson, *Scholars of Byzantium* (London, 1983). On relations between Byzantium and the west, there is a host of excellent collaborative volumes, such as J. D. Howard-Johnston, *Byzantium and the West, c.850–1200* (Amsterdam, 1988); J. Shepard and Simon Franklin (eds.), *Byzantine Diplomacy* (Aldershot, 1992); B. McGinn and W. Otten (eds.), *Eriugena: East and West* (Notre Dame, Ind., 1994); and A. Davids (ed.), *The Empress Theophano: Byzantium and the West at the Turn of the First Millennium* (Cambridge, 1995). On the Sasanians and other peoples further east, D. Sinor (ed.), *The Cambridge History of Early Inner Asia* (Cambridge, 1990) and B. A. Litvinsky (ed.), *History of Civilisations of Central Asia*, 3 (Paris, 1996) are comprehensive and see also the papers in Averil Cameron (ed.), *States, Resources and Armies* (Princeton, 1996) and D. M. Dunlop, *The History of the Jewish Khazars* (Princeton, 1954). On the

Slavs and their conversion to Christianity, see F. Dvornik, *Byzantine Missions among the Slavs* (New Brunswick, NJ, 1970); A. P. Vlasto, *The Entry of the Slavs into Christendom: An Introduction to the Medieval History of the Slavs* (Cambridge, 1970); and I. Ševčenkô, *Byzantium and the Slavs in Letters and Culture* (Cambridge, Mass., and Naples, 1992). On the Balkans and central and eastern Europe, apart from the relevant chapters in *The New Cambridge Medieval History*, Vols. II and III, see D. Obolensky, *The Byzantine Commonwealth: Eastern Europe, 500–1453* (London, 1971); Walter Pohl, *Die Awaren: Ein Steppenvolk in Mitteleuropa 567–822 n. Chr.* (Munich, 1989); J. V. A. Fine, *The Early Medieval Balkans: A Critical Survey for the Late Sixth to the Early Twelfth Century* (Ann Arbor, 1983); and Johannes Fried, *Otto III und Boleslaw Chobry*, 2nd edn. (Stuttgart, 1999). Moravia remains a source of contention: for a useful discussion, see M. Innes, 'Franks and Slavs, 700–1000: The problem of European expansion before the millennium', *Early Medieval Europe*, 6 (1997), pp. 201–16. For the north, see P. Sawyer, *Kings and Vikings: Scandinavia and Europe AD 700–1100* (London and New York, 1982) and S. Franklin and J. Shepard, *The Emergence of Rus, 750–1200* (London, 1996). On aspects of the south and west, see B. Kreutz, *Before the Normans: Southern Italy in the Ninth and Tenth Centuries* (Philadelphia, 1991) and T. C. Lounghis, *Les Ambassades byzantines en Occident depuis la fondation des états barbares jusqu'aux Croisades (407–1096)* (Athens, 1980).

Chronology

493	Theodoric the Ostrogoth defeats Odovacer and rules Italy
496–508	Conversion of Clovis to Catholicism
506	The Visigoths promulgate the *Breviary of Alaric*, an epitome of the Roman law Theodosian Code
507	The Franks defeat the Visigoths at Vouillé
c.511	*Lex Salica* issued
511	Death of Clovis and first partition of the Merovingian kingdom among his four sons
c.524	Boethius, *Consolation of Philosophy*
524	Execution of Boethius in Italy
526	Death of Theodoric the Ostrogoth
527–565	Reign of Justinian I, Byzantine emperor
c.532	The Easter Tables of Dionysius Exiguus are dated from the (supposed) year of the Incarnation of Christ and thus promote the Christian era .
533	Death of Gelimer, king of the Vandals
534	Byzantine army under Belisarius reconquers Vandal Africa Conquest of Burgundian kingdom by the Franks Justinian publishes the *Corpus Iuris Civilis*
535–536	The Byzantine general Belisarius recovers Sicily and invades southern Italy
536–561	Ostrogothic wars in Italy
537	Consecration of Justinian's church of Hagia Sophia in Constantinople
537–538	Cassiodorus compiles the *Variae*
c.540	St Benedict, *Rule* Silkworms brought to Byzantium from Central Asia, India, or China
c.540–565	Barbarini panel carved
540s	Franks rule lands north of the Po in Italy
542–543	Plague spreads west from Constantinople
c.550	Cosmas Indicopleustes' *Topographia Christiana*
552	Justinian's army, commanded by Narses, destroys Totila, the Gothic leader
c.552	Jordanes, *History of the Goths*
553	Totila's successor Teias is defeated

554	The last Ostrogothic military resistance collapses though some revolts in the north continue for a few more years
	Justinian issues the *Pragmatic Sanction* with measures to restore Italy as the westernmost province of the empire
c.560	Western Turks in alliance defeat Hephthalite Huns, become masters of Sogdia, continue migration westwards
561	The Byzantine general Narses occupies the north of Italy
	Second partition of Merovingian kingdom between the four sons of Chlothar I
563	Saint Columba founds the monastery of Iona on the island Hy given by the local Scottish king
567	Death of King Charibert and the redivision of the Merovingian kingdom, as a result of which the sub-kingdoms which became known as Neustria, Austrasia, and Burgundy emerged
568–569	The Lombards enter Italy
569–573	Byzantine embassies to western Turk Khagan in central Asia (described in Menander the Guardsman's *History*)
570	The Avars enter Pannonia
c.570–585	Leovigild conquers most of Spain for the Visigoths
582	Accession of Emperor Maurice in Byzantium
584	The Lombards establish permanent kingship
589	The conversion of the Visigoths to Catholicism from Arianism; Third Council of Toledo
590	Columbanus leaves Ireland bound for Gaul. There he founds the monastery of Luxeuil and inspires many Franks with his ascetic rigour
591	Gregory of Tours, *Histories*
597	Augustine of Canterbury converts the English king Æthelbehrt of Kent to Christianity
603–628	War between Byzantium and Sasanian Persia
610	Accession of the Emperor Heraclius in Byzantium
611	Persians capture Antioch
612	Foundation of the monastery of Bobbio
613	Chlothar II reunites the Merovingian kingdom with the assistance in particular of Arnulf, bishop of Metz and Pippin I. From the marriage later between Arnulf's son Ansegis and Pippin's daughter Begga the Carolingian family is descended

618/619– 628/629	Persians occupy Egypt
622	Mohammed leaves Mecca for Medina, beginning his *hijra* (emigration); beginning of Islamic calendar
623	The Frankish king Chlothar II creates the sub-kingdom for his son Dagobert in Austrasia
c.625–636	Isidore of Seville writes the *Etymologiae*
626	Avars, Slavs, and Persians besiege Constantinople
627–628	The Emperor Heraclius invades Persia and overthrows Chosroes II
632	Death of Mohammed. Abu Bakr becomes caliph
633–641	Arabs overrun Byzantium's Middle Eastern provinces and destroy the Persian empire
636	Arabs overrun Syria
637	Arabs overrun Iraq Arabs capture the Sasanian capital Ctesiphon
638	Arabs capture Jerusalem
639	Death of Dagobert, king of the Franks
642	Arabs conquer Egypt and begin conquest of North Africa
643	Rothari, king of the Lombards, issues his law code
651	Final defeat of Persians at Merv
654	The Visigothic king Recceswinth revises the *Liber Iudiciorum*, which includes many laws compiled by his father Chindaswinth
664	The Synod of Whitby resolves the Easter Question within the English church in favour of the Roman practice (namely, the cycle devised by Dionysius Exiguus)
674–678	Arab blockade of Constantinople
678–683	Cáin Fhuithirbe: earliest datable Irish law code proclaimed, dealing with the relationship between the church and kings
679	Barontus' journey to heaven and back
680	Bulgars cross lower Danube and occupy land between the river and the Haemus (Balkan) range
c.680	Peace concluded between Byzantium and the Lombards
681	The Visigothic king Ervig revises the *Liber Iudiciorum*
687	Battle of Tertry and Pippin II, mayor of the palace in Austrasia, assumes control of the Merovingian kingdom

690	Willibrord the Anglo-Saxon missionary leaves Ireland bound for Frisia
692	Completion of Dome of the Rock in Jerusalem, demonstrating Umayyad piety and power
695	On 21 Nov., Willibrord is consecrated bishop by Pope Sergius and thereafter establishes his see at Utrecht
	Wihtred, king of Kent, issues a law code, at about the same time as Ine, king of Wessex, issues his. Both are in English
698	Arabs capture Carthage
711	Arabs invade Visigothic Spain
713	Liutprand, king of the Lombards (712–744) makes the first of many additions to the Lombard law code
714	Death of the Carolingian Pippin II, mayor of the palace. His bastard son, Charles Martel, makes a bid for power in Francia against the Neustrian Franks, led by Ragamfred, and the Frisians
716	Duke Theodo of Bavaria asks the pope for help in the reorganization of the church in Bavaria
716–718	Arab assault on Constantinople
718	Charles Martel establishes control in Francia and thereafter rebuilds Frankish power in a series of military campaigns
	At the 'Battle of Covadonga' the Arabs are defeated by the Christian ruler of the Asturias and his army
722	The English missionary Boniface is sent to Germany as a newly consecrated bishop by Pope Gregory II
725	Bede completes his *On the Reckoning of Time*, which becomes a highly influential guide to calculation in the schools of western Europe
726	Emperor Leo III of Byzantium comes to the throne
730	Emperor Leo III orders the destruction of all icons in the Byzantine empire, allowing only crosses to remain, as being symbols, not images
731	Bede, *Ecclesiastical History of the English People*
732–734	Battle of Poitiers (which actually took place between Tours and Poitiers); Charles Martel defeats the Arabs and forces them to retreat southwards
735	The Franks conquer Frisia
c.736	Brude, king of the Picts, establishes Pictish rule over the Scottish kingdom of Dál Riata

737   Danevirk constructed across the Jutland peninsula by Danish rulers

741   Death of Charles Martel; Pippin III and Carloman succeed Charles Martel as mayor of the palace

Euloga law code in Byzantium

741/742   Bishoprics established in Erfurt, Buraburg, and Würzburg

742/743   *Concilium Germanicum,* presided over by the Englishman Boniface, archbishop of Mainz and Carloman, Frankish mayor of the palace in Austrasia, takes the first steps to reform the Frankish church

743   Carloman, mayor of the palace in Austrasia elevates the last Merovingian king, Chilperic III, to the throne

746   The Franks defeat the Alemans at Cannstadt

King Ratchis of the Lombards promulgates additions to the Lombard law code

747   Synod of *Cloveshoe* in Mercia and reforms, closely resembling the Frankish measures, are introduced into the English church

749   Liutprand, king of the Lombards, invades the Pentapolis. Pope Zacharias persuades him to leave

*c.*750   First wooden structures built at Staraia Ladoga on the River Volkhov; the settlement serves as a trading post, where Muslim silver was bartered for furs

Chrodegang, bishop of Metz, establishes a school for ecclesiastical chant at Metz which it is claimed is modelled on that of Rome

750   Abbasid caliphate established

751   Lombards capture Ravenna from Byzantium

Battle of Talas River establishes boundary between China and Abbasid caliphate in east

Pippin III, the Carolingian mayor of the palace, usurps the Merovingian throne

754   Pippin III, his wife Bertrada, and two sons Charles and Carloman, are anointed as the ruling family by Pope Stephen II (III) in Francia

Boniface, bishop of Mainz, is murdered by brigands at Dokkum in northern Frisia

Iconoclast council in Heireia

755   Capitulary of Herstal and reform of Frankish coinage by Pippin III who promotes the use of the new silver penny

756	The Umayyad 'Abd-al Rahman I seizes power in Córdoba
757	Tassilo, duke of Bavaria, swears fidelity to Pippin III at Compiègne
	Byzantine embassy to the Frankish court presents an organ to Pippin III
767	Gisela, daughter of Pippin III is betrothed to the Byzantine heir to the throne (later emperor) Leo IV. The marriage does not take place
768	Death of Pippin III
	Carolingian conquest of Aquitaine is completed by Charles and Carloman, sons of Pippin III, who succeed Pippin as kings of the Franks
771	Death of Carloman; Charlemagne is left as sole ruler of the Franks
773–774	Conquest of the kingdom of the Lombards by Charlemagne
776–798	Completion of the palace complex and baths at Aachen
778	Charlemagne's expedition to Spain. Roland, count of the Breton March is killed at Roncesvalles and is celebrated in the Old French poem, first written down in the eleventh century, the *Chanson de Roland*
782	Charlemagne has 4,000 Saxon prisoners executed after the Frankish defeat in the Süntel hills
780s and 790s	Scholars from Francia, England, Ireland, Italy, and Spain gather at Charlemagne's court
c.783	Paul the Deacon, *History of the Lombards*
785	Surrender of Widukind the Saxon to Charlemagne produces a temporary subjugation of the Saxons to the Franks
786	The papal legates report on the state of the church in England
	Lichfield is (temporarily) elevated to an archbishopric
	Beatus of Liebana, *Commentary on the Apocalypse*
c.786	Completion of great Mosque of Córdoba
787	Second council of Nicaea anathematizes the iconoclasts and defines the veneration to be accorded images
788	Annexation of Bavaria; Duke Tassilo and his family imprisoned in monasteries in west Francia
789	*Admonitio Generalis* of Charlemagne advocates an extensive reform programme for the Frankish church, with a stress on *correctio*

Brihtric, king of Wessex, marries Offa of Mercia's daughter Eadburh

Egbert of Wessex takes refuge at the court of Charlemagne

791   Defeat of the Avars by the Franks

792   Revolt of Pippin the Hunchback against Charlemagne

793   Theodulf of Orleans, *Libri Carolini* on the use of images in religious worship

Charlemagne attempts to link the Danube and Rhine/Main rivers by a canal dug between the Rednitz and Altmühl rivers. Napoleon also failed. This was a project not achieved until the late twentieth century

Viking sack of Lindisfarne

794   Council of Frankfurt. Charlemagne reforms the coinage and regularizes weights and measures. Adoptionism and Iconoclasm are condemned, but, due to a misunderstanding of the Greeks' arguments and definition of veneration, so are the acts of Nicaea II (787)

*c.*795–835 Viking hit-and-run raids on Ireland

796   Destruction of the Avar Ring by the Franks, and the plundering of the Avars' enormously rich treasure

Charlemagne writes to Offa, king of Mercia, concerning trading links and political exiles

798   Final subjugation of the Saxons by Charlemagne and the Franks after many years of campaigns

799   Charlemagne meets Pope Leo III at Paderborn

Anon., *Carolus Magnus et Leo Papa*

Theodulf of Orleans, *Contra Judices*

800   Charlemagne captures Barcelona

Charlemagne's letter, *De litteris colendis* is circulated concerning the encouragement of education in the schools of monasteries and bishoprics

The *Capitulare de villis* is issued by Charlemagne, concerning the organization of the royal estates

Charlemagne crowned emperor in St Peter's, Rome by Pope Leo III on Christmas Day

802   Caliph Haroun al Rashid of Baghdad sends an elephant, Abul Abaz, to Charlemagne

Charlemagne issues his programmatic capitulary on the administrative reorganization of the empire

806	Frankish control over Barcelona and the Spanish March, and (briefly) Pamplona, established
	Divisio regnorum: Charlemagne makes provision for the division of his realm, between his then three living sons, but not for the continuation of the imperial title, after his death
808	Further fortifications of the Danevirk in the Jutland peninsula
810	Pippin of Italy captures Venice and attacks Dalmatia
	Death of the elephant Abul Abaz while on campaign in Germany
811	Byzantine expedition against the Bulgars ends disastrously: the Emperor Nicephorus I is slain and his skull is turned into a drinking cup
	New ecclesiastical provinces are created, with Besançon, Tarentaise, and Embrun becoming archbishoprics. Cologne's metropolitian status is restored
812	Byzantium concludes a peace with the Franks in relation to Dalmatia and recognizes Charlemagne as emperor
812–814	Bulgars overrun Thrace and Macedonia
813	Charlemagne crowns his son Louis as emperor
	Reform councils of the Frankish church
814	Death of Charlemagne and accession of Louis the Pious
816	Peace concluded between Byzantium and Bulgaria
816/817	Aachen reform decrees promote the *Rule* of Benedict in monasteries of the Frankish empire
817	The *Ordinatio imperii* of Louis the Pious divides his empire between his three sons, Lothar, Louis, and Pippin, and makes the eldest, Lothar, co-emperor
	Pactum Ludovicianum: Louis the Pious confirms the pope in the possession of his papal states and patrimonies and guarantees the freedom of papal elections
	Revolt of Bernard, king of Italy. It fails; he is blinded and dies
817–824	Pope Paschal I builds the church of Sa Prassede in Rome
818–847	During the episcopate of Bishop Theodemir of Iria Flavia, the relics of St James are discovered at Compostela. Santiago subsequently becomes a major cult and pilgrimage site
*c.*820	Plan of St Gallen
822	Redaction of the polyptych of the abbey of Saint-Germain-des-Prés on the orders of Abbot Irmino

823	Birth of Charles the Bald to Louis the Pious' second wife Judith
824	*Constitutio romana* restores the role of the people of Rome in papal elections
	Independent kingdom of Pamplona established
824–830	Muslim raiders seize Crete and begin seizing strongholds in Sicily
825	Synod of Paris reiterates the Franks' condemnation of Greek views on images
	Dicuil, *De mensura orbis*
826	The Danish king Harald Klak is baptized at the court of the Frankish emperor Louis the Pious
827	Byzantine gifts to Louis the Pious include the works of pseudo-Denys the Areopagite
829/830	*Historia Brittonum* attributed to 'Nennius'
830s	Hungarians move into steppes north of the Black Sea
830	Revolt against Louis the Pious led by Counts Hugh and Matfrid
830–831	Anskar's mission to Sweden
c.831	Hamburg–Bremen becomes an archdiocese
833	Deposition of the Frankish emperor, Louis the Pious
	Public penance of Louis the Pious
834	Restoration of Louis the Pious
834–837	Annual raids by Vikings on the trading settlement of Dorestad
839	'Rhos' form part of a Byzantine embassy to the court of Louis the Pious
840	Death of Louis the Pious. Civil wars ensue between his surviving sons, Lothar, Louis the German, and Charles the Bald
840–841	Vikings establish a base at Dublin
841–843	Stellinga revolt in Saxony
841–871	Muslim emirate in Bari
842	Strasbourg oaths between Louis the German and Charles the Bald. In the record made of them by Nithard (d. 844), *History of the Sons of Louis the Pious*, writing soon thereafter, the oath sworn in 'Romance' is the earliest extended example of Old French

843	Treaty of Verdun and division of the Frankish empire between Lothar, Charles the Bald, and Louis the German
	Vikings attack Nantes. Many other places in the Frankish kingdoms are raided over the next 50 years
	Restoration of icons in Byzantium and Feast of Orthodoxy established
845	Vikings sack Hamburg
847–852	Pseudo-Isidorean canonical collection forged
848–849	Kenneth I, king of the Picts and Dál Riata by 842, makes Dunkeld his new ecclesiastical centre and places the relics of St Columba in the church there
855	Death of the Emperor Lothar. His 'Middle kingdom' is divided between his three sons, Lothar II, Louis II (in Italy), and Charles
856	Rhodri, king of Gwynedd, kills the Viking leader Horm
857	Æthelwulf of Wessex visits King Charles the Bald of the west Franks and subsequently marries Judith, Charles' daughter
858	Louis the German invades his brother Charles the Bald's kingdom
860	Rus attack Constantinople
	Gottschalk's views on predestination are condemned at the Synod of Tusey
*c.*861	Conversion of Khazars to Judaism
863	The missonaries Constantine-Cyril and Methodius sent to Moravia
	Otfrid of Weissenberg, *Evangelienbuch*
864	Conversion of Khan Boris of Bulgaria to Byzantine Christianity
	Subsequently he turns to Pope Nicholas I for spiritual leadership and accepts priests from the east Franks
	Edict of Pîtres: Charles the Bald reforms the west Frankish coinage
867	Mission of Ermanrich of Ellwangen to the Bulgarians
869	Constantine-Cyril dies in Rome. Methodius later returns to central European Slavs as papal emissary and continues with pastoral and translation work, championing the use of Slavonic as the language of the liturgy

Death of Lothar II, king of Lotharingia; his kingdom is claimed by his uncle Charles the Bald, king of the west Franks, who is crowned king at Metz

869–870   Council of Constantinople. Khan Boris accepts loose religious affiliation with Byzantium

Conversio Bagoariorum et Carantanorum

870   Treaty of Meersen: Charles the Bald and Louis the German divide Lotharingia between them

Rastislav is deposed as ruler of Moravia and is succeeded by Zwentibald/Svatopluk

*c.*870   Beginning of Norse settlement in Iceland

873–874   The magnificent Westwork at Corvey is built

874   Peace concluded between east Franks and Moravians

875   Charles the Bald, king of the west Franks (840–877), is crowned emperor in Rome by Pope John VIII. The pope is presented with the *Cathedra petri* (a throne of oak with ivory panels depicting the labours of Hercules) and a life-size silver crucifix

875/876   Byzantines reoccupy Bari, and regain other strongholds in southern Italy

876   Death of Louis the German

8 Oct. Battle of Andernach, Charles the Bald, king of the west Franks is defeated by his nephew Louis the Younger of the east Franks. Eastern Lotharingia is divided between Louis and his brother Charles III the Fat

877   6 Oct. Death of Charles the Bald. He is succeeded by his son Louis the Stammerer

Death of Rhodri Mawr, major king in Wales

878   Syracuse falls to Muslims

Battle of Edington; King Alfred defeats the Viking leader Guthrum and establishes his chain of fortified burhs

Vikings winter in Dyfed, Wales

879   Boso becomes king of Provence

880s   Ohthere the Norwegian rounds the North Cape and reaches the White Sea

Later (*c.*890) he recounts his journey to King Alfred of Wessex

880   Death of Carloman, king of the east Franks, whose territory is acquired by his brother Louis the Younger

Louis the Younger, king of the east Franks, invades the kingdom of the west Franks and is conceded western Lotharingia by the treaty of Ribemont

Louis the Younger defeats the Vikings at Thiméon on the Sambre river

881	Louis III, king of the west Franks, defeats Vikings at a battle at Saucourt
	Ludwigslied (a poem in Old High German) celebrates the victory of a Frankish king called Louis over the Vikings
	Eulalia Sequence. The oldest extant poem in Old French
882	Death of Louis the Younger
884	Æthelred, king of Mercia submits to Alfred of Wessex
	Carolingian empire briefly reunited under Charles the Fat
885	Death of Methodius. His pupils are oppressed by east Frankish clergy; some flee to Bulgaria
885–886	Viking siege of Paris
886	Photius, patriarch of Constantinople is obliged to vacate his office for the second time. He dies some years later
	King Alfred of Wessex occupies London
887	Charles the Fat relinquishes throne (and dies the following year). He is succeeded by Arnulf in east Francia
888	Arnulf acknowledges Odo, Rudolf, and Berengar, elected kings of the west Franks, of Burgundy, and of Italy respectively. Only Berengar is a Carolingian family member
894	Pechenegs defeat Hungarians
	Baptism of Borivoj, ruler of the Bohemians
895	Council of Tribur
	Haesten's army of Danes ravages south Wales
896	Arnulf crowned emperor by Pope Formosus
897	Pope Stephen VI has the rotting corpse of his predecessor Formosus exhumed and tried for perjury, breaking canon law, and coveting the papacy. Formosus is declared guilty and the body is flung into the Tiber
898	Odo, king of the west Franks, succeeded by the Carolingian Charles the Simple
899	8 Dec. Death of Arnulf; he is succeeded by Louis the Child
c.900	Rus establish themselves on Middle Dnieper and thereafter trade regularly with Byzantium
902	The Vikings are driven from Dublin

904	Leo of Tripoli, Muslim pirate chief, sacks Thessalonica
905	Magyars/Hungarians begin to raid western Europe
907	The Magyars defeat a Bavarian army at the Marchfeld near Bratislava
*c.*907	First written trading privilege granted by Byzantium to Rus, followed by more elaborate treaties
910	Foundation of Cluny
911	County of Rouen ceded to Rollo the Viking by Charles the Simple, king of the west Franks. Over the next 80 years the territory expands and becomes the duchy of Normandy
	Death of Louis the Child, the last Carolingian king of the kingdom of the west Franks
	Conrad of Franconia elected king of the east Franks
914	A Viking fleet arrives in the Severn estuary from Brittany, ravages Wales and captures Bishop Cyfeiliog, who is ransomed
*c.*914	Byzantine religious mission to Alans, nomads living to the north of the Caucasus
915	Berengar of Friuli, great-grandson of Louis the Pious, crowned emperor by Pope John X
917	Sitric the Viking king reoccupies Dublin
918	Death of Conrad I; Henry I 'the Fowler' of Saxony elected king
919	The Viking leader Ragnall from Dublin takes York and becomes king of Northumbria
922	Ibn Fadlan's visit to the middle Volga
929/925–972	Czechs dominate the Bohemian plain
929	Boleslav I, king of Bohemia, kills his brother Wenceslas. The latter is later recognized as a saint and becomes the Czech national saint
	Abd-ar-Rahman III establishes caliphate at Córdoba
930	Otto, son of Henry I 'the Fowler', marries Edith, sister of Æthelstan of Wessex
936	7 July. Death of Henry I
	His son Otto I succeeds him and on 8 Aug. is crowned at Aachen
937	Foundation of monastery of St Maurice, Magdeburg

	Battle of *Brunanburh*: the kings of Scotland and Strathclyde ally with the Norse to fight King Æthelstan of Wessex. The battle is celebrated in a poem incorporated into the *Anglo-Saxon Chronicle*
948	Bishops appointed to sees at Schleswig, Ribe, and Aarhus in Denmark
940s and 950s	Various northern leaders visit Constantinople and are baptized, including the Hungarian chieftain Bulcsu and Princess Olga of the Rus
949	Liudprand of Cremona's first embassy to Constantinople, later described in his *Antapodosis* ('Tit-for-Tat')
*c.*950	*De administrando imperio* compiled under the direction of Constantine VII Porphyrogenitus
951	Otto I crowned king of Italy and marries Adelheid, widow of Lothar, king of Italy
953	Otto I's brother Bruno is made archbishop of Cologne
954	Death of Eric Bloodaxe, Viking ruler of York
955	Otto I of Saxony defeats the Hungarians at the Battle of the Lech. He executes their leaders, including the Christian Bulcsu
957	Division of the English kingdom between Edgar and Eadwig
958	Gorm, king of the Danes, buried at Jelling
959	England reunited under King Edgar
961	Byzantium reconquers Crete
962	Otto I crowned emperor in Rome by Pope John XII
	Ottonianum confirms the donations of Pippin III and Charlemagne and the freedom of papal elections
965	Conversion of King Harald Bluetooth of the Danes to Christianity
966	Baptism of Miezko I, king of Poland
967/972–999	Prague is made a bishopric during the reign of Boleslav II
968	Establishment of Magdeburg as a new archbishopric in eastern Germany
	Poznán in Poland becomes a bishopric
	Liudprand of Cremona's embassy to Constantinople on behalf of Otto I, described immediately afterwards in his *Relatio de Legatione Constantinopolitana*
969–971	Prince Sviatoslav tries to establish a new centre of Rus power on the lower Danube

*c.*970	*Regularis Concordia*
972	Death of Prince Sviatoslav of the Rus and many of his warriors at the Dnieper Rapids
	Marriage in Rome of Otto I's son Otto II to Theophano, niece of the Byzantine Emperor John I Tzimisces
973	Death of Otto I
982	Otto II is defeated by the Saracens in Calabria
983	Death of Otto II
	Slav uprising east of Elbe and the destruction of the German missionary churches there
*c.*985	First Scandinavian settlements in Greenland
987	Death of the last Carolingian king of the west Franks, Louis V. Accession of Hugh Capet
	Godfrid the Viking ravages Anglesey and takes 2,000 prisoners. This raid is one of many over the preceding 15 years
*c.*988	Prince Vladimir of Kiev adopts Byzantine Christianity. Mass baptism of citizens of Kiev in the river Dnieper
989	Maredudd ab Owain, king of Dyfed, pays a poll tax of a penny to the Vikings
990	Miezco I of Poland annexes Silesia and Little Poland
*c.*990	First church built at Roskilde in Denmark
991	Death of the Empress Theophano. Her mother-in-law Adelaide is left as sole regent for her grandson Otto III
992	Byzantine chrysobull granting privileges to Venetian vessels
995	Waik (Stephen) of Hungary marries Gisela of Bavaria
996	Otto III pays his first visit to Rome and has his cousin Bruno elected as Pope Gregory V
	Otto III crowned emperor in Rome
997	Adalbert of Prague is martyred by the Prussians
998	Otto III's second visit to Rome. He deposes the anti-pope John Philagathus
999	Otto III's former tutor, Gerbert, archbishop of Rheims becomes Pope Sylvester II
	Death of Olaf Tryggvason king of Norway who promoted the conversion of his people to Christianity
	Unsuccessful revolt of Sitric Silkenbeard, Viking king of Dublin, who is defeated by Brian Boru, king of Ireland

1000	The Icelanders accept Christianity
	Otto III and Boleslaw of Poland venerate relics of St Adalbert at Gniezno
	Gniezno elevated to an archbishopric
	Coronation of King Stephen of Hungary with a crown sent by the pope
	Otto III visits Aachen and opens the tomb of Charlemagne
*c.*1000	Earliest churches built on Greenland
	First landings of Scandinavians on the North American seaboard
1002	Death of Otto III

Maps

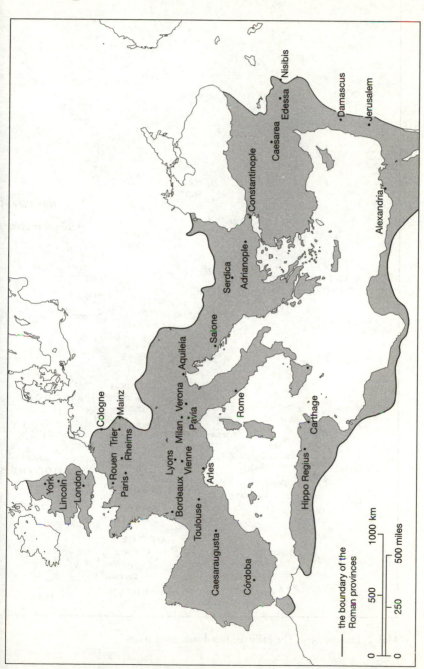

Map 1 Europe c.400: The late Roman empire

Map 2 Europe *c.*526: The early medieval successor states

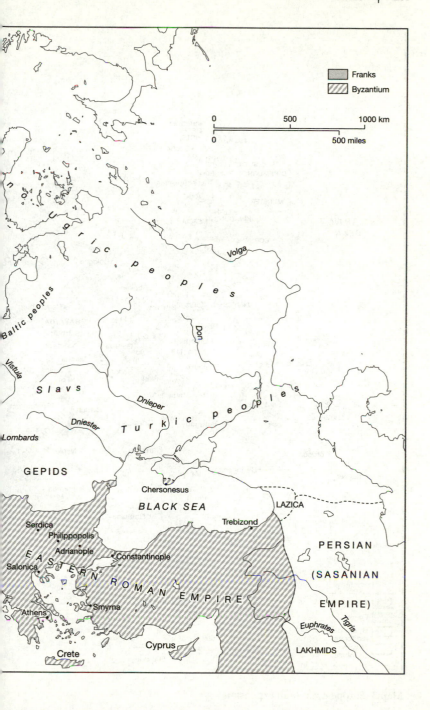

Franks
Byzantium

0   500   1000 km
0   500 miles

Volga

Don

Ugric peoples

Baltic peoples

Vistula

Slavs

Dnieper

Dniester

Lombards

GEPIDS

Turkic peoples

Chersonesus

BLACK SEA

LAZICA

Serdica

Philippopolis

Adrianople

Trebizond

PERSIAN

Salonica

Constantinople

EASTERN ROMAN EMPIRE

(SASANIAN

Athens

Smyrna

EMPIRE)

Euphrates

Tigris

Cyprus

Crete

LAKHMIDS

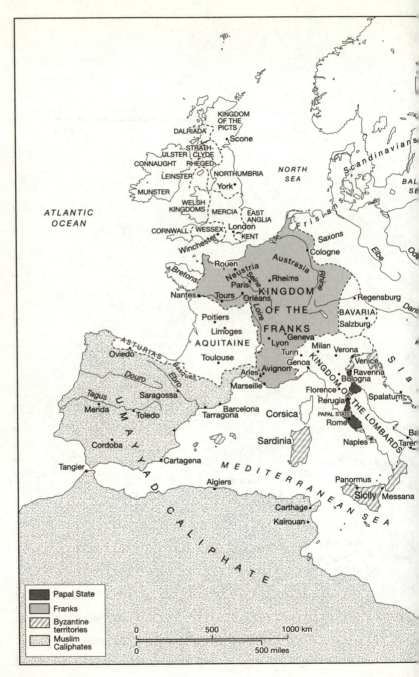

Map 3 Europe *c.*732: Arab expansion

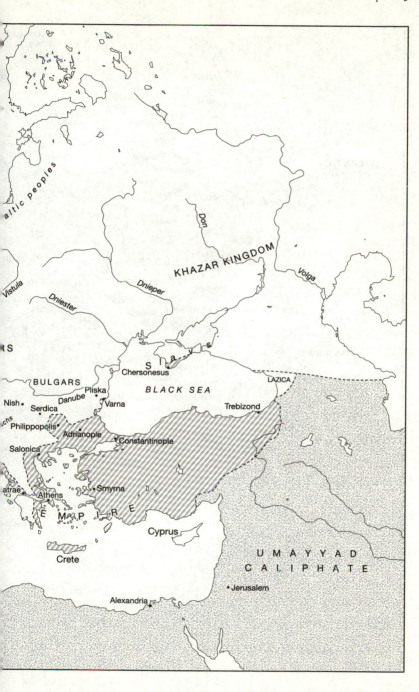

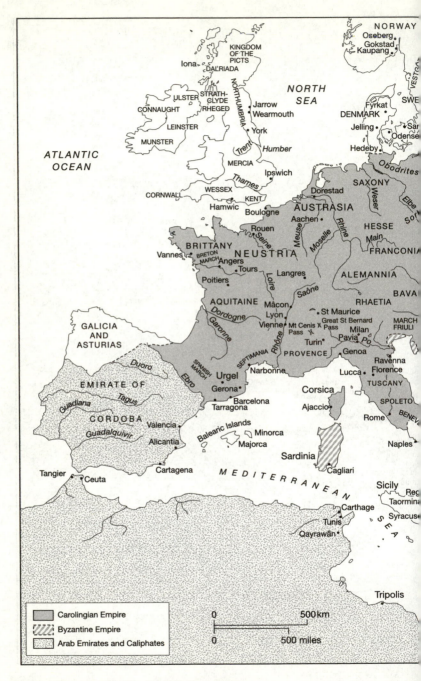

Map 4 Europe *c.*814: The Carolingian empire

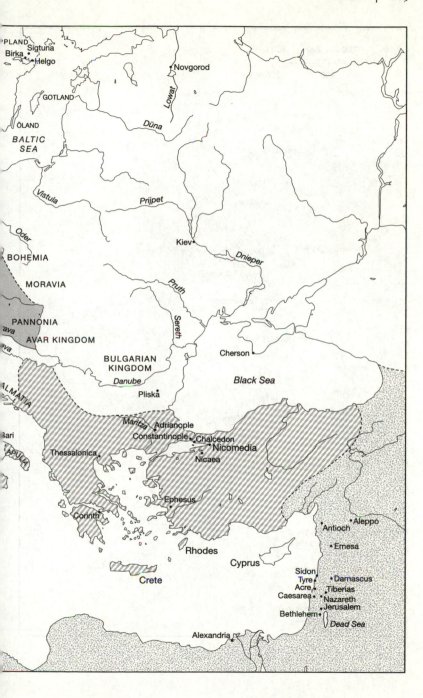

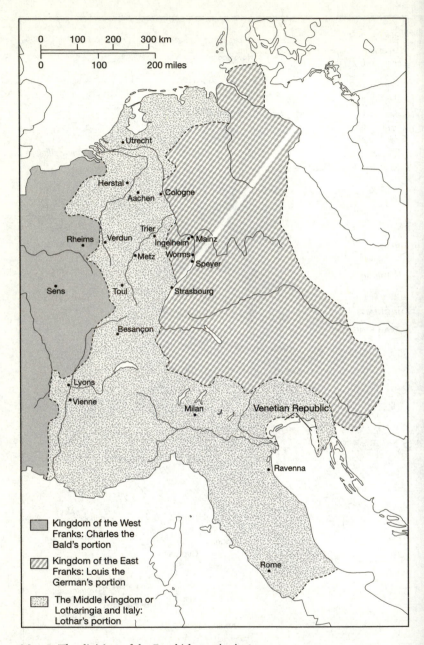

Map 5 The division of the Frankish empire in 843

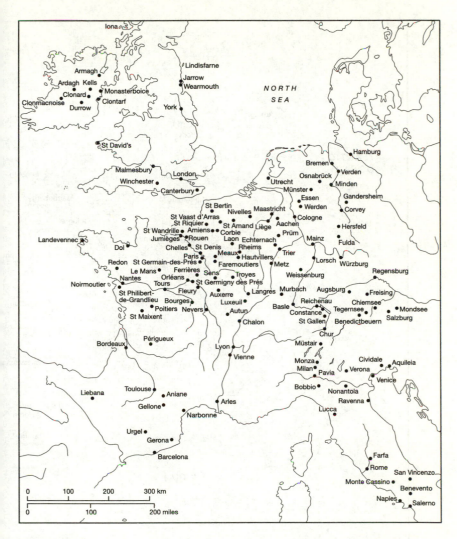

Map 6 Early medieval Europe: Monastic and cathedral centres of learning and culture

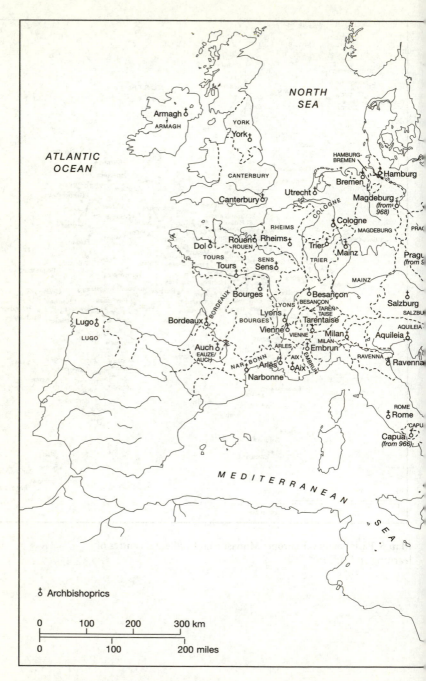

Map 7 The ecclesiastical provinces of Latin Europe (reflecting changes made in 811)

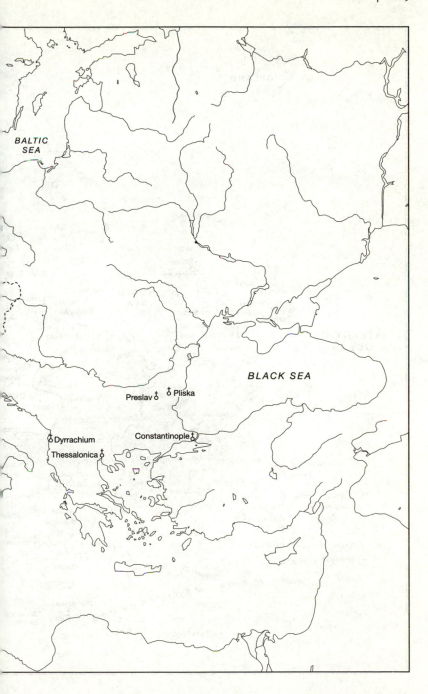

Map 8 Europe *c.*1000

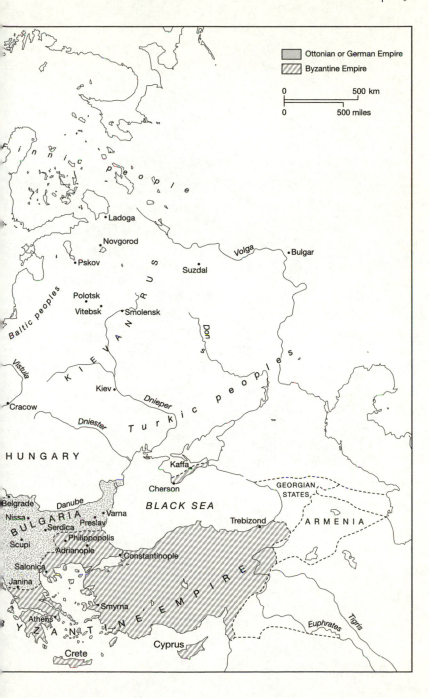

Ottonian or German Empire
Byzantine Empire

0   500 km

0   500 miles

Finnic peoples

• Ladoga

• Novgorod

Volga   • Bulgar

• Pskov

• Suzdal

Baltic peoples

Polotsk

Vitebsk   • Smolensk

K I E V A N   R U S

Don

Vistula

• Kiev   *Dnieper*

Cracow

Dniester

T u r k i c   P e o p l e s

H U N G A R Y

Kaffa

• Cherson

GEORGIAN
STATES

Belgrade   *Danube*

Nissa   B U L G A R I A   • Varna

BLACK SEA

Trebizond

A R M E N I A

Serdica Preslav

Scupi   • Philippopolis

Adrianople • Constantinople

Salonica

Janina

Euphrates

Tigris

• Smyrna

B Y Z A N T I N E   E M P I R E

Athens

Cyprus

Crete

Index